# TIDEWATER VIRGINIA FAMILIES:
A Magazine of History and Genealogy

Virginia Lee Hutcheson Davis, Editor

VOLUME 1, MAY 1992 - FEBRUARY 1993

WILLOW BEND BOOKS
2013

# WILLOW BEND BOOKS
*AN IMPRINT OF HERITAGE BOOKS, INC.*

Books, CDs, and more—Worldwide

For our listing of thousands of titles see our website
at
www.HeritageBooks.com

Published 2013 by
HERITAGE BOOKS, INC.
Publishing Division
5810 Ruatan Street
Berwyn Heights, Md. 20740

Copyright © 1992 Tidewater Virginia Families

All rights reserved. No part of this book may be reproduced or transmitted in any form or by any means, electronic or mechanical, including photocopying, recording or by any information storage and retrieval system without written permission from the author, except for the inclusion of brief quotations in a review.

International Standard Book Numbers
Paperbound: 978-1-58549-661-7
Clothbound: 978-0-7884-6879-7

# TIDEWATER VIRGINIA FAMILIES:
## A Magazine of History and Genealogy

### TABLE OF CONTENTS

| | |
|---|---:|
| By Way of Introduction | 1 |
| The Counties of Tidewater Virginia | 3 |
| Thomas Butler of Tuckoman, King William County | 15 |
| Yeocomico Church, Cople Parish, Westmoreland County | 22 |
| Tithables, Lancaster County, 1659 | 24 |
| Civil Appointments, Charles City County, 1780-1787 | 28 |
| Petition, Caroline County, 1821, Reedy Church and Bull Church | 33 |
| Will of James Cathon, 1696, Warwick County | 37 |
| Miller Family Bible, Hanover County, 1824-1894 | 39 |
| Parrish Family Graveyard, King and Queen County | 41 |
| BOOK REVIEWS: | 42 |
| AND ANNOUNCEMENTS: | 43 |
| SEARCH: | 44 |

Volume 1 Number 1                                May/June 1992

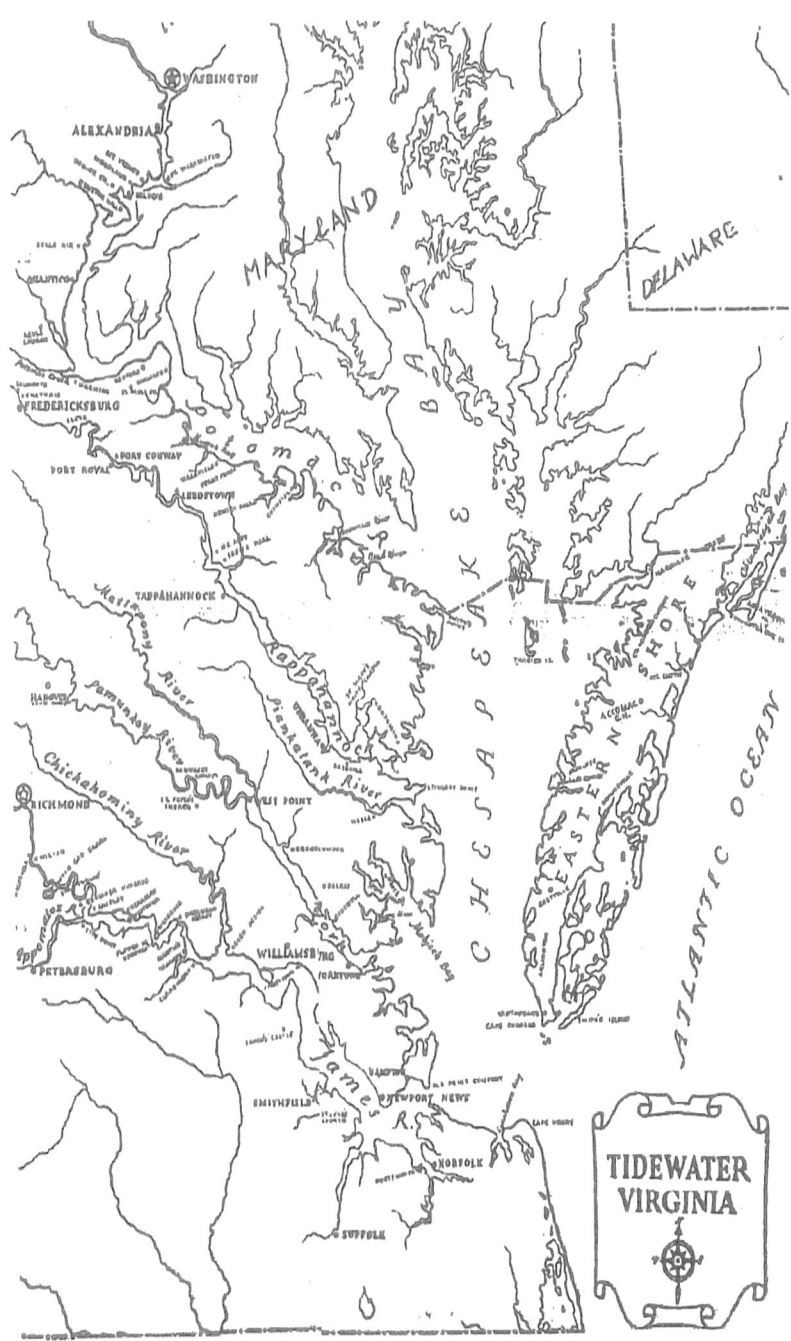

## By Way of Introduction

*TIDEWATER VIRGINIA FAMILIES: A Magazine of History and Genealogy* has come about as an outgrowth of the book, *TIDEWATER VIRGINIA FAMILIES: A Social History* privately printed by the author and the second edition, *TIDEWATER VIRGINIA FAMILIES* published in 1990 by the Genealogical Publishing Company. This magazine will not be limited to the families nor the area presented in the book, but will explore new research and information concerning tidewater Virginia.

When one looks over the list of counties in the tidewater that have lost their records to courthouse fires, war and the ravages of time, it is realized that all of the possible sources of information must be searched to piece together the lives of the early settlers of Virginia. The goal of this magazine is to offer records that have not been printed, and are relatively inaccessible to the public. It is because additional information has continued to come to the attention of this writer that it is felt that a real service can be rendered by making this information available.

It is planned that county court records, not generally available to the public will be included in the magazine. There are loose wills, deeds, chancery suits, powers of attorney and many other court records that need to be made public. Bible records, church records, cemetery records and gravestone inscriptions are often found locally and need to be shared. Often times the history of an old home or church also provides genealogical information, and if not that, then insight as to where an ancestor lived and worshipped.

It is an awesome task for one individual to gather all the information that the researcher seeks, and from all of the sources available. The editor earnestly requests your indulgence in her efforts to balance the material presented geographically and in content. She also earnestly solicits material from any interested researchers and subscribers.

Queries from subscribers are also solicited, and will be published on a space-available basis. Many times an individual unlocks a door to a new family member through his quest for information about an ancestor.

The editor will be glad to acquaint the reading audience with new publications. A complimentary copy of a book recently published will elicit a review by the editor, and good publicity for the author. The subject matter of the book should relate to the counties considered in this publication.

It is the fervent hope of the editor that this publication will make a real contribution to the preservation of the early history of tidewater Virginia and the dissemination of that history to those who are interested in learning of their culture and ancestry. By living just seventy-five miles from the most distant courthouse in the area presented, the editor also hopes that an added perspective can be given the reader from an intimate knowledge of the area.

Any such research into the early history of an area is a "labor of love", and it is hoped a lasting contribution. It is hoped that *TIDEWATER VIRGINIA FAMILIES* will be a coming together of those of us who have their origins in colonial tidewater Virginia. May it be a joint venture, discovering ancestors, relationships and a shared heritage.

              Virginia Lee Hutcheson Davis

## The Counties of Tidewater Virginia

One can visualize an imaginary line that follows the coastline of Virginia from south to north. It is known as the fall line, and crosses the rivers that feed into the Chesapeake Bay, at the point at which they become navigable. Count off the rivers: the James; the Pamunkey and the Mattaponi, which become the York; the Rappahannock and the Potomac. Each creates a finger of land, known locally by the names: "the Peninsula", "the Middle Peninsula" and "the Northern Neck". There is, additionally, "the Eastern Shore", the peninsula that lies between the Chesapeake Bay and the Atlantic Ocean.

There are five major geographic regions of Virginia: the tidewater, the piedmont, the Blue Ridge, the Valley of Virginia and the Allegheny Mountains. The tidewater is the sandy coastal plain between the Atlantic Ocean and the fall line of the rivers. This is the point at which these rivers cease to be affected by the tidal flow and are no longer navigable. It was here that the first settlers of Virginia created their homes and livelihoods from the wilderness. The rivers provided an easy means of local transportation, and a means of transporting their goods to and from England.

The settlers fanned out along each side of the James, along the coast and up each of the other rivers. It was felt that settlements some distance from the Chesapeake Bay were safer, because of the perceived threat of piracy. As the settlers became more familiar with their new land, they ventured farther inland and farther up the rivers. Still the rivers provided them with the means of travel, and communication with their neighbors and with their English homeland.

While there are counties south of the James, as well as the counties of the Eastern Shore, that are categorized as tidewater Virginia, this publication will explore the area that lies north of the James River, that is by definition, east of the fall line, and is thus identified as tidewater Virginia. These counties, as they evolved were: Caroline, Charles City, Elizabeth City, Essex, Gloucester, Hanover, Henrico, James City, King and Queen, King George, King William, Lancaster, Mathews, Middlesex, New Kent, Northumberland,

Richmond, Warwick, Westmoreland and York. These were the counties that were in existence at the end of the eighteenth century.

The identity of many of these counties began as another entity, and the counties were known by different names at different times in history. Some of the counties no longer survive as counties but have been incorporated into their adjacent cities and now assume that corporate identity. It is important to understand the history and evolution of these Virginia counties in order to appreciate the origins and lives of these early settlers. It is also mandatory that one have this information to locate the early homes of ancestors and the surviving records about them.

As a geographic area grew in population and new political needs must be met, a petition for the formation of a new county would be submitted to the General Assembly. Not only were political and business interests of significance, but it was also a consideration that the courthouse be within reasonable travel distance of the population. Records of the counties are still kept in that county of origin, with the records of the more recently formed counties beginning at the date that the county was chartered by the General Assembly. It is very important to keep this in mind when searching the colonial records of Virginia.

It is imperative that the researcher have an understanding of the history of the evolution of Virginia counties to pursue research in the counties in which they are interested. While the information presented here can be found in a number of places, it seems of importance that it be offered as an introduction and a concise reference to the readers of this magazine. Since this publication will explore the counties of tidewater Virginia it is essential to have the history of these counties at hand.

Those researchers with a long acquaintance of colonial Virginia records will be aware of the great frustration and also the great sense of reward found in searching for ancestors who had their origins in Virginia. Those researchers who are just beginning to explore these counties will likely have a great sense of frustration that is ill-defined and ever-present. The explanation is that a number of the counties of Virginia have lost their early records; in fact, in some cases, most or all of those records that preceded the Civil War period have been lost to posterity. In some cases the loss is due to the destruction of the courthouse, in some cases it may be due to the ravages of wars: the Revolutionary, the War of 1812, or the Civil War. In other cases, individual record books have been removed, misplaced or destroyed, so that there are gaps in the continuity of the records. In counties where it appears that most of the records have survived, this may be deceptive and a void exists where record books, or pages in record books have been lost.

In some of the states with colonial records, the state legislature has required that all of the colonial records be housed in the appropriate state hall of records or archives. In Virginia each county has the prerogative of housing its records within the county court record repository. This means that the records may be found at the county courthouse, in the keeping of the clerk of the circuit court. In this case copies of these records are housed in the Virginia State Archives. In other instances the Virginia State Archives has been selected as the repository of all of the colonial records of a given county. All of which is to say that there is no mandate that the county court records of Virginia be uniformly located in a specified repository. It will be the mission of this introduction to attempt to offer definitive information about, not only the existence, but the whereabouts of the tidewater Virginia county records.

The early settlements of the colony of Virginia were first gathered into four large corporations: Warwick River, Elizabeth City, Accawmack and James Citty. Each corporation contained one or more boroughs in 1619, and was represented by two burgesses in the General Assembly. This organization was not effective because of the geographic distances and agricultural nature of the population. In 1634 the political units designated as plantations and hundreds[1] and represented by thirty-two burgesses in the Assembly, were divided into eight shires and were to be governed as the shires of England. These

---

[1]The hundred was a division of an English county. Originally it was probably one hundred hides of land, or enough land to support one hundred households. Corresponding land divisions were designated in the colonies. The name, such as Bermuda Hundred, still survives in Virginia.

shires, or counties, were called: Accawmack, Charles City, Charles River, Elizabeth City, Henrico, James City, Warrosquyoake and Warwick River.

The shire of Accawmack (Accomac) lay wholly within the Eastern Shore of Virginia. Warrosquyoake (Isle of Wight) lay on the south side of the James River and encompassed the area extending from Chuckatuck Creek to Lawnes Creek. The other six shires formed the genesis of the tidewater Virginia counties from which the counties of this publication evolved. It must be kept in mind, however, that Charles City, Elizabeth City, Henrico and James City also originally were extended to include land on the south side of the James River.

Elizabeth City on the south side of the James became New Norfolk County in 1636. James City lost its area on the south side of the James River to Surry County in 1652. The southern portion (or western as it appears on the map) of Charles City became Prince George County in 1702. Henrico County on the south side of the James became Chesterfield County in 1749. The subsequent history of these counties south of the James will not be presented in this introduction. The records of these counties prior to the dates of these divisions may be included in the exploration of these counties.

Elizabeth City County

Elizabeth City County was named for Elizabeth, the daughter of James I. Its boundaries remained unchanged except for the loss of the territory south of the James. It became extinct in 1952 when it was incorporated into the city of Hampton. Hampton had originally been the county seat, and remains the repository of the old county records. Hampton was established by an act of the assembly in 1680 and was designated a port in 1708. It was first incorporated as a town in 1849. In 1952 it not only took over the county of Elizabeth City but the town of Phoebus.

James City County

James City County was named for James I. Originally "James Citty" referred to the settlement that became know as "Jamestown". Land south of the James became Surry County, then after the formation of New Kent and York counties a portion of these became a part of James City County. Williamsburg is now the county seat of James City County.

Warwick County

Warwick County became designated as such in 1642, after having been identified first as Warwick River, and then in some land patents as Denbigh County after the parish name. It may have been named for the county of Warwick in England. Warwick County became extinct in 1952 when it became the city of Warwick. The name was lost when it was consolidated with the city of Newport News in 1958. Denbigh was the county seat. The records of Warwick County are now maintained in the city of Newport News.

Henrico County

Henrico County was named for Henry, Prince of Wales, the oldest son of James I. It first lost territory on the north side of the James to Goochland County in 1727, then on the south side in 1749. When the city of Richmond was chartered, Henrico County surrounded it on the north side of the James. Early residents of what came to be Richmond, settled in what was then Henrico County. The colonial records of Henrico County are housed in the Virginia State Archives. Other records are at the Henrico County Courthouse, with a city of Richmond address.

Charles City County

Charles City County should not be confused with the original shire of Charles River, the latter is extinct, while the county of Charles City is well and thriving. It was named for Charles I of England and provided the home of many notable Virginians. Its area was enlarged in 1637, then diminished in 1702 when the area south of the James was cut off. The county courthouse is located at Charles City.

Charles River County

The name Charles River was changed to York County in March 1642.

York County

York County was probably named in honor of James, duke of York, the second son of Charles I. The county seat of York County is Yorktown. By the year 1651, Gloucester County had been formed from the eastern part of York County that lay on the north side of the York River.

Gloucester County

Gloucester County was formed in 1651 and probably named for the English county. It may briefly have encompassed the area of Lancaster County south of the Rappahannock River. It lost territory to Mathews County in 1791. The county seat is Gloucester.

Mathews County

Mathews County was formed from Gloucester in 1791, a relative newcomer to tidewater Virginia. It was named for Thomas Mathews, of Norfolk, the speaker of the Virginia House of Delegates at the time the county was formed. The county seat is Mathews.

While York County appears on early maps to lie south and east of James City County, New Kent County was formed from upper York County.

New Kent County

New Kent County was formed in 1654 and was either named for the English county of Kent or for Kent Island in the Chesapeake Bay. William Claiborne, a secretary of the colony, had been driven from Kent Island by Lord Baltimore and settled in the area before the county's formation. New Kent County was the forerunner of a number of Middle Peninsula counties. The county seat is at New Kent.

King and Queen County

King and Queen County, lying within the Middle Peninsula, was formed from New Kent County in 1691. Without identifying them by name, the county was named for William III and Mary II, who were called to the throne of England in 1688. The county seat is King and Queen Courthouse.

King William County

Also lying within the Middle Peninsula was King William County, taken from New Kent and King and Queen counties in 1701. The county was named for King William III. The county seat is King William.

As the settlers pushed further into the wilderness it became apparent that new county divisions were necessary, and new county seats need be established. Each of the petitions from the inhabitants read like a litany of pleas: "Whereas many Inconveniences attend the upper Inhabitants of the County......by reason of their Great distance from the Courthouse and other places usually appointed for Public Meetings......"[2]

Hanover County

Hanover County, geographically located at the top of the Peninsula, was formed from New Kent County in 1720. In a roundabout way, the county was named for George I of England. At the time of his accession to the throne he was elector of Hanover in Germany. The county seat is Hanover.

Caroline County

Caroline County adjoined Hanover County on the north and was formed in 1727 from part of King William County, but also took a part of its territory from King and Queen and Essex counties. An additional area from King and Queen was added later. The county was named for Caroline of Anspach, the consort of George II of England. The county seat is Bowling Green.

Northumberland County

Northumberland County was not one of the eight original shires, but was formed quite early, about 1645, from the Indian district of Chickacoan. Chickacoan was the early Indian name for the region between the Potomac and Rappahannock Rivers that included the area now know as the Northern Neck. The county was probably named for the English county of the same name. While Northumberland County gave up land to other counties it has remained a county in its own right, with the county seat at Heathsville. Lancaster County very shortly became a separate entity.

---

[2]*Virginia Magazine of History and Biography*, Vol. XXIII, July, 1915, 254-55. Original manuscript copies of nine Acts of Assembly found in the Public Record Office in London.

Lancaster County

Lancaster County was formed in 1651 from Gloucester and Northumberland counties. It encompassed land on both sides of the Rappahannock River. The county seat is located at Lancaster. Very early the residents of the south side of the Rappahannock felt exceedingly inconvenienced by the location of the courthouse and petitioned the assembly to be relieved of the burden of travel across the river. The county of Middlesex was formed very shortly.

Middlesex County

Middlesex County was formed about 1669 and was named for the county of the same name in England. The earliest records of Middlesex County are those maintained in Lancaster County. The county seat is located at Saluda.

Westmoreland County

Westmoreland County was formed from Northumberland County in 1653, and named for the English county of the same name. A part of King George County was added to its area later. The county seat is Montross.

Essex County

The early records of Essex County are found under the county name of Old Rappahannock. The county was named for the Rappahannock River, which in turn was named for the Indian tribe of the same name. The county was formed in 1656 from Lancaster County. This county is not to be confused with the contemporary county of Rappahannock that was formed in 1833. The records of Old Rappahannock County are housed with those of Essex County, as the former was abolished in 1692 when Richmond and Essex became separate entities. It is likely that Essex was named for the English county of the same name. The county seat is Tappahannock.

Richmond County

Richmond County was formed in 1692 from Old Rappahannock County. It may have been named for the duke of Richmond, or for the English borough of Richmond. The early records of Richmond County are those of Old Rappahannock County. The county seat is Warsaw.

King George County

King George County was formed from Richmond County in 1720, and named for George I of England. Part of Westmoreland County was added later. The county seat is King George.

## The Geographic Locations

The Peninsula:

Charles City County, Elizabeth City County (City of Hampton), Hanover County, Henrico County, James City County, New Kent County, Warwick County (City of Newport News) and York County.

The Middle Peninsula:

Caroline County, Essex County, Gloucester County, King and Queen County, King William County, Mathews County and Middlesex County.

The Northern Neck:

King George County, Lancaster County, Northumberland County, Richmond County and Westmoreland County.

District Courts:

City of Fredericksburg, King and Queen County, Northumberland County, City of Richmond and City of Williamsburg.

Virginia Lee Hutcheson Davis

References:

Hening, William Waller. *Statutes at Large of Virginia*. Vols.I-XIII. New York. 1823.

Meyer, Virginia M., and John Frederick Dorman. *Adventurers of Purse and Person*. Richmond: Dietz, 1987.

Nugent, Nell Marion. *Cavaliers and Pioneers*, Vol.1. Baltimore: Genealogical. rep. 1991.

Robinson, Morgan Poitiaux. *Bulletin of the Virginia State Library*, Vol.9, Nos.1,2 and 3. Baltimore: Genealogical. rep.1992.

Salmon, Emily J. *A Hornbook of Virginia History*. Richmond: Virginia State Library. 1983.

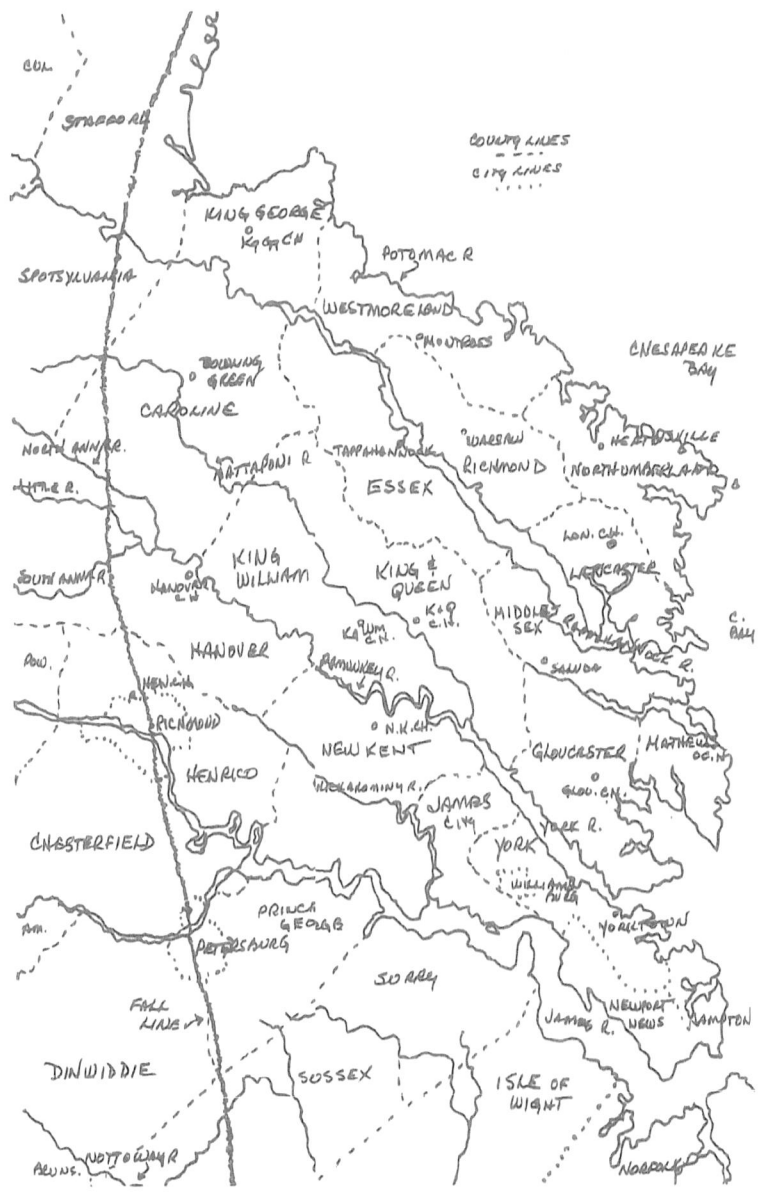

Tidewater Virginia 1985

## Thomas Butler of Tuckoman, King William County

*Butler, Col. Thomas, late of King William County, deceased, his executor, Thomas Butler, will sell his plantation called Tuckoman in King William County.*[1]

This interesting notation was abstracted from the *Virginia Gazette and General Advertiser* for September 9, 1795. It provided the first definitive information as to the location of the plantation of Thomas Butler at the time of his death.[2] Thomas Butler was the son of Samuel Butler of King William County and was probably born about 1734.[3] He died there in late 1794.[4]

As well as can be established, Thomas Butler lived between Judy Swamp and Mehixon Creek,[5] near Dabney's Mill, at least until 1784. The King William Land Tax Records credit him with 600 acres of land from 1782 until 1784. It is inferred that this land was the same land described earlier as adjoining the land of George Dabney and shown on

---

[1]Headley, Robert K., Jr. *Genealogical Abstracts from 18th-Century Virginia Newspapers*. Baltimore: Genealogical. 1987. p.51.

[2]The life of Thomas Butler, his father and grandfather are presented in detail in Davis, Virginia Lee Hutcheson. *Tidewater Virginia Families*. Baltimore: Genealogical. 1990. pp.157-175.

[3]The Keith Patterson Papers. Virginia Historical Society. Richmond, VA; The Josephine Green Fountain Papers, Halifax County Library, Halifax, NC; Chesterfield County Will Book 1, pp.232-233; Chesterfield County Deed Book 2, pp.176-177.

[4]Granville County, NC Deed Book T, pp.396-397; King William County Land Tax Records and Personal Property Records, 1794-1796.

[5]*Genealogies of Virginia Families: Virginia Magazine of History and Biography*. Vol.II. Baltimore: Genealogical. 1981. pp.647-648.

a plat of the land of George Dabney.[6] The Dabney land lay at the forks of the roads to Manquin and Dabney's Mill, with the Pamunkey River nearby. All of the known activities of Thomas Butler during his adult life appear to have taken place in this general area, and with individuals who had associations in or near Aylett.

By the year 1787, Thomas was credited with 450 acres of land, along with the notation in the alterations that Thomas had never listed fifty acres. From 1787 until the year 1794, only the land transfers (alterations) were given in the King William Land Tax Records. In 1792 Thomas sold 458 acres to James Govan, along with this information was the notation that Thomas had gained eight acres by the survey of the land. It would appear from this information that Thomas had removed himself from the Mehixon Creek area.

It is interesting that Thomas Butler was never credited with the 1030 acres of land belonging to Tuckoman until after his death. The land was listed in the name of Thomas Butler, Sen. in 1795 and in the name of John Butler in 1796, with the notation "Thomas' Est." following the name. This same year the land was sold to James Price.[7]

The advertisement that appeared in the *Virginia Gazette and General Advertizer* reveals much about the life style of Thomas Butler and about his plantation:

"To Be Sold...
Agreeable to the last will and testament[8] of Colonel Thomas Butler, deceased, on Wednesday the 30th day of September next on the premises.

---

[6]*GVF:VMHB*. 647-648.

[7]King William County Land Tax Records, 1782-1797.

[8]The will did not survive among the King William County records. It has been related that a copy of the will survived with his descendants in Granville County, NC; however, it seems to have disappeared and no record could be found among the court records relating to the disposition of his land in Granville County.

That well know Tract of land called Tuckoman lying in King William County pleasantly situated on the Pamunkey River twelve miles below the courthouse of the said county and eight miles above West Point; containing by a late survey Eleven hundred [sic] and Thirty acres, five hundred and thirty of which is high land and the balance marsh; about three hundred acres of the high land cleared and the residue in prime wood, on which is an excellent new two-story dwelling house, 36 by 34, a new kitchen, dairy, meat house, and corn house, all of which has been built within the last four years; there is also an excellent fishery, together with an abundance of wild fowl on the land. It is unnecessary to detail further particulars on the advantages of the seat Above described possesses as it is presumed that any person willing to become a purchaser will first view the premises. The land will be shewed by Thomas Butler who lives five miles above, to any person inclined to purchase. The terms of payment will be one third in one year one third in two years and the remaining in three years the purchaser giving bond and approved security to the executor.

Also will be sold on the same place and day all the stock of horses cattle sheep and hogs, household and kitchen furniture and plantation utensils. Cash will be required on all sums not exceeding five pounds, nine months credit will be allowed on all sums above five pounds giving bond and approved security to the executor."

The plantation Tuckoman has survived today. It is located on the west side of present-day State Route 30, east of Sweet Hall. It is a working farm, and while the present home dates back to the early 1800s, it is not the house in which Thomas Butler lived. It is set back from the highway, amid tall stately trees, magnolias and boxwoods and is clearly visible at the end of a long lane across cultivated fields. Tuckoman is privately owned and is not open to the public. The people in the area call it "Tuck'-o-mn", while those in the upper end of the county call it "Tuc-Kow'-mn".

The first record of the marsh called Tococomans (sic) occurs in the land patent of William Claiborne[9] in December 1657; it was described as lying adjacent to his plantation[10]. It appears that it was, in fact, a part of the original grand patent of Claiborne for 5000 acres in 1653.[11] This land was described as lying on the north side of the Pamunkey River in the Narrows, adjoining the land of Captain John West, thence in a westerly direction to a point of land where the said Colonel Clayborne (sic) landed the Army under his command in 1644. His plantation was called Romancoke.

Claiborne later gave the land of Tuckoman to his son, Captain Thomas Claiborne by deed of gift in 1673; it was a part of the original Sweet Hall dividend. After his death in 1732, the land passed to his son, Nathaniel Claiborne, who devised the land by will to his son, Thomas Claiborne. It seems that Thomas had continued financial problems and in 1772 offered the Tuckoman Tract for sale.[12] Robert Ruffin, of the Surry County Ruffins, was living at Windsor by 1768, with land on the Pamunkey River just above Sweet Hall and Tuckoman by Ruffin's Ferry.[13] It was his son, Sterling who apparently purchased Tuckoman

---

[9]William Claiborne was chosen by the Virginia Company as surveyor of the colony. He arrived in Jamestown in 1621 and was responsible for the laying out of the area known as New Towne. He was appointed to the Council in 1623, served as Secretary of the Colony (1625-1635, 1652-1660) and as Treasurer (1642-1660).
Jester, Annie Lash and Martha Woodroof Hiden. *Adventurers of Purse and Person*. NV: Princeton. 1956. pp.131-132.

[10]Land Patent Book 4, p.145; Nugent, Nell Marion. *Cavaliers and Pioneers*. Vol.I. Baltimore: Genealogical. pp.358-359.

[11]Land Patent Book 3, p.33; Harris, Dr. Malcolm H. *Old New Kent County Some Account of The Planters, Plantations, and Places in New Kent County*. Vol.II. Virginia: West Point. n.d. pp.601-605.

[12]Harris 601.

[13]Harris 606-607.

from Thomas Claiborne, for he was credited with 2000 acres of land in the land tax records of 1782.

The loss of the deeds and other records of King William County make it very difficult to follow exactly what really happened with the land. It seems from a deed dated 1792[14] that Henry Young deeded to Sterling Ruffin, 2000 acres of land lying on the south side of the road to West Point, on the south side of the Pamunkey River.[15] In 1796 Sterling Ruffin and his wife, Alice conveyed to John Butler of the City of Richmond, a part of the large tract. The conveyance was for 530 acres of high land and 500 acres of marsh contiguous to, known by the name of Tuckoman.[16] The record of this sale, as well as the sale by John Butler have survived.[17]

It is difficult to reconcile what has survived and is known from the county records with what is inferred from the description of the sale of the property of Thomas Butler. While it can be assumed that a deed to Tuckoman has not survived, no explanation can be found for the fact that land was deeded by Sterling Ruffin to John Butler in 1796, or that the Tuckoman acreage was not credited to Thomas Butler prior to his death. It would seem that he was in possession of the land and living on it from the year 1792. The date given for the construction of the home coincides with this date.

Dr. Harris related in his book that a cellar and some colonial type bricks were found where the early house stood, near where the Southern Railway (now Norfolk Southern Railroad) crossed the back

---

[14]King William County Records, 1700-1785, p.143.

[15]While the directions don't quite agree with a contemporary description of the land, it is the same land.

[16]King William County Records, Book 3, p.207.

[17]Book 3,140.

field.[18] A description of this house was found in an insurance policy of 1805:[19]

"William Ring, residing at Tuckoman, between the plantation of Robert Slaughter and G. W. P. Custis: Dwelling for $2500, Kitchen for $210, Dairy for $130. Wooden dwelling house 40 x 40 2 storeys underpinned with brick 3 ½ ft above ground; wooden kitchen 20 x 16 one storey."

This agrees with the description of the home of Thomas Butler, with perhaps an addition that increased the outside dimensions of the house. Dr. Harris further stated that this house burned during the occupancy of the Richards family, who acquired the plantation about 1828.[20]

Dr. John Richards inherited the home from his sisters, Eliza and Penelope Richards and bequeathed it to his son, Dr. Buchan Richards. It was while he was living in the home that it burned and the dwelling was built that now faces the King William Road. The property ultimately went to his son, then his niece, Mrs. Frank Holman. She was buried at Tuckoman on July 16, 1976. Tuckoman remains in her family.[21]

Some further notes about the activities of Thomas Butler of King William County, found in the Journal of Council of the State of Virginia[22]:

December 1776    Warrant to Captain Thomas Butler pay roll for his company of King William militia.

---

[18]Harris 603.

[19]Mutual Insurance Policy 1805 No.529-770-648.

[20]Harris 604.

[21]Harris 604.

[22]*Journals of Council of the State of Virginia*. McIlwaine, H R, ed. Vols.I, II & IV. Richmond: VSL. 1932. pp.279, 132, 158.

| | |
|---|---|
| March 1777 | Liston Temple appointed inspector at Aylett's and Todd's warehouses in room of Thomas Butler, resigned. |
| June 1778 | Thomas Butler among Commissioners named to hear petitions from persons damaged by destruction of King William records by fire. |
| November 1789 | Appointed sheriff of King William County in room of William D. Claiborne who declined acting another year. |
| January 1790 | John Hill appointed sheriff of King William County in room of Thomas Butler "who hath been unable to give bond according to law." |

So the threads of the life of Thomas Butler are picked up and woven into a part of the fabric. It is tantalizing to be able to visit the places that Thomas visited, to be familiar with the area in which he lived, and yet be unable to reconstruct his life. Many questions remain. It is believed that he married twice. The name of his wife, or wives, is not known. Nothing in the history of King William County or Thomas Butler reveals his closest associations, nor the name of the early home he made for his family[23].

Virginia Lee Hutcheson Davis

---

[23]Davis *TVF*. see Thomas Butler II.

## Yeocomico Church, Cople Parish
## Westmoreland County

A visit to Yeocomico Church, set in a grove of fine old oak trees, with abundant dogwood and red bud trees, delights the beholder. It is a place of quiet beauty that transcends time and reminds one, not only of his God, but of his heritage.

Yeocomico is one of the most historic churches in America. Among its congregations were persons associated with the founding of the Virginia, Plymouth, Amsterdam and Maryland colonies. The first church, one of the ancient outposts of Christianity in the New World, was a frame structure, built in 1655 on the site of the present church. The existing brick church was built in 1706 during the rectorship of the Reverend Samuel Gray, the bricks having been burned in a kiln on the grounds.

This beautiful little church stands within a completely rural setting, reminiscent of the setting of which it was a part when it was constructed in 1706. Forests and cultivated fields are its companions today, as were the forests and wilderness at that time.[24] It is two miles from the Yeocomico River, an estuary of the lower Potomac River. In the vicinity of "Old Yeocomico" in the Colonial period were the estates of such families as the Washingtons, Lees and Carters. Among the plantations in that section of Westmoreland County were Sandy Point, the home of Colonel George Eskridge, the guardian of Mary Ball; the home of Captain Henry Lee; Mount Pleasant, the home of George Lee and his wife Ann Fairfax; and Nomini Hall, the home of Councilor Robert Carter.

Yeocomico Church is built in the form of a cross, with the chancel in the east gable, surmounted by a Georgian window. It is an illustration of the transition that occurred in colonial architecture at the beginning of the eighteenth century. It is thought that the present form of the building is the result of the addition of the T-wing about 1730-

---

[24] It is on the west side of County Road 606 before the crossroads of Tucker Hill. Traveling west on State Route 202 from Callao, one turns northeast on County Road 604, then north on 606.

1740.[25] The old brick work is of special interest, being strangely inconsistent in its execution. There are no less than eleven sets of initials molded in the bricks, suggesting the participation of a number of workers. The construction date of 1706 is also molded into one of the bricks.

The large door in the south end of the church is the original door from the 1655 church and has a wicket door (a smaller door cut into a larger door) to be used in cold weather. This is a common feature of medieval English churches but a unique survival in this country. In the yard is a sundial bearing the date of 1717, which is as accurate today as it was then. Inside the church the brick floor and white woodwork and walls lend an air of simplicity and quaintness to the reverence of the setting. At the north end of the church is a gallery, said to have been the seating space for the early slaves and carriage drivers.

After the Revolutionary War and the withdrawal of the English clergy, the church was deserted and unused for some years. It was occupied by British soldiers during both the Revolutionary War and the War of 1812. Union soldiers occupied it during the Civil War. Despite all of this, the church has survived in a remarkably good state of preservation. Both the communion table and the reading desk, in the church today are pieces of original furniture, and have withstood the ravages of time.

The Reverend Alan B. Hooker is the Rector of the Cople Parish churches. The church is meticulously cared for by Mr. Samuel Gaskins, Jr. the present sexton. The grounds are as beautifully kept as the church itself, and are a tribute to a caring congregation and church family. The church cemetery is enclosed in an old brick wall and that part near the church building is the final resting place of a number of eighteenth century members.            Virginia Lee Hutcheson Davis

Taken from the Yeocomico Church Bulletin, Sunday, March 29, 1992 and used with the kind permission of the Reverend Alan B. Hooker and Cople Parish.

---

[25]Loth, Calder, ed. *The Virginia Landmarks Register*. 3rd Ed. Charlottesville: University. 1987. p.481.

## Tithables, Lancaster County, 1659

A list of all of the tithable males of Lancaster County was recorded for the assessment of the tax for the year 1659. A tithable was the male freeholder who was taxable. Widows were listed as heads of households, and the number of males who were eligible for taxation were listed with her name. Traditionally a tithe was considered to be one-tenth of a person's income, to be given to support the church. The tax in this case supported the business of the county. The expenses were listed in pounds of tobacco, as the medium of exchange, and divided among the total number of tithables in the county. Thus the individual tax assessment was that person's share of the total number of pounds of tobacco required to pay the county's expenses. For the year 1659 the individual assessment was 37 pounds of tobacco.

A list of the tithables is of value in identifying the county of residence of an individual at a given time.

At a court, Lancaster County, November 30, 1659.

Coll: Jo: Carter to collect for 105 tithables

| Name | No. | Name | No. |
|---|---|---|---|
| Coll: Jo: Carter | 30 | Richd Gorsuch | 05 |
| Mr Hawke | 01 | Mr fflower | 02 |
| Mr Math: Kempe | 10 | Nich George Sen | 01 |
| Wm Clappam Jun | 06 | Jo: Edwards | 02 |
| Edward Lundsford | 01 | Mr Connoway | 02 |
| Tho: Philips | 01 | Jo: Jones | 01 |
| Wm: Wignor | 01 | Walt Herd | 01 |
| Jn: Taylor | 01 | Will Cromp | 01 |
| Wm: Hutchins | 03 | Jo: Meredith | 03 |
| Wm: Clark Sen | 04 | Hugh Kinsey | 05 |
| Walter Dickenson | 05 | Tho: Powell | 02 |
| Howell Powell | 01 | Charles Kinge | 01 |
| Mr Ball | 04 | Arth: Clarke | 01 |
| Mr Roots | 04 | Will: Wroughton | 04 |

| | | | | |
|---|---|---|---|---|
| Sam: Tucker | 02 | | Will: Abbey | 01 |

Coll: Fleet to collect for 36 tithables

| | | | | |
|---|---|---|---|---|
| Mr Maidsson | 1 | | Richd the Irishman | 1 |
| Hugh Brent | 1 | | Ever Peterson | 3 |
| Willm Shirt | 1 | | Ebby Bonnison[3] | 5 |
| [n.o.] Tabb[1] | 4 | | Toby Horton | 4 |
| Sam: Sloper | 1 | | Robt Sison | 1 |
| [n.o.] Lippit[2] | 1 | | Coll: ffleet | 10 |
| Mr Lawson | 3 | | | |

Mr Potter 103 persons

| | | | | |
|---|---|---|---|---|
| Coll: Robt Smith | 25 | | Sir Hen: Chichley qt | 37 |
| Sander Smith | 2 | | Jo: Jackson | 4 |
| Mrs. Duncombe[4] | 5 | | Mr Jo: Curtys | 7 |
| Robt Osborn | 3 | | Will: Butcher | 3 |
| Sir Gray Skipwith | 5 | | Jo: Smith | 2 |
| Mr Potter | 8 | | Lambert Moore | 2 |

Leech to collect for 22 persons

| | | | | |
|---|---|---|---|---|
| Lt. Coll. Ellyott | 14 | | Mr Leech | 8 |

Mr Kempe to collect for 65 persons

| | | | | |
|---|---|---|---|---|
| Mr. Coks plantacon | 2 | | Jo: Bell | 2 |
| Tho: Hayward | 1 | | Jo: Needles | 5 |
| Will Harper | 2 | | Goodman Harper | 2 |
| Michl Hill | 3 | | Goodman Waterman | 2 |
| Patricke Miller | 3 | | Arthur Nash | 3 |
| James Bonner | 5 | | Mr Kempe | 5 |
| Mr Wadding | 3 | | Rowland Haddaway | 3 |
| Mr Walterton | 6 | | Mr Rigsby | 5 |
| Jo: Richards | 2 | | Mr Keeble | 4 |

| | | | |
|---|---|---|---|
| Edward Webb | 1 | Mr Carborrow | 2 |
| Mr Bonen[t] | 4 | | |

Mr Corbyn to collect for [illeg.] persons

| | | | |
|---|---|---|---|
| Tho: Kidd | 2 | Tho: Chatwyn | 2 |
| Mr Wyllis | 2 | Robt. Taylor | 3 |
| Mr Holart | 3 | Mr Perrott | 8 |
| Richd Lewys | 4 | Mr Marsh | 8 |
| Jo: Welsh | 5 | Widd Segar[5] | 3 |
| Tho: Williams | 2 | Dan: Johnson | 2 |
| Andrew Butcher | 1 | Mrs Montague[6] | 4 |
| Jo: Vause | 4 | Mr Cocke | 4 |
| Will: Ludford | 1 | Will: Thompson | 2 |
| Hen: Nichols | 4 | Jo: Jadwyn | 2 |
| Robt Kempe | 2 | Jo: Hudson | 1 |
| Robt. Chowning | 3 | Mr Corbyn | 22 |
| Mr Patteson | 5 | Abraham Weeks | 3 |
| Wm. Copeland | 1 | James Macknum | 2 |
| Dan: Wilsh | 4 | Hen: Thatcher | [blot] |

Edward Dale to collect for 94 persons

| | | | |
|---|---|---|---|
| Mr Travers | 8 | Nich: Hale | 3 |
| Tho: Williams | 2 | Robt Pritchard | 2 |
| Bryan Stott | 1 | Jo: Sharpe | 3 |
| Jo: Simpson | 2 | Mr ffox | 14 |
| Tho: Stott | 2 | Jo: Haselwood | 5 |
| Mr Powell | 5 | Mr Edwards | 5 |
| Geo. Vezey | 3 | Mr Dale | 4 |
| Jo: Willis | 3 | Jo: Nichols | 1 |
| James Gates | 3 | Mick Arme | 2 |
| Will: Thomas | 1 | Mr Neesham | 5 |
| Hen: Pulman | 3 | Jo: Pine | 6 |
| Robt Pollard | 4 | Mr Merryman | 2 |

Hen: Davys          4          Mr Therriott          2

Transcribed by VLHD

Lancaster County Orders, Etc. No.3, 1656-1666. pp.101-105. Published with the kind permission of Dr. Louis H. Manarin, State Archivist.

1. Sparacio, Ruth and Sam. *Deed and Will Abstracts of Lancaster County, Virginia* McLean: Antient. 1991. p 122.

2. Listed in Sparacio (37) as Will:.

3. Listed in Nugent (355) as Eppy.

4. Listed in Sparacio (33) as widow of Thos.

5. Listed in Sparacio (30) as Widow of Oliver.

6. Listed in Sparacio (20) as Widow of Peter.

Cople Parish, Yeocomico Church, Westmoreland County, Virginia

## Civil Appointments
## Charles City County, 1780-1787
### Submitted by Minor Tompkins Weisiger

These Civil Appointments from the Executive Department provide information of the lives and business of the residents of Charles City County. They have been selected for the counties of tidewater Virginia, and particularly those counties for which the county order books do not generally exist. There are not files for every year, or for all appointments made within a year. They are transcribed rather than presented as abstracts, to provide all of the information possible. In some cases the actual signatures of the persons writing the notation will also be presented.

At a Court held for Charles City County Decr. 5. 1780

Freeman Walker David Minge & William Christian Gent. are by the Court recommended to his excellency the Governor[26] of this Commonwealth as proper persons to execute the Office of Sheriff of this County, the ensuing year.

*Mordecai Debnam C.C.C.*

A Copy Teste
Mordecai Debnam C.C.C.

---

[26]Governors of the Commonwealth of Virginia during the time of these Civil Appointments were:
    Thomas Jefferson, 2 June 1779-3 June 1781
    William Fleming, 4-12 June 1781
    Thomas Nelson, Jr. 12 June-22 November 1781
    David Jameson, 22-30 November 1781
    Benjamin Harrison, 1 December 1781-30 November 1784
    Patrick Henry, 30 November 1784-30 November 1786
    Edmund Randolph, 30 November 1786-12 November 1788
Salmon, Emily J. *A Hornbook of Virginia History*. Richmond: Virginia State Library. 1983. p.77.

Ch. City

I hearby certify that Freeman Walker & David Minge two of the above mentioned Gent. are dead Since the recommendation.

James New DC 4 March 1781

At a Court held for Charles City County December 6: 1780

John Major, Edward Marable, Joseph Vaiden & John West are by the Court recommended to his excellency the Governor as proper persons to execute the office of inspector at the publick warehouse at Kennons in the County.

A Copy  Mord: Debnam C.C.C.

At a court continued and held for Charles City County April the 4: 1781

The Court doth hereby recommend Otway Byrd, Henry Armistead, Stith Hardyman, Benjamin Edmondson & Henry Vaughan Gent. to his excellency the Governor of this Commonwealth, as proper persons to be added to the Commission of the peace, and Commission of Ayer & Terminer for this County.

A Copy Test Mord: Debnam C.C.C.

At a Court held for Charles City County the 5th day of April 1781

Philip Par[r] Edmondson Gent. is hereby recommended to his Excellency the Governor of this Commonwealth as a proper person to execute the office of Coroner of this county, according to law.

Teste Mord: Debnam C.C.C.
A Copy James New Cl Cur

At a Court held for Charles City County Augt. 7 1782

Henry Southall Peter Royster and Otway Byrd Gent. are hereby recommended to his excellency the Governor of this Commonwealth as proper persons to execute the offfice of Sheriff of this County for the ensuing year

            A Copy J New Cl Cur

At a Court held for Charles City County May 5th 1784

Philip Parr Edmondson, William Green Munford and Otway Byrd Gent. are recommended to his excellency the Governor as proper persons to Execute the office of Sheriff of this County for the Ensuing year

          A Copy  Peter Royster Cl. Cur.

[Notations made later on two copies of the same recommendations]
N.B. I do hereby Certify that the Two first Gentleman in the above recommendation are Dead and that this County at present is without a Sheriff. [n.d.]             Peter Royster

I hereby certifie that Mr Philip Parr Edmondson the person first Mentioned in the recommendation died the 22nd day of October 1784. His Excellency the Governor.

            Peter Royster Cl Cur
            Octor. 22nd 1784

At a Court held for Charles City County May 5th 1784

William Lightfoot William Royall & Joseph Vaiden are recommended to his Excellency the Governor as proper Persons to be added to the Commission of the Peace in this County.
         A Copy Peter Royster Cl. Cur.

At a Court held for Charles City County the 4th day of August 1784.

Edward Marrable, Joseph Vaiden Gent. and John Major are recommended to his Excellency the Governor as proper persons to serve as Inspectors of Tobacco at Kennons Warehouse in this County.
         A Copy Peter Royster  Clk Court

Charles City December Court 1784

Benjamin Harrison Esqr. by the Unanimous opinion of the Court is desired to be continued as Senior Majestrate [sic] in the Commission of the peace for this County, John Tyler, James Southall, John Colgin and Richmond Terrell, Gent are by the Court recommended as proper persons to be added to the Commission of the Peace for this County.
A Copy Peter Royster C,C,C,

At a Monthly Court held for Chas. City County 6th day of Decemr. 1786

John Harwood & Henry Vaughan produced Comms. from his Excellency the Governor appointing them Captains of the Militia in this County and took the usual oath prescribed by Law.
A Copy Peter Royster C,C,C,

Same Court:
Henry Edlow produced a Commission from his Excellency the Governor appointing him Ensign of the militia and took the usual oath according to Law.
A Copy P. Royster C,C,C,

At a Session Court held for Charles City County 4th day of Novr. 1786

Benjamin Harrison Gent. produced a Commission from his Excellency Patrick Henry Esq. our Governor & Chief Magistrate appointing him County Lieutenant for this County the same being read the said Harrison took the oath prescribed by Law
Peter Royster the same as Colonel of the Militia
Henry Armistead the same as Lieut. Colonel. do.
John Gregory the same as Major. do.
Stith Hardyman the same as Captain. do.
Wm. Royall, Charles Christian & Edmund Christian the same as Lieutenants. do.
A Copy Peter Royster C,C,C,

To His Excellency the Governor of Virginia
    The Petition of Gideon Bradley of Chas. City County Humbly Sheweth;
        That your petitioner being a single man took his neice to keep his house, but she proving a lewd woman, had two children, on which account he was presented by the Grand jury, & a fine of £50 laid on him, by the Worshipful Court of the County; your petitioner directly put the woman away, & soon after Intermarried with a respectable widow with several small children, whose maintenance intirely depend on his labour & industry. Now Sir, in case this heavy fine should be levied (or so much thereof as is unpaid) [interlined notation: being £17.15] on the few necessaries he's possess'd of, it will utterly disable him from supporting his poor helpless family, & moreover will (its very likely) distroy the Love & harmony which now Subsists between him & his wife; wherefore your petitioner humbly begs your Excellency would be pleased to consider his case, & grant him such relief as to you in your wisdom may seem meet; Yr petitioner shall pray be

[signed] Henry Southall
[signed] Wm Christian

Recd. Decr. 21. [17]86
Rejected Jan 15. [17]87

Transcribed by VLHD

*To be continued*

From the records of the Executive Department, Commonwealth of Virginia. Virginia State Library and Archives. Box 3, A-E. Pre 1790. Published with the kind permission of Dr. Louis H. Manarin, State Archivist.

Petition, Caroline County, 1821
Reedy Church and Bull Church

A Petition was presented to the Virginia Legislature on December 17, 1821 requesting that the property of the disestablished Anglican Churches, Reedy Church and Bull Church in Caroline County be returned to people of St. Margaret's Parish, Caroline County. It is presented in its entirety, not only for its historical interest, but also to identify the freeholders living in St. Margaret's Parish that may not be found by other means. This is a transcription of the original document which contains the original signatures of the petitioners.
"The petition of the freeholders and housekeepers of St. Margaret's Parish in the county of Caroline to the legislature of Virginia. Your petitioners beg leave today before your honorable body the subject of churches so far as they are interested They represent that these are two Churches in St. Margarent's Parish one of which is called the Reedy Church has fallen; the other called the Bull Church is unfit for religious purposes being so far in a state of decay that it will not afford a shelter from snow, rain or inclement weather; and believing it impracticable and needless to have the said Churches rebuilt or repaired at this time, there being houses for religious worship conveniently interspersed throughout the sd. parish And whereas the general Assembly by their Act passed January 24th 1799 repealed all Laws relative to the late Protestant Episcopal Church and declared a true esposition of the principles of the bill of rights and Constitution respecting the same, to be contained in the Act entitled "An Act for establishing religious freedom" thereby recognizing the principle that all property formerly belonging to the said Church of every description, devolved on the good people of the Commonwealth on the dissolution of the British government here in the same degree in which the right and interest of the said Church was derived therein from them. And whereas by one other act passed January 12th 1802 entitled "An Act concerning the Glebe lands and Churches within this commonwealth" have given the power to the Overseer of the Poor to sell Glebe Lands; but not the Churches; and have said in the sd. recited Act that nothing herein contained shall authorize a sale of the Churches Etc. Your petitioners

pray a sale of the Churches Etc. your petitioners pray the general assembly to pass an Act authorizing the Overseers of the poor to sell the ruins of the said Reedy Church and the Bull Church and the vestry houses belonging there for their benefit as the same were built by levies upon them and their property and that the proceeds of the Sale be applied in any way that a majority of the freeholders and housekeepers in said parish may direct and your petitioners will ever pray."

[Signed]

| | | |
|---|---|---|
| | | John Eubank |
| Benj Baughan Jr | Samuel Terrell | Benj Marshall |
| Benj Baughan Sr | Jno Terrell | Wm Burruss Sr |
| John Oliver | Patrick Bricuit | John Young |
| Henry Hill | Augustine Harris | Henry Morgan |
| Nathl Ware | George Madison | Hawes Coleman |
| Mathew Hundley | Winston Haley | Richard Pain |
| James Guy | Thomas Cleer | William Luck |
| Mau[blot] McDry | William Roots | Wm Newton |
| Richard Peatross | J D G Brown | Reuben Turner |
| Joseph Minor | Geo W Madison | Richard Hutcheson |
| Saml Lawrence | Wm Richison | Pholess[?] Samuel |
| Jno Hensley | Samuel Coleman | Archl Samuel |
| Joseph Tiller | Sen | Robert Cobb |
| Jno Haley | Henry Doggett | Mat Campbell |
| Geo. F Guy | Geo P Whitlock | John Jones |
| Flurry Seay | Saml Madison | Benjamin W Hurt |
| Elijah Priddy | James Dickens | H G Rainey |
| William Dunn | Walker Cobb | Thos H Burke |
| Gregory Moore | Rufus Chandler | John M Burke |
| Saml Burruss | James Madison | John Gatewood |
| Wm Norment | Isaac Butler | Nathaniel Young |
| Joseph H Laurence | James Young | Wm Green |
| Wm E Bower | Philip Thornton | Spilsbe Woolfolk |
| Charles Atkinson | as to Reedy Ch | Achillis Woolfolk |
| Thos T Harris | Robt Goodloe | Meriday Haley |
| Thomas Ship | as to Reedy Ch | F Dickinson |
| Timothy Chandler | Thomas Marshall | Thos Burruss |
| Zacheus Campbell | as to Reedy Ch | Wm H Peatross |
| Thomas Samuel | Wm D Coleman | Norborne P[illeg] |

| | | |
|---|---|---|
| Thos Marshall | as to Reedy Ch | George White |
| Jno P Samuel | Thos C Clayton | Thos Anderson |
| Jno. W Laughlin | Thomas B Coleman | as to Reedy Ch |
| Thos Wilson | as to Reedy Ch | Jos Flippo Jr |
| William Taliaferro | William Bell | as to Reedy Ch |
| John Smith | as to Reedy Ch | Moses Jones |
| Allen Apperson | Saml Terrell | as to Reedy Ch |
| Alfred D Brown | Jesse Terrell | James Harriss do |
| Wm Thompson | as to Reedy Ch | Elliott Campbell do |
| Pleasant Burruss | Christopher Terrell | Michael W Yates do |
| John Sutton Jr | William Campbell | James Gatewood do |
| John Size | William H Bullard | Wilson Swan do |
| Charles R Carr | John Goodloe | Wm White do |
| as to Reedy Ch | A[chilles] Duling | V Thacker do |
| William Penny | Lewis George | |
| Wml Burruss | | |

do is ditto as to Reedy Church

The history of both Bull Church and Reedy Church is obscure. Conflicting information is found about the formation of both churches, due to the significant loss of the early records of Caroline County. Bull Church has been reputed to be the oldest church in St. Margaret's Parish in Caroline County. It was built on land owned by Charles Yarbrough, it has been thought, about 1740[27]; however, it was not mentioned in the records until 1743, and Yarbrough did not acknowledge his deed to the vestry of the parish until 1747. Chesterfield Church[28] was mentioned in the Caroline County Court Order Books as early as 1732, and permission to build Reedy Church

---

[27]Mason, George Carrington. *Colonial Churches of Tidewater Virginia*. Richmond: Whittet. 1945. p.313.

[28]Chesterfield Church was built on the tract of land which lies south of the road leading from present day Ruther Glen to Carmel. Carmel is located at the intersection of US Routes 1 and 207.

was secured in 1741.[29] These were also churches in St. Margaret's Parish. Bull Church was located several miles west of what is now Penola, on the north side of the road leading from Ladysmith eastward. Reedy Church has been conclusively identified as having been located at what is now the intersection of County Roads 656 and 654[30]. It is believed that the present St. Paul's United Methodist Church was built on the location of the old Reedy Church.

Transcribed by VLHD

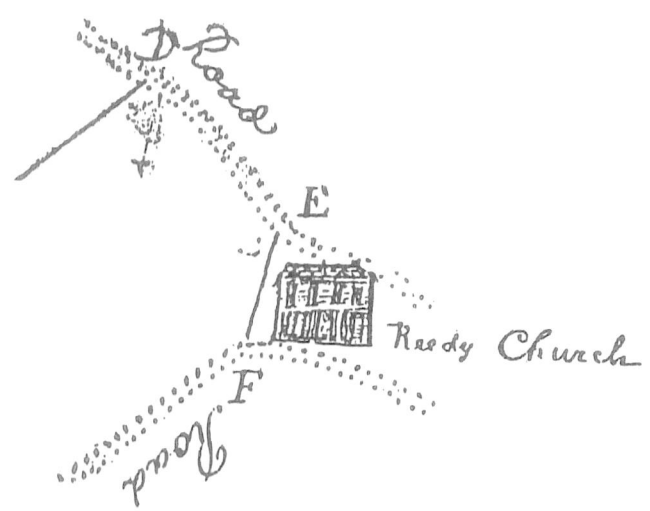

Sketch enlarged from Plat of land of Thomas Butler; 1820
Caroline County Court Records
Box 2, Folder 10, Plat S.

---

[29]Campbell, T Elliott. *Colonial Caroline*. Richmond: Dietz. 1954. pp.100-101.

[30]Davis. *TVF* (1989) pp.88,320,332. (1990) pp.69,276,285.

## Will of James Cathon, 1696
## Warwick County

I James Cathon of Warwk. county Cooper being Sick and weake of body but well in minde and understanding Doe make this my last Will and Testament in manner and form as followeth.

ffirst I Give and bequeath unto my Son William Cathon to him and his heirs for ever the plantation I now Live on ye land being bounded as followeth on a branch on ye west side of my house that runs to the broad[?] Swamp and So on ye Swamp side easerly unto ye Easerly ye branch of the fork that comes out of the main branch & So from thence to a Great pine that marked four ways & from thence my line to a Corner white Oake of William Norards[?] and to the branch again westerly 2:dg I Give and bequeath unto my Son John Cathon and to his heirs Lawfully begotten for ever all my Land on the west side of that branch which is my Son William Cathons bounds.

3dly: I give and bequeath unto my Son James Cathon and to his heirs for ever all my land thats Lying on William Cathons line and so to ye head of Waters Creek bounding on Peter Lawens Land but if it so happens that my Son James should dye without Issue or else not come to live on the said Land then my Will is that ye Land should desend to my Son William Cathon his heirs for ever.

4th: I give and bequeath unto my three Sons William John and James one hundred acres of Land which is in the Swamp bythe running Creeke to them and their heirs for to Supply them with timber about their occations for their plantacons use or they may Divide the Land between themselves if any one is agreived.

5th: My Will is that if my Sons William Cathon Sould dye without Issue then the Said Land which I gave hime to desend unto my Son John Cathon and his heirs for ever.

6th  All ye rest of my Estate after my just debts are paid I give & bequeath unto my Son Wm Cathon whom I make & appoint my whole & Sole Exec. of this my last Will & Testamt. In Testimony of what is writen on this & ye other Side I have here unto Set to my hand & Seal this 21th day of ye 4th Month called June 1696.

Signed and Sealed in presence of us
    James [his mark MF] Cathon
    Jno: [his mark IM] Matticoat Seal
    Jno: [his mark X] Spires Seal
    Ann [her mark A] Hopson

At a Court for Warwk. County Novr. 22d. 1697. This will was proved by ye Oaths of Jno. Matticoat and Jno. Spires & Ann Hopson ye Witnesses [illeg.] Probate hereby Granted Wm Cathon the Exer. hereby appointed.                         Col Miles Cary Cl. Cut.

                                    Transcribed by VLHD

Miscellaneous Records. Warwick County Deeds & Etc. 1695-1697. p.455. Virginia State Library and Archives. Published with the kind permission of Dr. Louis H. Manarin, State Archivist.

## Miller Family Bible
## Hanover County, 1824-1894

### James Miller Bible

Marriages

In Richmond Va

Decr. 8th 1847. By Revd. J. C. Stiles Jas. Miller to Susan J Reeve

In Ashland Va

Oct. 28th 1875 By Revd. M. D. Hoge F. M. Wright Jr. to Sue Daughter of Jas. & S. J. Miller.

In Ashland

Oct. 25th 1876 By Revd. M. D. Hoge. J. M. Leake to Lizzie daughter of Jas & S. J. Miller.

[In different handwriting]

In Ashland, Virginia, November 7th 1894 by Rev. B. A. Pendleton, Fleming Milton Fox to Fannie daughter of James & Sue J Miller.

Births

[In original hndwriting]

James Miller

Son of Hugh & Mary Miller born at Holmhead Stuartin Ayashire Scotland April 17th 1824.

Susan Joanna

Daughter of John F & E P Reeve born at French Hay Hanover Va. Ap 9th 1828.

Mary Eliza

Daugher of Jas & S J Miller born in Richmond Va Feby 12th 1849.

Hugh

Son of Jas & S J Miller born in Richmond Va April 3rd 1851.

Elizabeth (Lizzie)
Daughter of Jas & S J Miller born near Richmond Va Jany: 29th 1853.

Susan (Sue)
Daughter of Jas & S J Miller born near Richmond Va Sept 25th 1854.

James Caskie
Son of Jas & S J Miller born in Richmond Va Aug 6th 1857.

Fannie Martin
Daughter of Jas & S J Miller born in Chapel Hill N. C. June 27th 1862.

Margaret Caskie
Daughter of Jas & S J Miller born in Richmond Va Jany 11th 1868.

Roberta Bolling
Daughter of F M & Sue Wright born in Ashland Va May 21st 1878.

John Marion Leake
Son of J M & Lizzie Leake born in Ashland Va May 21st 1878.

Margaret Caskie Miller
Daughter of F M & Sue Wright born in Petersburg Va Jany 10th 1879

James Miller
Son of J M & Lizzie Leake born in Ashland Va Oct 1st 1879.

Transcribed VLHD

Miller Family Bible, Hanover County, 1824-1894. Virginia State Library and Archives. Accession Number 33775. Published with the kind permission of Dr. Louis H. Manarin, State Archivist.

## Parrish Family Graveyard
## King and Queen County

These inscriptions were transcribed in November 1991 by the editor. Some of the graves are enclosed with a wrought iron fence. Others are outside the fence. It appears that there are also unmarked graves. The graveyard is located in the yard of what is known as the "Old Garnett Home". The house appears to date back to the mid-to-late-1800s. It must post date 1860 since it is not listed in *Old Houses of King and Queen County*.[31] It is a two-story gambrel roof house with a story and one-half addition with gambrel roof, in a state of disrepair. The farm is cultivated, but the house is abandoned. It is located on County Road 656 (a dirt road) west of CR 610, north of Mascot in King and Queen County. These roads lie east of State Route 14.

Our Mothers Grave
Sally T Parrish
wife of James
　Parrish
and Mother of
Jno II & Euluara
　Parrish
born March 17, 1798
Died in March 1822

Mary E Smith
　wife of
Lewis O Smith
Sept. 8, 1839
Jan. 31, 1872

Mary Lewis
daughter of
L. O. & Mary
　Smith
July 6, 1871
Nov. 26, 1871
J. Adolphus Garrett
　1831-1912
Anne Smith Garrett
　1842-1912

---

[31]Cox, Virginia D and Willie T Weathers. *Old Houses of King and Queen County*. Richmond: Whittet. 1973.

## BOOK REVIEWS:

John P. Alcock, *Five Generations of the Family of Burr Harrison of Virginia, 1650-1800*, viii, 284 pp, appendices, map, index, end notes, bibliography, paper. 1991. $25.00 plus $3.00 shipping. Burr Harrison is known to have been in Westmoreland County in 1659, and even with the gaps in the county court records, his life has been documented well in Mr. Alcock's book. He and his wife have done meticulous research and have presented in well documented detail the lives of four generations of Burr Harrison, as well as the lives of Thomas Harrison, Cuthbert Harrison, Mathew Harrison, George Harrison, William Harrison and Benjamin Harrison. He also presents descendants in Kentucky and Ohio and Calvert (Harris) Harrison of Newberry County, South Carolina. Other families covered: Whitledge, Barton, Wallis, Linton, Bullitt, Fowke, Gibson, Gillison, Hunston, Peyton and Quarles. It is exciting to read such a detailed, readable and well researched account of this early Virginia family. Heritage Books, Inc., 1540E Pointer Ridge Place, Bowie, MD 20716. Call 301-390-7709.

Elizabeth Petty Bentley, *Index to The 1810 Census of Virginia*, xiii, 366 pp, cloth. 1980. $30.00 plus $2.50 shipping, first book; $1.00 each add. The book, as compiled by Elizabeth Bentley is in itself, an alphabetical listing of the heads of households in the 1810 Federal Census of Virginia; therefore no index is required. The last name of the individual, the given name, then the county of residence and the reference of the page number of the census schedule is presented. As is usual, this book provides a convenient tool for the location of the residence of the individual in question and further investigation of the microfilm copy of that census record. It also provides the necessary direction to pursue the records of that individual in his county of residence. The author has provided a comprehensive Foreword for an understanding of the information available from the 1810 census. The Genealogical Publishing Co., Inc., 1001 N Calvert St., Baltimore, MD 21202. Call 800-727-6687.

Morgan Poitiaux Robinson, *Virginia Counties: Those Resulting from Virginia Legislation, Bulletin of the Virginia State Library*. 1916. 283 pp, maps, indexed, cloth. Rep.1992. $25.00 plus $2.50 shipping, first book; $1.00 each add. It is especially appropriate that this book be reviewed in the first issue of *TIDEWATER VIRGINIA FAMILIES* since it has been used by the editor as a reference to present the history of the counties of tidewater Virginia to the new readers. As can be seen, it is imperative that the researcher understand the history and evolution of the counties that made up the Commonwealth of Virginia in earlier times. It is also necessary to know the disposition of these counties so that repositories of records can be located. A number of these early counties are now extinct, and some have now been cut off to form the territory of Kentucky and West Virginia. The book is an invaluable research tool. While the bibliography that is included was originally written in 1916, it too, provides good information about books that are available to further ones knowledge of these counties. It is clearly an authorative account of the origin of Virginia counties. The Genealogical Publishing Co, 1001 N Calvert St, Baltimore, MD 21202. Call 800-727-6687.

## AND ANNOUNCEMENTS:

Colonial Dames of America in Virginia, *The Parish Register of Christ Church, Middlesex County, Virginia, 1653-1812*. 1897. 341 pp, indexed, cloth. Rep. 1990. $19.95. Postage, one item $2.50, each add. $1.00. Clearfield Company, Inc 200 E Eager St, Baltimore, MD 21202. Call 410-625-9004.

Augusta B Fothergill, *Wills of Westmoreland County, Virginia, 1654-1800*. 1925. 229 pp, indexed, cloth. Rep. 1990. $17.50. Postage, one item, $2.50, each add. $1.00. Clearfield Company, Inc 200 E Eager St, Baltimore, MD 21202. Call 410-625-9004.

## SEARCH:

MASON, Colonel Enoc born c.1769, attorney in Stafford County. Interested in heirs. T Freeland Mason, Jr, 91 Blue Ridge St, Warrenton, VA 22186.

HURT, William, of Buckland, Charles City County mid-1600s. Daughter m. Philip Pendleton, after 1674. Request information about Hurt family. William Eldon Tinsley, P O Box 430, Pflugerville, TX 78660.

WADKINS, James, born in Georgia, living in Alabama 1855. m. Caroline Wahls before 1855. Information about parents and children. Virginia L H Davis P O Box 876, Urbanna, VA 23175.

TERRELL, Matthew, born 1769, prob. Hanover or Caroline Co. Interested in names of parents and brothers and sisters. M Maxine Connell, 412 Sunshine Ct, Warrensburg, MO 64093.

WRIGHT, John Durrett m. Virginia (Ellen) Henderson. c. 1850. Caroline Co. Seek information about Wright and Henderson families. Max Peatross, 1680 South 2350 E, Price, UT 84501.

*Coming in the Next Issue:*

*Records of the Tidewater Virginia Counties*

*Walter Chiles, The Father and Son*

*Civil and Militia Appointments*

*Property Claims from British Depredations*
*(Valuable for DAR Eligibility)*

# INDEX

Abbey
    Will: 25
Anderson
    Thos 35
Apperson
    Allen 35
Arme
    Mick 26
Armistead
    Henry 29, 31
Atkinson
    Charles 34
Ball
    Mary 22
    Mr 24
Baughan
    Benj 34
Bell
    Jo 25
    William 35
Bonen[t]
    Mr 26
Bonner
    James 25
Bonnison
    Ebby 25
Bower
    Wm E 34
Bradley
    Gideon 32
Brent
    Hugh 25
Bricuit
    Patrick 34
Brown
    Alfred D 35
    J D G 34

Bullard
    William H 35
Burke
    John M 34
    Thos H 34
Burruss
    Pleasant 35
    Saml 34
    Thos 34
    Wm Sr 34
    Wml 35
Butcher
    Andrew 26
    Will: 25
Butler
    Isaac 34
    John 16, 19
    Samuel 15
    Thomas 15-17, 19, 20, 21
Byrd
    Otway 29, 30
Campbell
    Elliott 35
    Mat 34
    William 35
    Zacheus 34
Carborrow
    Mr 26
Carr
    Charles R 35
Carter
    Coll: Jo: 24
    Councilor Robert 22
Cary
    Col Miles 38

Cathon
    James 37, 38
    John 37
    William 37, 38
Chandler
    Rufus 34
    Timothy 34
Chatwyn
    Tho: 26
Chichley
    Sir Hen: 25
Chowning
    Robt. 26
Christian
    Charles 31
    Edmund 31
    William 28
    Wm 32
Claiborne
    Nathaniel 18
    Thomas 18, 19
    William 18
    William D. 21
Clappam
    Wm, Jun 24
Clark
    Wm:, Sen 24
Clarke
    Arth: 24
Clayton
    Thos C 35
Cleer
    Thomas 34
Cobb
    Robert 34
    Walker 34

Cocke
    Mr 26
Coks
    Mr. 25
Coleman
    Hawes 34
    Samuel Sen 34
    Thomas B 35
    Wm D 34
Colgin
    John 31
Connoway
    Mr 24
Copeland
    Wm. 26
Corbyn
    Mr 26
Cromp
    Will 24
Curtys
    Mr Jo: 25
Custis
    G. W. P. 20
Dabney
    George 16
Dale
    Mr 26
Davys
    Hen: 27
Debnam
    Mordecai 28, 29
Dickens
    James 34
Dickenson
    Walter 24
Dickinson
    F 34
Doggett
    Henry 34

Duling
    A[chilles] 35
Duncombe
    Mrs. Thos. 25
Dunn
    William 34
Edlow
    Henry 31
Edmondson
    Benjamin 29
    Philip Parr 29, 30
Edwards
    Jo: 24
    Mr 26
Ellyott
    Lt. Coll. 25
Eskridge
    Colonel George 22
Eubank
    John 34
Fairfax
    Ann 22
ffleet
    Coll: 25
fflower
    Mr 24
ffox
    Mr 26
Flippo
    Jos Jr 35
Fox
    Fleming Milton 39
Garrett
    Anne Smith 41
    J. Adolphus 41
Gaskins
    Samuel, Jr. 23

Gates
    James 26
Gatewood
    James 35
    John 34
George
    Lewis 35
    Nich 24
Goodloe
    John 35
    Robt 34
Gorsuch
    Richd 24
Govan
    James 16
Gray
    Samuel 22
Green
    Wm 34
Gregory
    John 31
Guy
    Geo. F 34
    James 34
Haddaway
    Rowland 25
Hale
    Nich: 26
Haley
    Jno 34
    Meriday 34
    Winston 34
Hardyman
    Stith 29, 31
Harper
    Goodman 25
    Will 25
Harris
    Augustine 34

Harris
  Malcolm H 19, 20
  Thos T 34
Harrison
  Benjamin 31
Harriss
  James 35
Harwood
  John 31
Haselwood
  Jo: 26
Hawke
  Mr 24
Hayward
  Tho: 25
Henry
  Patrick 31
Hensley
  Jno 34
Herd
  Walt 24
Hill
  Henry 34
  John 21
  Michl 25
Hoge
  Rev. M. D. 39
Holart
  Mr 26
Holman
  Mrs Frank 20
Hooker
  Alan B. 23
Hopson
  Ann 38
Horton
  Toby 25
Hudson
  Jo: 26

Hundley
  Mathew 34
Hurt
  Benjamin W 34
Hutcheson
  Richard 34
Hutchins
  Wm: 24
Irishman
  Richd 25
Jackson
  Jo: 25
Jadwyn
  Jo: 26
Johnson
  Dan: 26
Jones
  Jo: 24
  John 34
  Moses 35
Keeble
  Mr 25
Kempe
  Mr 25
  Mr Math: 24
  Robt 26
Kidd
  Tho: 26
Kinge
  Charles 24
Kinsey
  Hugh 24
Laughlin
  Jno. W 35
Laurence
  Joseph H 34
Lawens
  Peter 37

Lawrence
  Saml 34
Lawson
  Mr 25
Leake
  J M 40
  J. M. 39
  James Miller 40
  John Marion 40
  Lizzie 40
Lee
  Captain Henry 2.
  George 22
Leech
  Mr 25
Lewis
  Mary 41
Lewys
  Richd 26
Lightfoot
  William 30
Lippit
  Will: 25
Luck
  William 34
Ludford
  Will: 26
Lundsford
  Edward 24
Macknum
  James 26
Madison
  Geo W 34
  George 34
  James 34
  Saml 34
Maidsson
  Mr 25

Major
    John 29, 30
Marable
    Edward 29
Marrable
    Edward 30
Marsh
    Mr 26
Marshall
    Benj 34
    Thomas 34
    Thos 35
Matticoat
    Jno. 38
McDry
    Mau[blot] 34
Meredith
    Jo: 24
Merryman
    Mr 26
Miller 40
    Elizabeth 40
    Fannie 39
    Fannie Martin 40
    Hugh 39
    James 39, 40
    James Caskie 40
    Lizzie 39, 40
    Margaret Caskie 40
    Mary 39
    Mary Eliza 39
    Patricke 25
    S J 39, 40
    Sue 39
Minge
    David 28
Minor
    Joseph 34
Montague
    Mrs 26
Moore
    Gregory 34
    Lambert 25
Morgan
    Henry 34
Munford
    William Green 30
Nash
    Arthur 25
Needles
    Jo: 25
Neesham
    Mr 26
New
    James 29, 30
Newton
    Wm 34
Nichols
    Hen: 26
    Jo: 26
Norard
    William 37
Norment
    Wm 34
Oliver
    John 34
Osborn
    Robt 25
Pain
    Richard 34
Parrish
    Euluara 41
    James 41
    Jno II 41
    Sally T 41
Patteson
    Mr 26

Peatross
    Richard 34
    Wm H 34
Pendleton
    Rev. B. A. 39
Penny
    William 35
Perrott
    Mr 26
Peterson
    Ever 25
Philips
    Tho: 24
Pine
    Jo: 26
Pollard
    Robt 26
Potter
    Mr 25
Powell
    Howell 24
    Mr 26
    Tho: 24
Price
    James 16
Priddy
    Elijah 34
Pritchard
    Robt 26
Pulman
    Hen: 26
P[illeg]
    Norborne 34
Rainey
    H G 34
Reeve
    E P 39
    John F 39
    Susan Joanna 39

Richards
    Buchan 20
    Eliza 20
    Jo: 25
    John 20
    Penelope 20
Richison
    Wm 34
Rigsby
    Mr 25
Ring
    William 20
Roots
    Mr 24
    William 34
Royall
    William 30
    Wm. 31
Royster
    Peter 29-31
Ruffin
    Alice 19
    Robert 18
    Sterling 18, 19
Samuel
    Archl 34
    Jno P 35
    Pholess[?] 34
    Thomas 34
Seay
    Flurry 34
Segar
    Widd 26
Sharpe
    Jo: 26
Ship
    Thomas 34
Shirt
    Willm 25

Simpson
    Jo: 26
Sison
    Robt 25
Size
    John 35
Skipwith
    Sir Gray 25
Slaughter
    Robert 20
Sloper
    Sam: 25
Smith
    Coll: Robt 25
    Jo: 25
    John 35
    L. O. 41
    Lewis O 41
    Mary 41
    Mary E 41
    Sander 25
Southall
    Henry 29, 32
    James 31
Spires
    Jno. 38
Stiles
    Rev. J. C. 39
Stott
    Bryan 26
    Tho: 26
Susan
    James 40
    S J 40
    Sue 40
    Susan 40
Sutton
    John Jr 35

Swan
    Wilson 35
Tabb
    Humphrey 25
Taliaferro
    William 35
Taylor
    Jn: 24
    Robt. 26
Temple
    Liston 21
Terrell
    Christopher 35
    Jesse 35
    Jno 34
    Richmond 31
    Saml 35
    Samuel 34
Thacker
    V 35
Thatcher
    Hen: 26
Therriott
    Mr 27
Thomas
    Will: 26
Thompson
    Will: 26
    Wm 35
Thornton
    Philip 34
Tiller
    Joseph 34
Travers
    Mr 26
Tucker
    Sam: 25
Turner
    Reuben 34

Tyler
    John 31
Vaiden
    Joseph 29, 30
Vaughan
    Henry 29, 31
Vause
    Jo: 26
Vezey
    Geo. 26
Wadding
    Mr 25
Walker
    Freeman 28
Walterton
    Mr 25
Ware
    Nathl 34
Waterman
    Goodman 25
Webb
    Edward 26

Weeks
    Abraham 26
Welsh
    Jo: 26
West
    John 29
White
    George 35
    Wm 35
Whitlock
    Geo P 34
Wignor
    Wm: 24
Williams
    Tho: 26
Willis
    Jo: 26
Wilsh
    Dan: 26
Wilson
    Thos 35

Woolfolk
    Achillis 34
    Spilsbe 34
Wright
    F M 40
    F. M., Jr. 39
    Margaret Caskie Miller 40
    Roberta Bolling 40
    Sue 40
Wroughton
    Will: 24
Wyllis
    Mr 26
Yates
    Michael W 35
Young
    Henry 19
    James 34
    John 34
    Nathaniel 34

# TIDEWATER VIRGINIA FAMILIES:
## A Magazine of History and Genealogy

## TABLE OF CONTENTS

| | |
|---|---:|
| From Virginia | 52 |
| Records of Tidewater Virginia Counties | 53 |
| Walter Chiles, Father and Son | 67 |
| Mattaponi Baptist Church and Cemetery King and Queen County | 73 |
| Civil Appointments, 1786-1799, Charles City County | 80 |
| Will of Gideon Macon, 1767, New Kent County | 88 |
| Losses Sustained from the British Depredations Gloucester County | 90 |
| The Stiff Family Bible, 1777-1856, Middlesex County | 96 |
| Book Reviews | 99 |
| Announcements | 100 |
| Search | 101 |
| Index | 103 |

Volume 1 Number 2                August/September 1992

From Virginia............

It is hoped that the enthusiasm of all of the subscribers of *TIDEWATER VIRGINIA FAMILIES* has carried over to the first issue of the quarterly. With issue number two in hand, it is time to let your editor know of your impressions. It may not be possible to act upon them all, but they will be gratefully received. By now you know that the editor is not infallible (i.e., typos), but also, it is hoped, recognize the dedication to accuracy and appropriate documentation. It is promised that the former will be vigilantly monitored, and the latter adhered to with diligence.

Some readers have felt that the magazine has "class", others that it has "tooth". Let it be said simply, the format is designed to be traditional and tasteful. More important the print style is meant to be readable and the paper has been selected not only because of the tint, but because it is acid-free and of archival quality.

It may not be apparent immediately in the content of the quarterly, but all of the family names in which subscribers have expressed an interest are being cross-referenced by family name, county and subscriber name. This information will be used in searching for family data in the various counties. With your permission the listings can be printed in a future issue.

This brings up a further point of the economics of the editor's correspondence. All of the present subscribers have courteously included a stamped envelope when they have sought information from the editor. To insure a response, it is requested that this be a standing policy.

There is a certain sense of history and continuity in actually seeing the originals of these old records. When one finds an original signature it evokes a relationship not otherwise felt. There are certain original documents that the editor has found and transcribed in the magazine that contain original signatures. If a subscriber would like to have a xeroxed copy of an original document, the editor will be glad to comply at the rate of $1.00 per page. Keep in mind that those records transcribed from county court record books are copies and do not contain original signatures (except the signature of the county clerk). The editor is not ignoring requests when a sought-after will is not presented; its a matter of what has been preserved!

Thanks for your enthusiasm and support, we'll enjoy the magazine together.........

VLHD

## Records of Tidewater Virginia Counties

"I'm sorry, the early records of this county were burned. We only have scattered information about the inhabitants of this county at an early date." This is a familiar statement, made by the clerks of a number of tidewater Virginia county courts (as well as a number of other Virginia county courts). The lack of records, in many cases, for the length of the time preceding the Civil War, make research in Virginia very difficult. No wills may have survived for several generations of Virginians whose families continued to live in the same general area. There is no documented record of the children of many of the inhabitants. Since deeds may have also been destroyed, there is little hope of finding descriptions of relationships in land transfers. It requires a great deal of ingenuity to piece together family relationships. It also requires a good knowledge of what information is available.

In some counties where the preponderance of pre-1865 records have been lost, the county court order books have survived[1]. They are the record of any and all business brought before the court and they are the most intriguing and frustration of all of Virginia's early records. They contain considerable genealogical information, but are difficult and time consuming to study. Many do not have indexes, and if they do, they generally relate only to court cases, listing the plaintiffs and defendants, more or less alphabetically.[2]

The land tax and personal property tax records are generally available from the initial order requiring the recordation of these lists (1782). They are not extant for all of the tidewater counties, and the records for all of the years have not necessarily survived in those counties in which there are records.

---

[1]The county court order books contain brief entries of the court proceedings, grand jury presentments, the laying of the county levy, provision for the processioning of lands and the commissioning of court officials. The entries may be very brief or may contain valuable genealogical information, depending upon the clerk in office at any given time. In any case, they provide evidence that events of legal significance occurred, and when.

[2]Clay 14.

The largest concentration of "burned record" counties is on the peninsula southeast of Richmond along the James and York Rivers. Of the twenty counties explored by *TIDEWATER VIRGINIA FAMILIES*, three-fourths have suffered varying degrees of damage or loss of records. There is no complete listing of extant records for counties that have suffered extensive record destruction. The Virginia State Library has photocopies of most known materials, but originals are scattered in many different collections. In instances where counties suffered from Civil War loss rather than destruction, there is always a chance that records will find their way home (by the hands of some interested individual).[3]

This listing of the counties of tidewater Virginia, the history of their records, and the records that have survived today will be of interest and invaluable assistance to the researcher.[4] While it is not a comprehensive listing of the colonial records that have survived, it does present an understanding of the limit or extent of those extant records of each county.[5] Research in the records of these counties must generally be conducted in either the county courthouse or the Virginia State Archives. Written permission must be obtained from the appropriate clerk of the county circuit court to view many of the original documents housed in the Virginia State Archives. The history of the counties and the contemporary location of the records is given in the article *Tidewater Virginia Counties*.

It is the stated purpose of this magazine to help the researcher in exploring the unpublished records of these counties where they are available. It is hoped that supplementary records that can be found and published will also aid the researcher in establishing relationships among their early ancestors and the early Virginia settlers.

---

[3]Clay 14-15.
[4]See the two Virginia State Library and Archives books listing the records available at the Virginia State Library for research, listed in References.
[5]The dates presented in this account are as accurate as can be determined. The dates of the establishment of the counties may vary by a year or two, depending upon which source of information is used. The dates of the extant early records are approximations.

Caroline County

While the county was formed in 1727, the earliest court records date only from 1732. At the time of the Civil War the court records of Caroline County were taken to Richmond for safe keeping. During the last days of the war, Richmond's supplies of military interest to the Union Army were burned by the retreating Confederate Army when it evacuated Richmond on April 3, 1865. The fire raged out of control and the financial and business districts of Richmond were destroyed. Among the losses were the records of those counties that had transported their court records to Richmond to save them from the invading army. Most of the records prior to 1863 for Caroline County were destroyed in the fire.

The Caroline County court order books survived (left behind at the courthouse) and are basically intact for the years:[6] 1732-1789, 1799-1824 and 1862-1863. Minute books survive for the years: 1770-1781, 1787-1791, 1794-1796, 1815-1819, 1847-1851 and 1858-1866.

Scattered wills have survived for the years 1742, 1762-1830 and 1794-1897. Some plats are also bound in the book of wills, 1777-1840. One of the most productive sources of information is the collection of chancery court suits from 1780-1850.[7] These are original documents and must be viewed at the Virginia State Archives. Other scattered court and miscellaneous records are available, generally dating from the early 1800s.

Charles City County

While the history of Charles City County goes back to the 1634 shire of Charles City, the early records of Charles City are lost to posterity. Records were destroyed, badly damaged or stolen during the Civil War. There are Charles City County court order books for the

---

[6]See abstracts by John Frederick Dorman.
[7]For a listing and abstract of these see: Hopkins, William Lindsay, *Caroline County Court Records and Marriages, 1787-1810*. Virginia: Richmond. 1987.

years: 1672-1673, 1677-1679, 1731-1751, 1758-1762[8] and fragments of the years: 1650, 1680, 1682, 1685 and 1722-1723. These inclusive dates do not mean that all of the consecutive dates of court order entries are available. There are gaps.

Inventories, estate appraisements and audits have survived, in part, for the years, 1782-1859; some guardian accounts have survived for the years 1782-1893. A Record of Wills, Etc., 1724-1731 is contained in one volume; a will book for 1789-1808 has survived, along with some items dated 1788-1868. Deeds and related papers survive for the years 1784-1897, but again, there are only scattered items. A volume entitled Deeds, Wills, Orders, Etc., 1655-1665 is extant. Most of the other records post date the Civil War period.

Elizabeth City

The history of Elizabeth City begins with the shire formed in 1634. The extant records of the county are much later. The Elizabeth City and Hampton area was strategically located at the end of the peninsula and access from the Chesapeake Bay to the rivers of Virginia. The town of Hampton was sacked and burned during each of the wars, with considerable record destruction in the Revolutionary War, the War of 1812 and again in the Civil War. Almost nothing remains of the records prior to 1688. The surviving records of a later date are of two general types, the court order books, and the books of deeds, wills and indentures. Sometimes the two are found in separate halves of one volume.[9]

There are Elizabeth City County order or minute books (titles vary) for 1731-1747, 1755-1769, 1784-1788 and 1798-1816. The titles of the record books for deeds and wills vary but are extant and on microfilm, in part, for the years: [1684]-1699, 1715-1730, 1737-1756, 1758-1771, 1787-1806, 1809-1818 and 1820-1835. There is a General

---

[8]See the works of Dr. Benjamin B. Weisiger, III for the abstracts of the Charles City County records.
[9]Starkey, Marion L. *The First Plantation, Hampton and Elizabeth City County, Virginia, 1607-1887.* Hampton: Houston. 1936.

Index to Deeds, Wills, Etc., 1758-1899 and an Index to Will Books, 1800-1875 (which doesn't mean that all of the wills are extant). Other records for the county are extant but are generally from a later date.[10]

Essex County

As has been recounted in the history of Essex County it began in 1656 as Old Rappahannock County and continued as Essex County beginning in 1692. There have been dedicated clerks in the county courthouse, and the county was removed from the invasions of the various wars, thus most of the records are extant. They have also been carefully restored. While one cannot follow chronologically all of the events in the lives of its inhabitants, generally, the records provide a good account of the residents.

Old Rappahannock County Records begin in 1656, with both deeds and wills extant. Court order books, deed and will books are also extant for Essex County. The original records are to be found at the courthouse, copies and microfilm are in the Virginia State Archives. There are also some original loose records in the archives collection. Time has claimed a few volumes, invariably the one most sought, but research in the Essex County records is rewarding.[11]

Gloucester County

Gloucester County dates from 1651, but its extant records, by and large, begin over two hundred years later. All of the early records were destroyed by fire in 1821, and most of the records from that date until 1865 were destroyed in the fire in Richmond. An inspection of the listing in the *Preliminary Guide* shows that generally the records of the county begin subsequent to the Civil War. Tax accounts for the years

---

[10]See *A Preliminary Guide to Pre-1904 Municipal Records*.
[11]Embrey, Alvin T. *Indexes to Records of [Old] Rappahannock, 1654-1692 and Essex [Counties], 1692-1700*. 11 Volumes. Recent work in abstracting the records of Essex County has been done by John Frederick Dorman and later by Ruth and Sam Sparacio of McLean VA: Antient Press.

1770-1771 and Surveyors Book A, 1733-1810 and No. 1, 1817-1852 have survived.

Hanover County

Hanover County began its history in 1720. Its early records have not survived, following the fate of other records removed to Richmond for safe keeping during the Civil War. Two old books bound in rawhide, dating about 1730 remained in the clerk's office and were not destroyed. Specifically, Deeds, Wills, Etc. 1733-1735 and 1783-1792 are extant. Court papers (including fiduciary and suit papers) 1805-1870 and deeds, 1735 and 1749, as well as deeds removed from other court papers and dated 1744-1855 in the number of twenty-five items are extant. Will Book, 1831-1850 and wills and inventories removed from court papers, 1792-1858 are extant. This information is deceptive, in that there are many gaps in the dates of the material that has survived.

Henrico County

While the history of Henrico County dates to an original shire, the early records have not survived. It is understood that the records were destroyed when Arnold invaded the city (Richmond) during the Revolutionary War. All records prior to 1655 and most of the records prior to 1677 were destroyed at that time. The records that survived were those removed from the courthouse and stored at Powhatan Furnace.[12] The records of the circuit court were destroyed in the evacuation of Richmond during the Civil War.

The earliest order book (which also includes wills) begins in 1678 and continues to 1701, other order books are: 1707-1714, 1719-1724, 1755-1769, 1737-1746, 1823 and 1781-1816.[13] Records prior to 1781 are not in continuous order, but subsequent records are intact. Wills have survived beginning with 1781-1787 and 1802-1822. There are eight items of wills not probated, 1819-1899. An index of colonial

---

[12]Robinson 80.
[13]See abstracts of Henrico County records by Dr. Benjamin B. Weisiger, III

records, 1677-1739 is extant and miscellaneous court records from 1650-1807 have survived. There are deeds (titles of the books vary) dated: 1677-1692, 1688-1704, 1706-1718, 1725-1737 and 1744-1767, also 1767-1774. The original records of Henrico County are housed in the Virginia State Archives.

Many early residents identified as having lived in the city of Richmond, actually lived in Henrico County. Unless one is certain of the exact place of residence it is important to search the Henrico County records as well as those of the city of Richmond.[14]

James City County

The settlement at Jamestown marks the earliest date of James City County. The extant records reflect no such early date. The records of the colony were first burned during Bacon's Rebellion in 1676. This was not the end of the destruction of the records of James City County, all of the subsequent records were destroyed in 1865. Today the only records that predate the Civil War are contained in Tax Book, 1768-1769, 1 volume. Extant records of the early colony must be found scattered among those records and manuscripts that have survived in other places (eg. personal papers and records kept in England).

King and Queen County

King and Queen County came into existence in 1691; its records went out of existence during the Civil War. The records were first destroyed in a courthouse fire in 1828, then subsequent records were destroyed by fire in 1865. It is hard to realize that none of the early history of a county has survived. Even when one is told that it is a

---

[14]The town of Richmond was established in the county of Henrico in 1742. In 1779 an act was passed moving the seat of government from Williamsburg to Richmond. There were at that time only 150 to 160 houses, and between 700 and 800 inhabitants in the city. The area that came to be known as Church Hill was located in Henrico County and continued to be so into the 1800s. Richmond was incorporated as a city in 1842. Sanford 12,18. Salmon 158.

burned record county, it takes a trip to the courthouse to understand what this means. There are virtually no records extant prior to the 1850s. A plat book for 1823-1878; some tax accounts, 1779, 1786-1787; the Sheriff's Tax Book, 1821; a tax assessor's book, 1841-1842; and the Chancery Order Book 1831-1858 complete the list of earlier records.

King George County

King George County had its inception in 1720. The early records of the county are housed in the county courthouse, and are in excellent condition. Will Book A-1 was found[15] and returned to the county a few years ago, making the records of wills complete. Record-keeping differed in King George as there were separate volumes kept for each category of court record. Wills beginning 1721, deeds beginning 1721, inventories, bonds, appraisements, etc.[16] are extant. There are some missing and some mutilated pages, otherwise the records are intact. The original Marriage Register covers the years 1786-1850. Copies of the court records are to be found in the Virginia State Archives. There are four volumes of Orders and Judgments, dating 1721-1790. Will Books Nos. 1-3, [1752]-1846, in the number of three volumes are extant. There are additionally, Fiduciary Accounts (No. 3) and Orphans Accounts, 1739-1765 (1 volume) and Inventories [Book 1], 1721-1744 (one volume). Found on microfilm are: Deed Books Nos. 1-19, 1721-1868 and Will Books Nos. 1-4, [1752]-1904.

King William County

Formed in 1701, King William County was rich in early history. A disastrous courthouse fire in 1885 destroyed all of the early records; an earlier fire had already caused the destruction of early records.

---

[15]George Harrison Sanford King abstracted the records of this book under the title *King George County, Virginia Will Book A-1, 1721-1752*. Private printing. 1978.

[16]A complete set of Embrey's Index is located in the clerk's office, newly photocopied and bound. *General Index to Deeds, Trusts, Releases, Wills, Court Orders, Etc., 1721-1924*.

Except for charred pieces of some deed books, nothing remains. A dedicated clerk gathered the blackened and water soaked records that remained and had them bound as they were. If one is very lucky, one may find a record of the individual sought. There are four of these volumes. The record shows that there are Record Books [deeds, wills, etc.] Nos. 1-19, 1701-1884, 19 volumes. With this time span, most of the records relate to time after the early fire.

Lancaster County

Lancaster County was formed in 1651 and its history is well preserved in the county records. Records of wills go back to 1653, with a general index dated 1669-1950. A similar General Index of Records is dated 1652-1881. Deeds, etc. [also wills and orders; titles vary] begin with No. 1, 1652-57, then follows Nos. 2, 4, 6-7, 9, 11-19 and 21, 1654-1702, 1666-1782 and 1699-1800 (also Wills, 1661-1787).[17] Original records are to be found at the courthouse.

Mathews County

The early history of Mathews County (formed 1791) lies with that of Gloucester County, with its early records destroyed. An inspection of the listing of records in *The Preliminary Guide* would indicate that many of Mathews County's own records are also missing. Once again the prudent clerk of the court sent the court records to Richmond during the Civil War, and they were lost to the ravages of the fire that devastated Richmond. None of the court order books nor the will or deed books survived prior to 1865. Plat Books for 1817-1868 are extant. Several Fee Books beginning in 1795 are available on microfilm, but not for consecutive years. There are a few assorted court records extant, such as an Executor's Bond Book, 1795-1824.

---

[17]See abstracts by Ruth and Sam Sparacio.

Middlesex County

Middlesex County was separated from Lancaster County in 1669 and many of its early records are intact. During the War Between the States the records were securely packed and concealed in the Dragon Swamp, which makes up the headwaters of the Piankatank River. While the Union Army broke into the courthouse, they did not find any papers of value.

Extant for researchers today are Order Books: 1673-1680, which include deeds and wills; 1680-1694; 1732-1737; 1740-1744; and 1782-1783 (one volume, which includes deeds; 1745-1767, which includes wills and inventories); 1769-1784, including deeds and executions; 1764-1786, 1694-1705; 1705-1826; and 1767-1769. Deeds, Etc., 1687-1750; Miscellaneous Records, 1752-1831; Deed Books Nos. 2-[4], 1679-1720; Deed Books, 1740-1785; and Deed Book No. 11, 1791-1799. One volume of Surveys, 1735-1807 is extant. Original records are in the office of the clerk of the circuit court. General Indexes to Deeds, Volumes A and 1, 1675-1897 is on microfilm.

Wills, Etc., 1675-1798 and Will Books [A]-H, 1698-1734, 1740-1793-1795-1798 are extant. There is also a General Index to Wills, 1675-1950 on microfilm.[18]

New Kent County

New Kent County was the mother county of a number of later counties, being chartered about 1654. Its early history is lost to posterity. There are no early records. The Brick House, the early courthouse, was burned during Bacon's Rebellion. To add to the loss, John Price Posey had the courthouse at New Kent burned in 1787, because he "had a grudge against the sheriff". He was hanged for this. Still later, the accumulated records were sent to Richmond during the Civil War. This completed the destruction of the New Kent County records prior to 1865.

---

[18]See the abstracts of Middlesex County wills by William L. Hopkins, also those by Ruth and Sam Sparacio.

Northumberland County

The history of Northumberland County began in 1645, with its creation from the district of Chickacoan. Even though there was a courthouse fire in 1710, many of its early records have survived, and have been carefully preserved for posterity. The original records are in the clerk's office at the courthouse.

Deeds and Orders are dated 1650-1652; Record Books [deeds, wills and fiduciary accounts] are contained in twenty-three volumes and date 1652-1672, 1706-1729, 1738-1787; District Court Wills, dated 1789-1825 and Order Books, 1652-1770, 1773-1783, contained in seventeen volumes are extant.

Richmond County

Richmond County became a separate political entity in 1692. Its records date from that time. After the dearth of records in so many of the tidewater counties, it is exciting to find listing after listing of records that have survived and been preserved in Richmond County. Order Books, Nos. 1-15 and 21 encompass the years 1692-1762 and 1779-1794. Deed Books Nos. 1-16 for the years 1692-1793 are found in fifteen volumes. Wills and Inventories, 1699-1717, 1796-1797 and Will Books Nos. 4-7 and 9, 1717-1787, 1794-1822 are extant. There is a General Index to Wills, 1699-1950 on microfilm, as are Will Books 4-11, 1717-1879.

Warwick County

Warwick River was in existence as one of the eight original shires, but the records of Warwick County have not survived from that early date. Almost all of the records prior to the Civil War were destroyed during the Civil War. There are two volumes of county court minutes from the dates 1748-1762, but the court orders do not begin until 1867. Some fiduciary records are extant from the late 1600s, and a will book for 1648-1651 has survived. Scattered wills for the late 1600s and early 1700s are extant, but they number only ten items. Twelve items of deeds from this era have survived. For the most part the records of Warwick County post date 1865.

Westmoreland County

Westmoreland County became a separate entity in 1653. There are order books beginning with 1662-1664, and continuing, though not consecutively: 1675-1688, 1690-1746, 1750-1764, 1776-1795, 1797-1801 and 1804-1818.[19] Books entitled Deeds and Wills, with varying titles are numbered 1-10 and encompass the years: 1653-1671, 1691-1699, 1701-1709 and 1717-1803 (twenty-one volumes). Wills may be found as loose papers for scattered dates in the 1700s (forty-one items), as well as Liber S, 1747-1753 and a microfilm entitled Wills, 1755-1800 (one reel).

York County

York County, by name, began in 1642, prior to that time it was known as Charles River, the shire. The early records of York County have survived and the books entitled Deeds, Orders and Wills, Nos. 1-11 and 13 can be found beginning in 1633. There are twenty-five volumes dated: 1633-62, 1665-1702, 1706-10. Deed books, 1741-1754 and 1760-1880 are also extant. Wills continue in Wills and Inventories Nos. 18-20, 22, 23; 1732-1759.[20] Many other records have survived, and even though all of the records are not chronologically extant, there are many available for research, however difficult the early ones are to read.

\* \* \* \* \*

Initially the importance of keeping records in the colony of Virginia was not recognized, or if it was thought to be so by individuals, the hardships of survival made it a lesser priority. Through the years, while many court clerks were very dedicated persons, some were not and records were lost. Many times those who were dedicated did what

---

[19]See Abstracts by John Frederick Dorman.
[20]See abstracts by Dr. Benjamin B Weisiger, III and Lindsay O. Duvall.

they thought was prudent to protect the county court records, only to have the forces of nature or man thwart their efforts. The miracle is, after all, not that so much has been lost of the heritage of Virginia, but that after over three hundred and eighty years, so much survives. This is the challenge and charge to the researcher.

Virginia Lee Hutcheson Davis

References:

Clay, Robert Young. *Virginia Genealogical Sources*. Address before The Detroit Society for Genealogical Research (pub.). Richmond: Virginia State Archives. 1980.

Conversations with Clerks of County Circuit Courts (1992).

Hart, Lyndon H. III, J. Christian Kolbe. *A Preliminary Guide to Pre-1904 Municipal Records*. Richmond: Virginia State Archives. 1985.

Ray, Suzanne Smith, Lyndon H. Hart III, J. Christian Kolbe. *A Preliminary Guide to Pre-1904 County Records*. Richmond: Virginia State Archives. 1985.

Robinson, Morgan Poitiaux. *Bulletin of the Virginia State Library, Virginia Counties*. 1916. Baltimore: Genealogical. 1992.

Salmon, Emily J., ed., *A Hornbook of Virginia History*. Richmond: Virginia State Library. 1983.

Sanford, James K., Ed., *Richmond Her Triumphs, Tragedies and Growth*. Richmond: Metropolitan. 1975.

Virginia Bar Association, Annual Report. *Virginia Local Public Records in the Offices of the Clerks of County and City Courts of Record*. Richmond: Richmond Press. 1929.

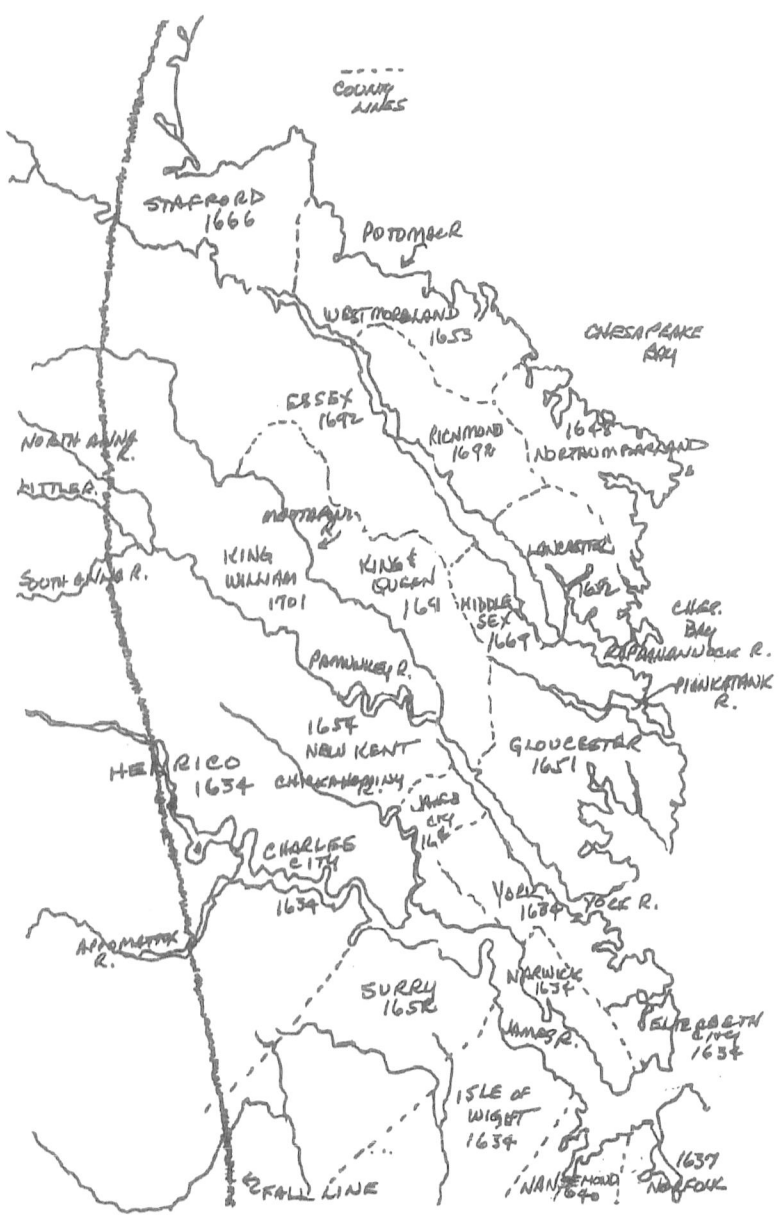

Tidewater Virginia 1702

# Walter Chiles, Father and Son

## Virginia Lee Hutcheson Davis

There are many theories about the lives of the two Walter Chiles, father and son, of Jamestown and about their wives and children. It is very difficult to identify the two men in relation to their individual activities, and even more difficult to be sure of who they married and accurately identify their children. This article is an attempt to bring together information that has been gathered from primary sources and to present a documented account of the two men. While it is tempting to resort to earlier printed material and the inferences drawn by earlier researchers, and to accept the earlier accounts of their lives, this article is an effort to rectify some of these misconceptions. While this may not be the final answer with regard to these two men, it is felt that it presents a more accurate picture than some that have been drawn in the past.

It would be simple to go to the records of England and resolve the issues of the identity of Walter Chiles, who patented land in Charles City County; when he was born and who he married. While work has been conducted among the English records, definitive inferences cannot at this time be drawn. Many of the parish records of the period in question simply are not extant. Marriage and baptismal records that might identify Walter and his wife and children do not seem to be available. This makes it even more difficult to follow the continuity of his life in Virginia. With the further loss of the early records of the counties of residence of the two Walter Chiles in the colony of Virginia, it makes it almost impossible to be certain of conclusions that are drawn.

Of all the families that this researcher has studied, the Chiles family has prompted the most discussion and provoked the most questions. There seem to be descendants of Walter Chiles in every corner and they all would like to be able to reconstruct the lives of the father and son in Virginia. So would this humble descendant, and the following is an attempt to do so.

## Walter Chiles of Charles City and James City Counties

### The Bristol Background of Walter Chiles of Virginia

No documentation has been found to positively identify Walter Chiles of Charles City County with the apprentice and parish records of

Bristol, England, concerning two Walter Chiles named in the records there.[a]

Walter Chiles served on *The Blessing* from September 1636 to June 1637, spending fourteen weeks in Virginia.[b] This information has been found in a deposition given by him on July 24, 1637. He identified himself as Walter Chiles of Bristol, a cloth worker, aged 29, or thereabouts. He served as an assistant to Henry Tutton, then the purser of *The Blessing*.

Two Walter Chiles (Childes) of that period have been discovered in the Bristol area records:
> Walter Childe son of Walter Childe of St. Mary Redcliff Parish was born March 20, 1608/9.[c]
> On April 1, 1632 Walter Chiles was recorded as "admitted to the liberties of this city [Bristol] for that he was the son of John Chiles".[d]

It appears that Walter Childe of St. Mary Redcliff Parish may have died prior to 1647, from the will that has been found of Richard Childe of Poddington, Bedfordshire.[e] No birth record has been found for the Walter Chiles of Bristol, the son of John Chiles. The entry of the marriage of a John Chiles of Temple Parish, Bristol on February 6, 1603/4 is found in those parish records, but not the birth record of Walter Chiles presumed to be his son, and born in 1608/9.

The land patents indicate that Walter Chiles, merchant, patented land on May 2, 1638, on the Appomattox River in Charles City County.[f] He claimed as headrights, Henry Tutton, Jon. Gerry, Jon. Shaw and Sarah Cole. On March 1, 1638/9 he repatented the 200 acres and an additional 200 acres for the personal adventure of himself, his wife, Elizabeth Chiles, and his sons, William and Walter (so identified in the patent).[g]

Conclusions...........
Just as no documentation has been found to conclusively identify Walter Chiles of Charles City County with those found in the records of Bristol, England, of the approximate same time; no records have been found to positively identify the Walter Chiles of the deposition as the same person who executed the land patent of 1638 in Charles City County. While the proximity of the dates has led researchers to assume they were one and the same person; this cannot be definitively established.

Henry Tutton was named in both court records associated with Walter Chiles. In the deposition, Walter Chiles was hired to serve under Henry Tutton, the purser of *The Blessing*; however, in the land patent, it is implied that Walter Chiles paid the passage of Henry Tutton and claimed him as a headright. While it may be accepted that Henry Tutton was named as a headright in the land patent of Walter Chiles, this does not conclusively imply that they were the same Walter Chiles.

## NOTES

a. Brame, Arden, Jr. *The Augustan Society Omnibus*. "The English Birth and Ancestry of Walter Chiles". 1987. Book 7, pp.102-109 (*English Genealogist*, Issue 19, pp.16-23).
b. High Court of Admiralty Libels and Depositions, (PRO Class HCA 13, 24 & 30), Public Record Office, London.
c. Brame 103; St. Mary Redcliff Parish Records.
d. Brame; Bristol Burgess Book, 1632-1633, p.221.
e. Brame. *Omnibus*. Book 12, 110; Mrs. V T C Smith, West Indies: Smith Collection, Vol. 15, pp.110-111.
f. Nugent, Nell. *Cavaliers and Pioneers*. Baltimore: Genealogical. 1991. Vol. I, p.87; Land Patent Book 1 Part II p.551.
g. Nugent I 103-104; L P Bk 1 P II 625.

## Walter Chiles (I) of Charles City County

Walter Chiles patented land in Charles City County on the Appomattox River on May 2, 1638 and on March 1, 1638/9. He brought to the colony of Virginia with him, his wife, Elizabeth and his sons, William and Walter (so identified in the land patent).[a]

Walter Chiles served as a Burgess from Charles City County for the Assembly terms, 1641, 1642 and 1643.[b]

By 1645 Walter Chiles represented James City County as a Burgess, and again in 1646 and 1649.[c] He purchased the Kemp House in Jamestown on March 23, 1648.[d]

Lef't Colonel Walter Chiles, member of the House of Burgesses was elected Speaker of the House, July 5, 1653.[e]

The bill of sale for the ship, *Leopoldus*, to Walter Chiles was dated July 12, 1653.[f]

Walter Chiles (I) died in 1653, as stated in the deed signed by Susanna Chiles, widow and executrix of Walter Chiles (II), deceased and identified as the son of Walter Chiles.[1] This deed was dated November 20, 1673.[g]

---

[1]There are researchers who have questioned the implications (and relationship of the persons involved) of the sale of the Kemp House by Susanna Chiles Wadding to John Page. The deed clearly states that Susanna was acting as the executrix of her husband's estate, and it was his wish, as stated in his will, that his property be sold.

Conclusions............
It appears that the above sequence of events all relate to the same Walter Chiles, since land was patented and repatented (1638, 1639, 1642, 1649)[h] in Charles City County in his name, and in each case, it was additional acreage with the same identification. He later served as a burgess from that county. He also later purchased land and a home in Jamestown and served as a burgess from James City County. He was identified as father to Walter Chiles in both a land grant (dated 20 May 1670),[i] in which Walter Chiles was identified as the son and heir, and the deed conveying the Kemp House property (November 20, 1673).[j]

The son, Walter Chiles (II) was evidently the son of Elizabeth. There is no further record of the son, William. No surviving records have been found to indicate when Elizabeth Chiles died. As stated before, no records have been found among the parish records of England that have been examined, that give the marriage date of Walter and Elizabeth; or the birth dates of Walter and Elizabeth, the parents, or Walter and William, the sons.

Walter Chiles may have married a second time and his wife may have been Alice Lukin. No concrete evidence has been found to document this, but as existing information is evaluated this possibility does exist. Although most researchers have concluded that the daughter of John Page was Mary Page, and that she married Walter Chiles, the son; this is not supported in the evidence at hand. It is believed that those researchers may have misinterpreted the identification by John Page of John Chiles and Elizabeth (Chiles) Tyler, as grandson and granddaughter, and taken these relationships literally, when in fact they were relationships that, today would be designated as step-grandchildren. Alice Lukin may have, then, married John Page as her second husband.

*To be continued*

# NOTES

a. L P Bk 1 II 551,625.
b. Hening, William Waller. *Statutes at Large.* Vol. 1, Richmond: Pleasants. 1807. p.239; Stanard, William Glover. *Colonial Virginia Register.* Baltimore: Clearfield. 1989. p.61.
c. Hening 322,358.
d. The Virginia Papers, Ambler Mss #4, Library of Congress; Duvall, Lindsay O., *Virginia Colonial Abstracts*, Series 2, Vol. 4, Easley: Southern. 1979. p.3.
e. Duvall 377-379.
f. Duvall 382-383.
g. The Virginia Papers, Ambler Mss, Folio 24, Library of Congress.
h. L P Bk 1 II 551,625,859; Bk 2 193.
i. L P Bk 6 413; Nugent II 112.
j. Ambler Mss 24.

## Mattaponi Baptist Church and Cemetery
### King and Queen County

### The Church

The first Lower St. Stephen's Church was succeeded by the existing second church of that name, the magnificent cruciform structure of colonial brick, long known as Mattapony Church.[1] The date of the construction of this church has not been definitively established, due to the loss of the King and Queen County court records, as well as the parish register and vestry books. St. Stephen's Parish was formed from Stratton Major Parish in c.1674, and the present church is believed to be the second on the same site.[2] It is believed that it was constructed during the second quarter of the eighteenth century.[3]

The church is an impressive example of that architecture reserved for the larger, more important Anglican parish churches, laid in Flemish bond with glazed headers and entrances framed with pedimented frontispieces of gauged and molded brick. The structure was abandoned after the Revolution and owes its preservation to the fact that it was taken over by a group of Baptists in 1803. It has survived a fire that destroyed the interior in 1922, but the interior was rebuilt and the exterior restored to its original beauty.

The Bible that was in use in 1733 is still owned by the church. The original colonial baptismal font was given to Old Fork Church in Hanover County and thus remains in an Episcopal church. It is of interest that the Mattaponi congregation in recent years asked for the return of the font, to which the Fork Church congregation replied that they would be glad to return the font if the Mattaponi Church would use it for its original purpose.

---

[1] Mason, George Carrington. *Colonial Churches of Tidewater Virginia*. Richmond: Whittet. 1945. pp.304-307.

[2] Rawlings, James Scott. *Virginia's Colonial Churches: An Architectural Guide*. Richmond: Garrett. 1963. pp.113-116.

[3] Loth, Calder, ed. *The Virginia Landmarks Register*. 3rd Ed. Charlottesville: University. 1987. p.218.

Mattaponi Church stands on the west side of State Route 14, about eight miles north of King and Queen Courthouse, still in a rural setting, almost but a clearing in a forest. Early eighteenth century tombstones may be found close to the north and east sides of the church.

## The Cemetery

A stone from 1708 with an interesting inscription in Latin lies just outside the north doorway.[4]

Set in the triangle of the southeast corner:

Here lies the Body
of George Braxton Esq
who Departed this Life
the first Day of July 1748
in the 71st year of his age
leaving Issue a son & two daughters
He died much lamented
Being a good Christian, a tender Parent, a kind Master and a friendly charitable neighbor

These are both flat sarcophagi set close to the church.

Here lies the body
of Mrs Mary Braxton who departed this Life the 17th day of September Anno Domini 1736 AE atis 34 [sic] She was the Daughter of the Hon. Robert Carter Esq. President & Treasurer of His Majesty's Council of this Colony Her death is much lamented by
All who knew her
Being a Good Christian a kind wife a tender Mother and a charitable neighbor
She left Issue two sons
George born January 13, 1734
Carter born September 16, 1736

Inscriptions are presented in the order of stones adjacent to each other. Only those stones that predated the twentieth century are presented, except where there were family groupings.

---

[4] Rawlings 116.

Heavy wrought iron fence enclosure:

Nannie & Juliet
only
daughters of
Rev A & S J Bagby
Aged
respectively 9 & 13 years

Sarah J
wife of
Rev Alfred Bagby
Febry 18, 1834
Jany 9 1888

John N son of
H R & Jessie
Pollard
1870-1871

Woodward
John Brockenbrough
Aug 19 1849
Apr 11 1930
His Son
Bell Jeter Woodward
Oct 29 1878 March 13 1955

R N Pollard
June 8, 1847
Aug 23, 1926

Mattie E Gresham his wife
March 9 1849
April 13 1917

Alfred
Rev Alfred Bagby DD
son of
John & Elizabeth Bagby
Past[or] Mattaponi Church
1855-1890
Founder Baptist Church
West Point Va
Author History
King & Queen County Va
June 15, 1828 Nov 14, 1925

Thomas Pollard
son of
John & Juliet Pollard
1829-1852

Dr R H Woodward
Born
Sept 11, 1825
Died
Oct 31, 1864

Sue C Davies
Wife of
Dr Richard H Woodward
and
Landon N Davies
Daughter of
Col John & Juliet
Jeffries Pollard
July 21, 1837
December 20, 1910

John Pollard
who died Sept 19th 1877
in the 75th year of his age

Juliet Pollard
wife of
Col John Pollard
Born
September 10, 1807
Died
September 4, 1874
Aged
66 years 11 months & 24 days

William H Pollard
1794-1858

Catherine R Pollard
1766-1843

Joseph Pollard
1759-1836

In wrought iron fence:

John C Hall
March 12 1861
March 28 1936

Rilee
Mary E Walton
wife of
W C Rilee
Born Dec 9, 1839
Died July 12, 1915

Landon Davies
born at Hail Western
Gloucester Co Va
August 12th 1829
Died
Saluda, Middlesex Co
April 19th 1890

P T Woodward
Born
April 6, 1821
Died
January 3, 1892

Mary Elizabeth Woodward
Relict of P T Woodward
Dau of
John Pollard
Born 1827
Died 1900

Loulie Cooke
wife of
John Hall
April 1867
Feb 1899

Father
Franklin Hall
Born April 9, 1835
Died Oct 11, 1909
Mother
Born May 27 1837
Died April 7 1913

In group:

        W G Wright          Mary L Wright
        born in                  wife of
  King and Queen Co Va       Wm G Wright
      Dec 28, 1819         Born in Essex Co
         Died              February 27, 1834
      Dec 7, 1897       Died September 16, 1880

        B S Wright
          Born
      May 20, 1872
    Died Oct 9, 1908

In wrought iron fence:

        Sudie M          Rev Joseph M Hart
   Beloved wife of             Born
    Rev J M Hart           Feb 19, 1842
    Jan 31, 1850             Died
    Jan 2, 1901            Aug 11, 1914

                       Mary C
                       wife of
                    Rev J M Hart
                Born July 26 1850
               Died May 10 1883

On a shaft:
     Our Father          Ida Carlton Smith
  Cornelius Carlton        Sept 5 1854
   March 28 1826         Sept 7 1909
    June 2 1887

    Alice Carlton
    Jan 31 1856
    Sept 27 1881

New stone, concrete curbing:

Wm Shepherd Dix
Nov 5 1829
July 4 1896

Mary Agnes His Wife
May 22, 1840
Mar 21, 1887

James M Jeffries
born within sight of this spot
June 25, 1809
Died West Point Va
April 6, 1890
He was Judge of the 9th Circuit
of Va 21 years
Died at his post of duty
in his 82nd year

Malvina Mason
Beloved wife of
James M Jeffries
Born Dec 3, 1814
Died May 31, 1883

Elizabeth Teagle
child of
Raleigh Travers
and
Elizabeth S Daniels
Born 23 July 1836
Died 13 Sept 1837[?]

John Thomas Vaughan
Apr 24, 1894
June 24, 1894

Maggie
daughter of
A F & M E Scott
died Novr 17 1883
Aged 15 years

M E Scott
wife of A F Scott
Born Northampton Co Va
Decr 6 1825
Died in Essex Co
June 14, 1879

Father
David A Powers
1833-1882

Mother
Harriet Cooke Powers
1835-1913

Brother
Rev John A Powers
1856-1880

C C Shepherd
1866-1887

William Todd
son of
Bernard & Elizabeth Todd
Born Oct 13, 1778
Died Dec 28, 1855

Capt Joseph H Drudge
1826-1878

Addie Carlton Drudge
February 6, 1869
January 7, 1893

Richard E Lumpkin
May 28, 1824
June 14, 1896

William S Fitzhugh
October 15 1854
February 25 1898

William B Todd
only son of
William & Maria P Todd
Born Jan 29, 1809
Died Sept 20, 1855

Mary Reed Drudge
wife of
Capt Joseph H Drudge
Died 1870

Edward Gresham
Born Sept 22, 1818
Died Mar 9 1873

Isabella Mann
Wife of
Edward Gresham
Born Nov 5, 1818
Died Aug 23, 1892

Transcribed by VLHD May 1992

Mattaponi Baptist Church from the church bulletin, May 1992, contributed by Virginia Coleman, Walkerton.

# Civil Appointments
## Charles City County, 1786-1799

### Submitted by Minor Tompkins Weisiger

*A continuation of Civil Appointments from the Executive Department from Volume 1 Number 1, page 32.*

His Excellency Patrick Henry Esq$^r$
Sir:
From my connection with Mr Otway Byrd, I take the Liberty in his absence of informing your Excellency that this County is without a Sheriff, as will appear by the inclosed Certificate_I expect Mr Byrd in Charles City on Tuesday--The Election commences on Wednesday - The shortness of the time, & the Death of Col$^o$ Munford, at so critical a period, will, I hope excuse this from

       Sir__
    Your very humble serv$^t$

Nesting
Charles City County April 2$^d$ 1786        G Dunbar

Charles City County J:$^c$.

This day John Cocke made oath before me James Southall a Justice of the Peace for the County aforesaid. that the Sloop Union of Virginia whereof George Knowles is at present Master. being a vessel of fifty seven tons burthen [burden] was built at Sandy Point in the year one thousand seven hundred & eighty seven and that William Lightfoot & John Cocke of said County. at present are sole owners thereof. given under my hand this 22$^{nt}$ day of May 1787

           *James Southall*

At a Session Court held for Charles City County 2nd day of May 1787 Furnea Southall produced a Comm$^n$ from his Excellency the Governor appointing him Captain of the Militia in this County having taken the Oath according to Law

         A Copy  Peter Royster C,C,C

At a Court held for Charles City County 6$^{th}$ day of June 1787 Henry Southall Gent produced a Comm$^n$ from his Excellency the Governor appointing him Capt. of the Militia in this County who Qualified thereto according to Law
John Bradley & Hardyman Irby produced the same as Ensigns...and Qualified according to Law

         A Copy  Peter Royster C,C,C

    The COMMONWEALTH OF VIRGINIA
 To all to whom these Present Letters shall come, greeting:

Know ye that the Court for the County of Charles City having nominated Stith Hardyman Gentleman to be Sheriff for the said County, our Lieutenant Governor, with the advice of the Council of State, doth hereby constitute and appoint him the said Stith Hardyman Gentleman, Sheriff for the said County.
In testimony whereof, these our letters are sealed with the seal of the Commonwealth and made patent. Witness Beverley Randolph Esquire our said Lieutenant Governor in the absence of the Governor at Richmond, on the 28$^{th}$ day of June in the year of our Lord, one thousand seven hundred and eighty seven and eleventh of the Commonwealth.
  Seal      Bev[everley Randolph, signature torn]

At a Court Held for Charles City County the 6$^{th}$ day of June 1787
Stith Hardyman, Benjamin Edmonson & William Christian Gen$^t$. are by the Court Recommended to his Excellency the Governor as proper persons to act in the office of Sheriffs for this County.

         A Copy  Peter Royster C,C,C

At a Quarterly Session Court begun and held for Charles City County the 1st day of August 1787

                    Present

  Benj. Harrison     William Christian]
  James Southall     John Colgin ]Gent$^a$
  Richm$^d$ Terrell     William Royall ]

On the motion of Otway Byrd Gentleman sheriff of this County setting forth that he was left out of the Order of recommendation of Sheriffs made in June last that he had not continued in the said Office two years the Court certifies to the Executive that it was not the intention of that Court to leave the said Byrd out of the said Order of recommendation, but the said omission was occasioned by inattention and that the said Byrd ought to stand first in the said Order of recommendation, in order that he may continue two years in this said Office.

                A Copy
               Peter Royster CCC

Reverse side:
Sir,
   The within ordinance meets with my consent if agreeable to Law, I have the honour to be Sir

              Your most Obe$^d$; Serv$^t$

Charles City
August y$^e$ 6 1787           Stith Hardyman
The Hon$^{ble}$ Beverley Randolph Esq L$^t$ Governor


We the subscribers Gentlemen Justices, who were absent from Court on the first of August, but were present at the Nomination of June Court, do perfectly agree to the justice of the recommendation in favour of M: Byrd & are of opinion he is intitled to the Sheriffs Office for two years

Charles City Aug$^{st}$..y$^e$..3$^d$ 1787

              Henry Southall
              Jos. Vaiden

I do certify that the above named Gentlemen Justices together with those inserted in the ordinance of the first of this instant formed a majority of the Court of June last.

Peter Royster Ct Cur

Charles City County Court                                               April 1790

Benjamin Edmondson this day produced a Commission from his Excellency the Governor and Council, appointing him Sheriff of this County; whereupon the said Edmondson with his securities entered into the several bonds required by law

A Copy   Otway Byrd CC

No date given

Ordered that Henry Vaughan, William Southall, Wyatt Walker, John Bradley, Edward Warren and Samuel Demovill[e] are in the opinion of the Court, fit Persons to be recommend to his Excellency the Governor, and council to be added to the commission of the peace for this county

A Copy Teste Otway Byrd CC

Charles City County Court                                               June 1791

Henry Duke is by the Court recommended to his excellency the governor and counsil as a fit person to be commissioned a Coroner in this County

A Copy   Otway Byrd CC

Charles City Court                                                       July 1791

Benjamin Edmondson. William Christian, and William Lightfoot Gent: are by the Court recommended to his Excellency the Governor and Council as fit persons one of whom to be commissioned Sherif of the County for the insuing year according to law.

A Copy   Ro: Munford   D.C.

Charles City County                                        July 1791

Ordered that Benjamin Edmondson, William Christian and William Lightfoot Gent: be recommended to his excellency the Governor and Council as fit persons, one of whom, to be commissioned Sheriff of this County.
                                                A Copy Otway Byrd CC

The above recommendation seems to correspond with the Commission Book
                                                    Sam: Coleman.

Charles City County Court                                 April 1792

William Christian this day produced a commission from the Governor and council appointing him Sheriff of this County. whereupon he qualified according to law.

*Teste Otway Byrd C.C.*

Otway Byrd's compliments to M: Coleman, will thank him, if the Executive should commission the Gentlemen recommended, if he will take the trouble to forward the commission by an early day in March. as many removals from the commission of the peace of this County have taken place within two years, the business is often stoped, for want of members. Our Court of yesterday was composed of so few members, that they determined to defer the recommendation of their Militia Officers until March.
Charles City                                No signature [Otway Byrd]
Febry 22d 1793

Charles City County court                             February 1793

It appearing to the court that William Christian, Henry Southall, Benjamin Edmondson, William Lightfoot, William Royall, Joseph Vaiden, James Southall, John Colgin, Richmond Terrel[l], William

Randolph and John Dunbar are the remaining Justices in the commission of the peace of this county and from the deaths & removals of Benjamin Harrison of Berkley, Otway Byrd, Stith Hardyman. John Dunbar who is immediately about to leave the County. & John Gregory dec$^d$ that there is not a sufficient number to do the duties of the said county it is therefore ordered that Henry Vaughan, William Southall, Wyatt Walker, John Bradley, Edward Warren and Samuel Demoville be recoumended to his excellency the Governor and council as fit persons to be added to the commission of the peace of said County.

Charles City County Court      July 1793

Ordered William Christian, William Lightfoot and William Royall be recommended to his excellency the Governor and council as fit persons one of whom to be comissioned Sheriff of this County according to law.

A Copy   Otway Byrd   CC

Charles City County Court      July 1794

William Lightfoot, William Royall and Joseph Vaiden Gent: are by the Court recommended to his excellency the Governor and Council as fit persons one of whom to be commissioned Sheriff of this County for the ensuing year.

A Copy   Otway Byrd   CC

Charles City County Court                                    June 1796

William Royall, Joseph Vaiden, and John Colgin, Esq$^r$ are by the Court recommended to his Excellency the Governor and Council as fit Persons, one of whom, to be commissioned sheriff of this County for the ensuing year

                              A Copy Teste  Otway Byrd CC

Charles City County Court                                    June 1797

James Walker, John Royall, and William Graves are by the Court, recommended to his excellency the Governor, and Council as fit persons to be added to those in the Commission of the peace for this County.

                              A Copy Teste  Otway Byrd CC

William Royall, Joseph Vaiden, and John Colgin Gen: are by the court recommended to his excellency the Governor and Council, as fit persons, one of whom to be commissioned sheriff for this County for the ensuing year.

                              A Copy Teste  Otway Byrd CC

Charles City County Court                                    June 1799

Joseph Vaiden, John Colgin and William Randolph are by the Court recommended to his Excellency the Governor and Council as fit persons one of whom to be commissioned sheriff of this County for the ensuing year

                              A Copy  Ro. Munford dc

                              Transcribed by VLHD

From the records of the Executive Department, Commonwealth of Virginia. Box 3, A-E. Pre 1790. Archives and Records Division, Virginia State Library and Archives, Richmond, Virginia. Published with the kind permission of Dr. Louis H. Manarin, Virginia State Archivist.

Charles City County Courthouse
Built c. 1730

## Will of Gideon Macon, 1767
## New Kent County

In the name of God Amen I Gideon Macon of New Kent County being at this present of Sound perfect mind and memory praised be almighty God, and I well considering the uncertainty of this Mortal Life I do therefore make and ordain this my present Last will and Testament in Manner and form following that is to say first and principally I commend my Soul into the hands of almightety [sic] God hoping through the Merits of my Savior Jesus Christ to have full free pardone and forgiveness of all my Sins and to Inherit everlasting Life and my Body I commit to the earth to be decently Buried at the Discretion of my Executors hereafter named and as Touching the Desposal of all such Temporal Estate as it hath pleased Almighty God to bestow upon me I give and dispose thereof as followeth. Item I give to my son Edmund Macon my land One Negro Girl named Mildred one Negro named Jack and a negro Girl named Nancy Likewise a Yoke of Steers two Cows and two calves and eight pounds Cash to buy him a Feather Bed and furniture. Item I give to my dear and Loving wife Rebecca Macon One Negro wench named Bess One negro Boy named Billy Boller and a negro girl named Cate during her natural Life and then to be equally Divided between my Two Daughters Elizabeth Macon and Rebecca Walker Macon. Item I give all my Estate not heretofore given be it of what nature or Kind or Degree known or unknown Between my Two Daughters Elizabeth Macon Rebecca Walker Macon. In case my wife Should be with Child my Desire is that the child Should Share equally with my Two Daughters Elizabeth and Rebeckah Macon my will and Desire is that all the estate may Continue with my wife During her natural widowhood or the Childrens comeing to the age of Twenty one years or do marry in case my wife should marry my desire is that my Estate may be devided as before mentioned. I appoint my Dear and Loving wife Rebecca Macon and my Loving Brother Lancelot Macon Executors and Executrix of this my Last will and Testament Revoking all other wills before by me made In witness whereof I have hereunto set my hand and Seal this 25th Day of December One thousand seven Hundred Sixty and Seven.

Signed Sealed and Delivered            Gideon Macon Seal
In presence of            My will is that my Just Debts
Test William Townes            and funeral Charges be first paid
    William Langley

At a Court held for New Kent the tenth Day of August 1769
This Last will and Testament of Gideon Macon decd was Exhibited into court by the Exors therein named Sworn to by the said Exors and being proved by the oathes of William Townes and William Langley all the witness thereto subscribed is Ordered to be recorded

                         Test Will. Clayton Clerk
                         A copy Test Will B Clayton DCC

                         Transcribed by VLHD

Found in Amelia County Suit Papers, H-P Judgments: Macon & Others vs. Macon & Children.

Loose Papers, Wills from Burned Record Counties, 1729-1830. New Kent County. Archives and Records Division, Virginia State Library and Archives, Richmond, Virginia. Published with the kind permission of Dr. Louis H. Manarin, Virginia State Archivist.

## Losses Sustained from the British Depredations Within the Commonwealth of Virginia Gloucester County, 1782

### Contributed by Minor Tompkins Weisiger

Transcriptions of losses claimed from the British invasions are presented for the burned record counties to help researchers identify residents of those counties, where other information is lacking. The losses claimed also provide information about the economic and social status (and property) of the claimants. Clues to relationships can be found in the names of those submitting the claims for others, and in those proving the claims. The approximate dates of estates not settled may also be identified. It is understood that this information may be used to establish eligibility for some hereditary societies.

The General Assembly of Virginia enacted the following law in May 1782: *"Be it enacted by the General Assembly, That the courts of the several counties within this state shall and they are hereby empowered and required either to hold special courts, or to appoint so many of their own body as to them shall seem most proper, to collect and state, from the best proof the nature of the case will admit of, the various losses and injuries, both public and private, which have been sustained within their respective counties during the war, from the depredations of the enemy in their several invasions, and to state the same under so many different heads as such losses or injuries may consist of, and return their proceedings herein, together with the proofs made in support thereof, to the governor and council, to be by them laid before the next assembly."*[1]

At a Court held in Gloucester County pursuant to an Act of Assembly for ascertaining the Losses and injuries Sustained from the Depredations of the Enemy within this Commonwealth the 7[th] Day of September 1782.

---

[1]Hening, Whilliam Waller. *The Statutes At Large, A Collection of All of the Laws of Virginia.* Vol.11, Richmond: Cochran. 1823.p.27.

Present Francis Tomkies, Peter Beverley Whiting, Thomas Smith, Thomas Smith jun$^r$ Philip Tabb and John Whiting Gent.

Ed. note: The following is transcribed from the original that was tabulated in chart form, with the headings: *Sufferers names; Negroes what sort & ages; Horses Cattle & Sheep hogs; Houses, Tobacco, Grain, Spirits & other property.*

Henry Forrest/ negro Man a valuable Smith 20 years old proved by Jn Lewis

Thomas Whiting deced. his Estate/ James 20 y$^r$ old, Harry 22, Peter 20, Barnaby a Shoemaker 25, Jack 14, Jack 16, Bob 17, Laurence a Weaver 19 y$^r$ old, Jerry 28, Ben 20, Peter 20, Amos 22, Pompey 50, Bob 29, Betty 40, Suky 23, Hannah 4, Agatha 1, Grace 36/ 1 Horse 12 years old, 1 ditto 15 years old. Proved by Elizabeth Whiting & Jn$^o$ Seawell.

The Estate of John Thurston Gen$^t$. deced/ 1 negro man Phill 50 years old went to the enemy rel$^d$ and died in a few days/ 1 Horse 3 years old taken & not returned. Proved by Jn$^o$ Vaughan/ a Dwelling House 30 by 20 feet pulld down & destroyed. a Large & almost new Storehouse Burnt. A Dairy and Smoak House pulld down, a large Garden destroyed a parcel of new posts pails [pales] and rails & plank destroyed, a corn field about 45 barrels with the cribs & destroyed dwelling House Kitchen & Store house damaged.

Johanna Dunlap/ 1 negro man George 30 years old a good Gardener, one negro Child two years old a negro child two months old/ 20 Hogs 8 Sheep. Proved by Mrs Dunlap/ A House 12 by 16 feet sawed logs two of which were planks above and below, 35 Barrels Indian Corn 80 Dunghill fowl 38 Turkeys 3 narrow axes 4 rum H$^{hd}$. a deal of wearing apparel 4000 bundles corn blades.

John Seawell/ Negro Jacob 40 years old went to the enemy returnd and died within 2 hours after his return, Toby 25 y$^r$ old, Abraham 20, Dick 55, Peter 26/ 2 Draft Oxen, Proved by J Seawell himself/ 100

Barrels Indian Corn, 300 Bushels Barley in the Straw 60 Bushels Oats, 300 fowl of different Kinds, 1 Horse Cart.

John Vaughan/ 29 hogs 6 Cattle, Proved by J Vaughan himself/ 1 Dweling house 36 by 26 feet burnt down, Smoke house burnt, 1 Billiard house & table burnt 1 dwelling house 20 by 16 feet pulld down, ½ acre of pailing [paled fence] destroyed, 1 Kitchen 16 by 12 feet destroyed 1 cornfield 1600 hills with new fencing destroyed 1½ Lots with pailing destroyed 2 corn houses pulled down 5000 lbs. Lignum vita [light wood]. ab. 5£ worth of Blockmakers tools destroyed 1 feather Bed 5 bedsteads, 3 Tables, 7 chairs 150 fowl of Different Kinds.

Benjamin Cluverius/ Negro Sam 50 years old, Michael 26, Anibal 20, Peter 23, Aaron 25, Dick 20, Aggy 15/ 30 Sheep, Proved by Benjamin Cluverius himself/ 8 Hd$^d$ Tobacco, 30 Barrels corn, 200 Bushels Oats, 100 fowl of different kinds.

Gibson Cluverius/ 12 Sheep/ Proved by Benjamin Cluverius.

John Cluverius/ 1 Negro man Moses 45 y$^r$ old. 1 Boy 6 or 7 years old/ proved by Benjamin Cluverius.

Elizabeth Tool/ 1 dwelling house 24 by 16 feet proved by J. Vaughan.

William Briggs/ proved by J. Vaughan/ 2 Cattle/ 1 Kitchen 20 by 16 feet, 1 shop 16 by 12 feet 500 lbs. Lignum vita.

Elizabeth Seawell and John Seawell/ one negro man Will 26 y$^r$ old/ proved by Jn$^o$ Seawell/ Elizabeth Seawells own losses 100 fowl different kinds.

William Busbys Estate/ 1 negro Girl Rachel 4 y$^r$ old proved by Edw$^d$ Busby/ 10 head cattle, 20 hogs, Horse 9 years old/ 40,000 Cornhills & fencing round it destroyed.

Edward Busby/ proved by Edw$^d$ Busby himself/ 11 Cattle 7 hogs/ 15,000 Corn hills and fencing round it 1 Kitchen 12 by 8 feet, ½ Lot garden destroyed.

Banister Mour Est./ Proved by J. Vaughan/ a dwelling house 28 feet square pulld down a Kitchen 20 by 16 feet a Table Garden & some outhouses in Gloster Town.

Zachairah Shackelford/ proved by himself/ 3 Cattle 10 Sheep 1 hog 100 lb.w/ 200 bundles Fodder, 12 Turkeys.

Mildred Scott/ a negro man Ned 22 years old, Wilson a Lad 17, Jenny a woman 40, Frank a Girl 4, Dick a boy 2, Robin a boy 3/ proved by John Scott/ These negroes Mrs Scot has only her Life in [interest].

John Scott/ 1 negro Lad Squire 17 y$^r$ old/ proved by himself.

Thomas Todds Estate/ 1 negro man Antony 21 y$^r$ old, James 24, Order 15/ proved by Phil Tabb Gen$^t$.

George Booth/ 1 negro man Charles 21 y$^r$ old/ proved by J. Scott.

Matthew Anderson/ a Negro man York 40 y$^r$ old, Peter 30/ proved by F Tomkies Gen.

Judith & Massey Cleaver/ negro woman Philis 55 y$^r$ old, Rachel 25, Nanny 10, 2 small ones 5 or 6 years old.

James Bentley/ Negro man James 30 y$^r$ old good sawyer, Bob a Lad 17, Winny woman 30 a good Cook/ proved by Tho$^s$ Hughes.

John Minter/ 1 negro man James 35 y$^{rs}$ old a Carpenter & very likely/ 16 sheep proved by Thom$^s$ Smith Gen.

Archibald Brainly/ 13 sheep proved by Thom$^s$ Smith Gen.

Thomas Smith Gen^t/ Dick a Carpenter 25 y. old, James Ditto 30, Tobey a Carpenter & Cooper 35, Dick 18, Peter 18, Esson 16, Jenny 35, James a Shoemaker 35, Abbey 15, Sue a house Servant 30, Daniel d° 18, Abram d° 18, Robin 20, Rose 14, Ben 50, Will body Servant 15 Joe 30/ proved by Thomas Smith jun Gen^t/ 1 new canoe 24 feet long 30 inches wide.

Francis Tomkies Gen^t/ 1 negro woman Lucy a house Servant 30 Kate d° both likely/ proved by Thomas Hughes and Jn° Throckmorton.

John Hughes Jur/ 1 negro man Jerry a good Sawyer & rough Carpenter 28 y^r old/ proved by Thomas Hughes & Jn° Throckmorton.

William Meichant [sic]/ 1 negro man Ralph 26 y^r old/ proved by James Carter and Jn° Elliott.

James Carter/ 1 negro man Samson 21 yr old/ proved by James Carter and Jn° Elliott.

John Elliott/ 1 negro man George 28 y^r old a good Sawyer and served 2 y^rs with the Blacksmith/ Trade proved by J Elliot & Jas Carter/

Peter B Whiting Gen./ proved by J. Vaughan/ 1 dwelling house in Gloucester town 74 by 24 feet in bad repair part Brick part wood.

William Vaughan/ 1 negro man Dellaware 15 y^r old/ 4 head Cattle/ 22 Barrels Corn proved by himself.

John Hobday/ a negro man Lewis 45 y^r old a negro woman 60/ proved by Wm Vaughan/ a Seine value £10. 100 fowl different kinds Carpenters Tools the value of £7.10.

Nathaniel Watlington/ Sworn to by himself/ 3 Cattle, 3 hogs/ 80 Bushels Oats 10 Barrels Corn.

George Hunley by the Enemy Curison [incursion]/ a negro woman Jane 40 y^rs old, Lewis 20, Alice a Girl 12/ proved by J. Belliaps [sic].

Thomas Coleman P Estate/ 1 negro man Sam 20 years old/ proved by Jo Coleman.

Transcribed by VLHD

*To be continued*

From The Legislative Department, House of Delegates, Office of the Speaker. Correspondence. Losses sustained from the British. May 1783. Archives and Records Division, Virginia State Library and Archives, Richmond, Virginia. Published with the kind permission of Dr. Louis H. Manarin, Virginia State Archivist.

# The Stiff Family Bible
## Middlesex County, 1777-1856

Inside Cover:   Thomas H. Stiff 1861-1921
James Willard Stiff 1856

Thomas H. Stiff son of William N. Stiff and Sarah his wife was born the 12th day of March 1797  married the 7th of September 1837

James M. Stiff Son of William Stiff and Sarah his wife was born the 14th day of December 1798

Mary Stiff daughter of William Stiff and Sarah his wife was born the 29th day of October 1800

William Stiff Son of William N. Stiff and Sarah his wife was born the 13th day of September 1802

Edmond Stiff son of William N. Stiff and Sarah his wife was born the 7th day of June 1805

Robert Stiff Son of William N. Stiff and Sarah his wife was born the 29th day of September 1807

Walter Stiff Son of William N. Stiff and Sarah his wife was born the 27th day of March 1809

Lewis S. Stiff Son of William N. Stiff and Sarah his wife was born the 24th day of January 1811

George Stiff Son of William N. Stiff and Sarah his wife was born the 14th day of January 1813, Departed this life the 23rd July 1836

Andrew Stiff Son of William N. Stiff and Sarah his wife was born the 13th day of March 1815

Sarah E. C. Stiff daughter of William N. Stiff and Sarah his wife was born the 18th day of February 1817, Departed this life 2 October 1834

Benjamin Stiff Son of William N. Stiff and Sarah his wife was born the 2nd day of April [n.d.given], Departed the life 30th April 1842

William I. L. Bennett son of Smith Bennett and Elizabeth B. Bennett his wife who was Elizabeth B. Stiff, daughter of James Stiff, Dec., was born the 8th day of September in the year of our Lord 1821 married to Adaline Miller daughter of Isham Miller and Nancy his wife the 1st day of January 1845.

Thomas H. Stiff and Elizabeth B. Bennett who was Elizabeth B. Stiff daughter of James Stiff, dec., was born 10 June 1801 and married the 7th day of September 1837

Frances Sarah Elizabeth Stiff daughter of Thomas H. Stiff and Elizabeth his wife born 24 August 1842

Sally Healy daughter of Thomas Healy, dec., was born 10 February 1777 and departed this life between 3 and 4 o'clock on the morning of the 1st day of November 1835 after being the wife of William N. Stiff. 39 years 9 months 3 days and the mother of 12 children, 10 sons and 2 daughters

James Stiff son of James Stiff, dec'd, was married to Susannah Wood the [blank] day of March 1796 and departed this life the 25th August 1819

Susannah Stiff wife of James Stiff, dec., and daughter of [blank] Wood departed this life the 27th day of December, 1836 (or 1830) 58 years 11 months

Frances M. Stiff daughter of James Stiff and Susannah his wife was born 13 January 1797 and departed this life 9 October 1829

James W. Stiff son of James Stiff and Susannah his wife was born 10 January 1799 and departed this life 31 December 1834

Susanna B. Stiff Daughter of James Stiff and Susannah his wife was born the 18th day of February 1807 and departed this life the 21st day of February 1833

Mary F. Stiff daughter of James Stiff and Susannah his wife was born the 3rd day of July 1804 and departed this life 15 October 1812

Sarah [blank] Stiff daughter of James Stiff and Susannah his wife was born 11 August 1810 married 5 January 1832 departed this life 8 April 1837

John S. Stiff son of James Stiff and Susannah his wife was born 12 June 1812 married 3 February 1835 and departed this life 22 April 1845

Lucy A. Stiff daughter of James Stiff and Susannah his wife was born 14 March 1814 and departed this life the 15th September 1834

Copied by Helyn Hatton Collison, May 1990

The Stiff Family Bible , 1777-1856. Bible Records. Accession Number 33828. Archives and Records Division, Virginia State Library and Archives. Richmond, Virginia. Published with the kind permission of Dr. Louis H. Manarin, Virginia State Archivist.

## BOOK REVIEWS:

Peter Wilson Coldham, *Emigrants in Chains: A Social History of Forced Emigration to the Americas of Felons, Destitute Children, Political and Religious Non-Conformists, Vagabonds, Beggars and other Undesirables, 1607-1776*. 188 pp. charts, appendices, bibliography, hardcover, $19.95 + $2.50 ship. 1992. Peter Coldham is the author of a number of standard books on Anglo-American genealogy and emigration. This book is not composed of lists of emigrants, but is, as the name states, a social history. It is authoritative, enlightening and fascinating reading. He presents many facts about the population of emigrants to the colonies that have either been ignored, or misrepresented. While a particular ancestor may not be identified, it provides insight about a social phenomenon little understood. Supported by a great array of documentary evidence and first-hand testimony the reader learns of the reception of these transportees into the colonies; their lives are graphically presented and make for engrossing reading, great enlightenment and a much better understanding of the peopling of the American colonies. Genealogical Publishing Co, 1001 N Calvert Street, Baltimore, MD 21202. Call 800-727-6687.

Bruce Roberts, *Plantation Homes of the James River*. xii, 116 pp. index, full color plates, map, guide, cloth, $29.95, paperback, $16.95. 1990. Bruce Roberts is senior travel photographer for *Southern Living* and some of his award winning photography is in the permanent collection of the Smithsonian Institution. He takes us on a magnificent photographic tour of fourteen of the famous colonial Virginia plantations along the shores of the Lower James River from Richmond east to Jamestown and Williamsburg. The photographic presentations are superbly executed and truly exciting. His selection of homes evidences a common bond of history, but each plantation home reflects the individual characteristics of the men and women who built and lived in the homes. They also reflect the dedication and appreciation of those present owners who have restored these plantations and now share them with the public on various occasions. The text is written in such a manner that, without sacrificing any of the sense of scholarly writing, or authenticity of the history, one becomes a visitor to the plantation. For those researchers of colonial tidewater history, the book provides insight, not only into the architecture and style of these plantations, but also the culture and society of their ancestors in tidewater Virginia. University of North Carolina Press, P O Box 2288, Chapel Hill, NC 27515. Call 919-966-3561.

*Heads of Families at the First Census of the United States, Taken in the Year 1790, Virginia*. 189 pp. index, map, introduction, 8½ x 11, soft cover. Government Printing, Washington, 1908. Reprint, GPC, Baltimore, 1992. $22.50 + $2.50 ship. The returns of the First Census of the United States with a complete set of schedules of each state were filed in the State Department, but unfortunately are not now complete. The returns for Virginia, among other states, were destroyed during the War of 1812. This publication is an effort to reconstruct the census returns for Virginia from other existing records (taxpayer lists) of the inhabitants during that time frame. Presented are the Virginia state enumerations for the years 1782, 1783, 1784 and 1785 of heads of families and the number of taxable persons for whom they were responsible. Not all counties are represented in each year, but this provides the most comprehensive listing of the residents of Virginia during that time period. This book is a must as a reference to identifying persons and their county of residence. Genealogical Publishing Company, 1001 N Calvert Street, Baltimore, MD 21202. Call 800-727-6687.

Virginia Lee Hutcheson Davis, *Tidewater Virginia Families: Bell, Binford, Bonner, Butler, Campbell, Cheadle, Chiles, Clements, Cotton, Dejarnette, Dumas, Ellyson, Fishback, Fleming, Hamlin, Hampton, Harnison, Harris, Haynie, Hurt, Hutcheson, Lee, Mosby, Mundy, Nelson, Peatross, Pettyjohn, Ruffin, Short, Spencer, Tarleton, Tatum, Taylor, Terrell, Watkins, Winston and Woodson.* xiv, 730 pp. index, maps, illus., facsimiles, cloth, 8½x11. $75.00 + $2.50 ship. "*Tidewater Virginia Families* is a book which should be examined by every serious student of family history and genealogy even if they have no family in Tidewater Virginia. It is a formidable synthesis of genealogy, family history and social history which is destined to serve as a bench mark for all future publications of this genre. In addition to extensive research into primary sources, the author has drawn heavily upon published histories and social histories in order to flesh out and provide context for her ancestors' lives and accomplishments...Where possible, Mrs Davis also includes information about the siblings of each direct ancestor which provides valuable clues for possible connections with other Virginia families." From the Western New York Genealogical Society, Vol. XVIII, No. 2. Genealogical Publishing Company, 1001 N Calvert Street, Baltimore, MD 21202. Call 800-727-6687.

Ed. note: I have included this because a number of subscribers, who are not acquainted with the book, have expressed interest in families presented in the book.

## ANNOUNCEMENTS:

*Historic Air Tours,* Peninsula Tour: View the entire historic triangle of Jamestown, Williamsburg and Yorktown. James River Tour: Discover the splendor of the James River Plantations. Hampton Roads Tour: Experience Virginia's maritime history. Tours $30.00 to $45.00 per person. Call for same day or advanced reservations. 804-253-8185. Mitchell Bowman, P O Box 681, Williamsburg, VA 23187.

*Mathews County, Virginia, US Census, 1810, 1820, 1830, 1840.* 93 pp. general index, foreward. $16.00 + $2.50 ship. *1850 Federal Census, Mathews County, Virginia.* 65 pp. includes all schedules. $15.00 + $2.50 ship. These two publications have been abstracted by Dr Stephen E Bradley, Jr and are available from the Mathews Historical Society, The Tompkins Cottage, P O Box 855, Mathews, VA 23109.

*Virginia, Atlas and Gazetteer.* Topographic maps of the entire state of Virginia. 80 pp, 11"x15½", full color, index. 1989. Item #5503H. $14.95 plus ship. DeLorme Mapping Company, P O Box 298, Freeport ME 04032. Call 800-225-5669, Ext.1035.

**SEARCH:**

CREEDLE/CRIDDLE. Seeking information about this family in Virginia before 1780.
FLOYD, John and Morris, residents of King & Queen and King William counties, 1700-1750. Seek information.
EARNEST family, Hanover Co prior to 1800. Seek information.
SANDERS family, James City Co c.1625, later in Nansemond Co. Seek information. Dr Susan C Slaymaker, 11463 Mother Lode Cir, Gold River, CA 95670.

SEAT/SEATE/SEATS, Nathan, m 1798 Halifax Co, Sarah Pryor, d 1835. Seek information or documentation of parents and children. Joan Seat Ellis, 10200 W Providence Rd, Richmond, VA 23236.

WINGFIELD, Ann, m c.1727 Robert Wingfield (b c.1697, New Kent Co, d c.1769, Louisa Co). Seek documentation of maiden name of Ann, d c.1787. Betty W Wingfield, 602 Holbein Pl, Richmond, VA 23225.

CHILES, Hezekiah, in Spotsylvania Co in 1754, witness will of George Musick with Henry Chiles and Henry Marsh. Exchange information with anyone researching ancestors of Hezekiah. Julia Brown Hazelwood, 1631 Spartan Ln, Athens, GA 30606.

BATCHELDER, CHOWNING, STRINGER, WARE, HUGHES, ABBOTTS, WATTS, WETHERSBY, also DANIEL, LAUGLIN, DICKERSON, ANDREWS families. Exchange information. Marie Stringer Kaehler, 1977 S Broadway, Grand Junction, CO 81503.

LONG, Capt John, b 1755, lived in KY then St Louis area, m 1782, Elizabeth Bennett. Children born in Port Royal VA (Isabella b 1783, Nancy b 1787, William b 1789, John b 1792). Need info. Wanza Barker Merrifield, 808 Sugar Maple, Ponca City, OK 74604.

ELLIS, Hezekiah, lived Gloucester Co before 1717. Seek parents and siblings. m Mary, d 1726, Middlesex Co. Issue: John, Elizabeth m Gordon, Mary m Maderas, Anne m Jolley, William, Hezekiah, Robert, Sarah m Davidson and dau. m Thomas Faulkner. Ellis O Moore, 984 Esplanade, Pelham Manor, NY 10803.

DILLARD, Nicholas, King & Queen, Caroline Co, d 1742. Issue (P): Lewis, George, Thomas, Nicholas (special interest), d c.1780, Halifax Co NC. Wish to contact descendants for Dillard history of family. Dorothy Dillard Hughes, 1908 18th St, Lubbock, TX 79401.

MCCOLGAN, Mary, b c.1823, VA, Seek parents and information. m c.1839, John Catlett, son of Lawrence and Elizabeth Conway Catlett, North Garden, Caroline Co. Son, Arthur Conway Catlett, b 1839. Mrs Jean Voss, 4505 Iola, Muskogee, OK 74401.

SIMMONS, William, James City Co, d 1678 and John, Surry Co, 1710, also John Simmons, York Co, 1714. Seek information about these Simmons, and those of 17 & 18 century VA for brief history.

MCGEHEE, Catherine m 1713, Thomas Butts (b 1669) New Kent Co. Seek information about Catherine, dau. (or grandau.?) of Thomas, King William Co? Also Thomas, land 1702, Kg Wm and William Machgehee, New Kent, 1689. Jean Butts Jones, 9209 River Rd, Richmond, VA 23229.

MILLNER, NOEL. Need information on when or where Cornelius Noel and William Millner left Essex Co. They moved to Bedford Co.
WINGFIELD. Will exchange information on the Wingfield family of Hanover County. T. Wingfield Millner, 1 Normill Landing, Newport News, VA 23602.

GRIFFIE, GRIFFITH families of King George and Hanover Co. Lewis Griffie was in Stafford & King Geo 1694, 1704 granted 414 a on Clayburn's Swamp, King Geo. Seek info. Mrs A Grant Fewsmith, Jr, 4167 Inman Court, Fort Worth, TX 76109.

PRICE, Col Warner W, son of Ann(a) Dejarnette and John L Price of Caroline/Essex/Cumberland, directed in codicil to will 28 Dec 1855 (Pr Edw WB 10:271/272): "sell Dejarnett tract land at $10/a, not to be cut apart". Location of land? Dorothy G Hankins, 101 Holdsworth Rd, Williamsburg, VA 23185.

EUBANK, Maj James Archer, b K & Q, 1813. Orphaned, raised by uncle (name unknown). Perhaps later lived near Richmond, m 1834 Cornelia Roane of "Prospect", Middlesex Co. Desire information on parents, siblings. Pat Perkinson, "Prospect", P O Box 174, Topping, VA 23169.

*Coming in the Next Issue:*

*Losses Sustained from the British Depredations*
*Parish Records that Have (and Have Not) Survived*
*Civil Appointments, Elizabeth City County*
*Walter Chiles II*

# INDEX

Abbotts
  family 101
Anderson
  Matthew 93
Andrews
  family 101
Bagby
  Elizabeth 75
  John 75
  Juliet 75
  Nannie 75
  Rev Alfred 75
  Sarah J 75
Batchelder
  family 101
Belliaps
  J. 95
Bennett
  Elizabeth 101
  Elizabeth B. 97
  Smith 97
  William I. L. 97
Bentley
  James 93
Booth
  George 93
Bradley
  John 81, 83, 85
Brainly
  Archibald 93
Braxton
  Carter 74
  George 74
  Mary 74
Briggs
  William 92
Busby
  Edward 92, 93
  William 92
Butts
  Thomas 102
Byrd
  Otway 80, 82-86

Carlton
  Alice 77
  Cornelius 77
  Ida 77
Carter
  Hon. Robert 74
  James 94
Catlett
  Arthur Conway 102
  Elizabeth 102
  John 102
  Lawrence 102
Childe
  Richard 68
  Walter 68
Chiles
  Elizabeth 68, 70, 71
  Henry 101
  Hezekiah 101
  John 68, 71
  Susanna 70
  Walter 67-71
  William 68, 70, 71
Chowning
  family 101
Christian
  William 81-85
Clay
  Robert Young 53
Clayton
  Will B 89
Cleaver
  Judith 93
  Massey 93
Cluverius
  Benjamin 92
  Gibson 92
  John 92
Cocke
  John 80
Cole
  Sarah 68
Coleman
  Jo 95
  M: 84

Coleman
  Sam: 84
  Thomas 95
Colgin
  John 82, 84, 86
Conway
  Elizabeth 102
Cooke
  Harriet 78
  Loulie 76
Creedle
  family 101
Criddle
  family 101
Daniel
  family 101
Daniels
  Elizabeth S 78
Davidson
  Sarah 101
Davies
  Landon 76
  Landon N 75
  Sue C 75
Dejarnette
  Ann(a) 102
Demoville
  Samuel 83, 85
Dickerson
  family 101
Dillard
  George 101
  Lewis 101
  Nicholas 101
  Thomas 101
Dix
  Mary Agnes 78
  Wm Shepherd 78
Dorman
  John Frederick 55, 64
Drudge
  Addie Carlton 79
  Capt Joseph H 79
  Mary 79

Duke
  Henry 83
Dunbar
  G 80
  John 85
Dunlap
  Johanna 91
Earnest
  family 101
Edmondson
  Benjamin 83, 84
Edmonson
  Benjamin 81
Elliott
  John 94
Ellis
  Anne 101
  Elizabeth 101
  Hezekiah 101
  John 101
  Mary 101
  Robert 101
  Sarah 101
  William 101
Embrey
  Alvin T 57
Faulkner
  Thomas 101
Fitzhugh
  William S 79
Floyd
  John 101
  Morris 101
Forrest
  Henry 91
Gerry
  Jon. 68
Gordon
  Elizabeth 101
Graves
  William 86
Gregory
  John 85
Gresham
  Edward 79
  Isabella 79
  Mattie E 75

Griffie
  Lewis 102
Griffith
  family 102
Hall
  Franklin 76
  John C 76
  Loulie 76
Hardyman
  Stith 81, 82, 85
Harrison
  Benj. 82
  Benjamin 85
Hart
  Lyndon H., III 65
  Mary C 77
  Rev Joseph M 77
  Sudie M 77
Healy
  Sally 97
  Thomas 97
Henry
  Patrick 80
Hobday
  John 94
Hopkins
  William L 55, 62
Hughes
  family 101
  John, Jur 94
  Thomas 94
  Thos 93
Hunley
  George 95
Irby
  Hardyman 81
Jeffries
  James M 78
  Juliet 75
  Malvina 78
Jolley
  Anne 101
King
  G. H. S. 60
Knowles
  George 80
Kolbe
  J. Christian 65

Langley
  William 89
Lauglin
  family 101
Lewis
  Jn 91
Lightfoot
  William 80, 83-85
Long
  Capt. John 101
  Isabella 101
  John 101
  Nancy 101
  William 101
Lukin
  Alice 71
Lumpkin
  Richard E 79
Machgehee
  William 102
Macon
  Edmund 88
  Elizabeth 88
  Gideon 88, 89
  Lancelot 88
  Rebecca Walker 88
Maderas
  Mary 101
Mann
  Isabella 79
Marsh
  Henry 101
Mason
  Malvina 78
McColgan
  Mary 102
McGehee
  Catherine 102
  Thomas 102
Meichant
  William 94
Miller
  Adaline 97
  Isham 97
  Nancy 97
Millner
  William 102

Minter
  John 93
Mour
  Banister 93
Munford
  Colonel 80
  Ro: 83, 86
Musick
  George 101
Negro
  Aaron 92
  Abbey 94
  Abraham 91
  Abram 94
  Agatha 91
  Aggy 92
  Alice 95
  Amos 91
  Anibal 92
  Antony 93
  Barnaby 91
  Ben 91, 94
  Bess 88
  Betty 91
  Billy Boller 88
  Bob 91, 93
  Cate 88
  Charles 93
  Daniel 94
  Dellaware 94
  Dick 92-94
  Esson 94
  Frank 93
  George 91, 94
  Grace 91
  Hannah 91
  Harry 91
  Jack 88, 91
  Jacob 91
  James 91, 93, 94
  Jane 95
  Jenny 93, 94
  Jerry 91, 94
  Joe 94
  Kate 94
  Laurence 91
  Lewis 94, 95
  Lucy 94
Negro
  Michael 92
  Mildred 88
  Moses 92
  Nancy 88
  Nanny 93
  Ned 93
  Order 93
  Peter 91-94
  Philis 93
  Phill 91
  Pompey 91
  Rachel 92, 93
  Ralph 94
  Robin 93, 94
  Rose 94
  Sam 92, 95
  Samson 94
  Squire 93
  Sue 94
  Suky 91
  Tobey 94
  Toby 91
  Will 92, 94
  Wilson 93
  Winny 93
  York 93
Noel
  Cornelius 102
Page
  John 71
  Mary 71
Pollard
  Catherine R 76
  Col John 75, 76
  H R 75
  Jessie 75
  John 76, 75, 76
  John N 75
  Joseph 76
  Juliet 76, 75
  R N 75
  Thomas 75
  William H 76
Powers
  David A 78
  Harriet 78
  Rev John A 78
Price
  Col Warner 102
  John L 102
Pryor
  Sarah 101
Randolph
  Beverley 81, 82
  William 85, 86
Ray
  Suzanne Smith 54
Reed
  Mary 79
Rilee
  Mary E 76
  W C 76
Robinson
  Morgan P. 58
Royall
  John 86
  William 82, 84-86
Royster
  Peter 81-83
Sanders
  family 101
Scott
  A F 78
  John 93
  M E 78
  Maggie 78
  Mildred 93
Seat
  Nathan 101
Seawell
  Elizabeth 92
  John 91, 92
Shackelford
  Zachairah 93
Shaw
  Jon. 68
Shepherd
  C C 78
Simmons
  John 102
  William 102
Smith
  Ida 77
  Thomas 91, 93, 94
  Thomas, jun 91, 94

Southall
  Furnea 81
  Henry 81, 83, 84
  James 80, 82, 84
  William 83, 85
Sparacio
  Ruth 57, 61, 62
  Sam 57, 61, 62
Starkey
  Marion L. 56
Stiff
  Andrew 96
  Benjamin 97
  Edmond 96
  Elizabeth B. 97
  Frances M. 97
  Frances Sarah Elizabeth 97
  George 96
  James 97, 98
  James M. 96
  James W. 98
  James Willard 96
  John S. 98
  Lewis S. 96
  Lucy A. 98
  Mary 96
  Mary F. 98
  Robert 96
  Sarah 96-98
  Susannah 97, 98
  Thomas 96, 97
  Walter 96
  William 96, 97
Stringer
  family 101
Tabb
  Phil 93
  Philip 91
Terrell
  Richmond 82, 84
Throckmorton
  Jno 94
Thurston
  John 91
Todd
  Bernard 79
  Elizabeth 79
  Maria P 79
  Thomas 93
  William 79
  William B 79
Tomkies
  F 93
  Francis 91, 94
Tool
  Elizabeth 92
Townes
  William 89
Travers
  Elizabeth 78
  Raleigh 78
Tutton
  Henry 68, 69
Tyler
  Elizabeth 71
Vaiden
  Jos. 83
  Joseph 84-86
Vaughan
  Henry 83, 85
  J. 92-94
  Jno 91
  John 92
  John Thomas 78
  William 94
Walker
  James 86
  Wyatt 83, 85
Walton
  Mary E 76
Ware
  family 101
Warren
  Edward 83, 85
Watlington
  Nathaniel 94
Watts
  family 101
Weisiger
  Benjamin B, III 56, 58, 64
Wethersby
  family 101
Whiting
  Elizabeth 91
  John 91
  Peter B 91, 94
  Thomas 91
Wingfield
  Ann 101
  family 102
  Robert 101
Wood
  Susannah 97
Woodward
  Bell Jeter 75
  Dr Richard H 75
  John B. 75
  Mary Elizabeth 76
  P T 76
Wright
  B S 77
  Mary L 77
  Wm G 77

## *TIDEWATER VIRGINIA FAMILIES:*
### *A Magazine of History and Genealogy*

### TABLE OF CONTENTS

| | |
|---|---:|
| From Virginia | 108 |
| The Parishes of Tidewater Virginia | 109 |
| Walter Chiles, The Son, James City County | 120 |
| Colonel John Page | 123 |
| A Brief History of Christ Church, Middlesex County | 127 |
| Civil Appointments, Elizabeth County, 1780-1804 | 131 |
| Will of William Sanders, 1793, Richmond County | 139 |
| Byrom Family Bible, 1816-1886 | 141 |
| The Grave of Jacob Lumpkin, 1708 | 142 |
| Tidewater Virginia Residents Identified in Deeds, Northampton County, North Carolina, 1759-1774 | 143 |
| Losses Sustained from the British Depredations Cloucester County, 1782-1783 | 146 |
| List of Marriages, 1794-1798, York County | 150 |
| Carlton Family Bible, 1804, King and Queen County | 152 |
| Book Reviews | 154 |
| Announcements | 156 |
| Search | 157 |
| Index | 161 |

Volume 1 Number 3       November/December 1992

## From Virginia............

It is heartwarming to find that *TIDEWATER VIRGINIA FAMILIES* is truly a collaborative venture. Subscribers have offered suggestions about records that should be preserved and presented to researchers. They have offered abstracts, family histories and records that they feel will be of interest to be published. It will take a while to assemble and include these, but it is exciting to have new material made available. There will never be too much or too many, so readers are encouraged to be contributors if they feel they have relevant material that they would like to share.

The archivists at the Virginia State Library and Archives are an integral part of this publication. Their professional competence, knowledge and insight are outstanding and invaluable. Their commitment to the preservation and dissemination of the information from the colonial Virginia records is beyond professionalism, and is truly a dedicated service. They offer insight concerning the use and interpretation of records that goes far beyond the necessary limits of their obligation to the public. Besides this they are patient and have a marvelous sense of humor. It is inadequate to say that their contributions are very much appreciated.

The editor and the publishing consultant have "settled in" with a workable schedule now, and it seems that this schedule will be helpful in planning, to the readers and contributors, as well as the staff of *TIDEWATER VIRGINIA FAMILIES*. The quarterly will go to the publishing consultant with its final contents in place the first of the month, two months prior to the publication date for that issue. The completed magazine will go to the printer one month prior to the publication date. This allows enough time for glitches and goblins to be eliminated. It is thus projected that each issue will be mailed on the first Tuesday of the first month of that issue. Postal requirements are such that the magazine should be in the hands of subscribers certainly by the end of the month of the mail date.

It is important to the editor that each subscriber receive the magazine within the stated time frame. Subscriber lists are checked and rechecked, the magazine does go out to each subscriber, and the editor would like to know if the postal service fails in its stated mission.

Please continue to express your thoughts and interest in the magazine...........

VLHD

## The Parishes of Tidewater Virginia I

The Church of England in the Colony of Virginia began when the first permanent colonists stepped ashore at Cape Henry on April 26, 1607. The colonists brought with them the Established Church with its canon law, as well as the common law of England. The Established Church of England was to be the ruling religious body in the new colony. The Virginia Company of London made a provision that each new settlement should become a parish and have its own minister. This was the beginning of the system of parishes in Virginia.

The Assembly of March 1655 ordered that all counties not laid out in parishes should be divided into parishes at the next County Court. As the settlements moved westward and northward up the James, York and Rappahannock rivers and their tributaries, new counties and thus new parishes were created. In many instances parishes and counties were coeval and coterminous, in some instances the parishes antedate the counties, in many instances there is more than one parish in a county, and in a few instances parishes cover parts of two counties. It must be remembered, however, that the western boundaries of the counties, and thus of the parishes were not definite, but extended in a westward direction as far as the settlement had proceeded.

It was required that there be a vestry held in each parish, for the enactment of levies and to oversee the parish business. The number of vestrymen was set at twelve and the most select men were appointed by the county court to serve. The parishes were an integral part of the county organization, with the churchwardens (officers of the vestry) required to report to the county court twice a year. Because the duties of the vestry were varied and reached into the everyday lives of the parishioners, the vestry minutes and registers (of births, marriages and deaths) provide important information about the lives of these people. The duties of the vestries included:

    The right to appoint their minister of the parish.
    The right to investigate moral offenses.
    The right to lay the parish levy.
    The obligation to care for the indigent of the parish.

The responsibility of the processioning of the land.[1]
The transaction of the business of the churches.
The responsibility of the recording of births and baptisms.[2]

A listing of the evolution of the parishes of colonial tidewater Virginia will help the researcher to identify the place of residence of early ancestors. Where the vestry books and registers have survived critical information about the early settlers may be found. In some of the burned record counties, this may be the only extant information available. In many of the parishes, neither the vestry book nor the register has survived. It is also important to note that there was not a consistency in the record keeping by either the clergymen or the clerk of the vestry, and records that may be found from one parish are disappointingly absent from another parish. This is especially true of the processioning returns.

This researcher has found the processioning returns to be invaluable in reconstructing the lives of the residents of St. Paul's Parish in Hanover County. One can plot the location of land, the life and death of the owner, and the passage from one generation to the next. For much of the same time frame, there are almost no court records available.

Where the parish vestry books and registers have survived they provide such a wealth of information about the lives of the inhabitants of that parish that one hopefully pursues this information in any county and parish from which one has identified ancestors. It seems such a

---

[1] The processioning of the bounds of every person's land was required every four years. It was this processioning that determined the record of land titles. The parishes were divided into precincts of convenient size and two freeholders for each precinct were appointed to conduct the processioning. It was accomplished in the presence of the land owner and two disinterested persons, who actually walked the land boundaries; they were then required to report to the vestry in writing, naming the persons and land involved.

[2] Act X of the early canons enacted between 1632 and 1649 required that a register of vital statistics be kept for each parish. A record of births and baptisms was kept and some of the ministers also recorded the dates of death or burial and of marriages; however, these latter records were not consistently kept.

simple task to find these records that one approaches it with great anticipation. It doesn't work that way. There are relatively few of these records that have survived from an early date. The Established Church continued during the Revolutionary period, and until 1784 when the Anglican Church was disestablished and the civil duties imposed on the vestries were assigned to other official groups in the counties.

The final damage occurred in 1802 with the seizure and sale of the Church's glebe lands, silver plate, bells and endowments, with few exceptions. This final dissolution of the Anglican Church meant that many of the records were no longer given a safe repository. Along with a listing of the parishes it is of value to list the vestry books and registers that have survived and been faithfully restored and transcribed for present day historians.

While the organization of the parishes has often followed the organization of the counties, originally there were a number of plantation parishes. This accounts for the large number of early parishes and their later extinction. These small parishes probably shared their minister and depended upon a reader to conduct divine services. These parishes later became a part of a larger parish.

The descent of the parishes will be presented chronologically within the organization of the original eight shires, or counties of the colony of Virginia. The dates of the existence of the parishes will be self-explanatory, with the dates of more recent parishes indicated by a date of inception that follows the termination or incorporation of an earlier parish. Presently existing parishes will be indicated by leaving the termination date blank. A listing of the parishes that were in existance in 1785, by county, will also be helpful to the researcher.

James City Parish, 1607
James City County (north side of the James River)[3]
Martin's Hundred Parish, 1618-1712

---

[3]Please be aware that this account deals only with the parishes that have evolved on the north side of the James River. James City County (as did Charles City and Henrico counties) extended to the south of the James and included early parishes that evolved into other parishes in a westward direction from those early parishes.

Chickahominy Parish, c.1632-1643
(Wallingford Parish, 1643-1720)
Wilmington Parish, 1658-1725
Blisland Parish, 1653[4]    (York County, 1653)
Middle Plantation Parish, 1633-1658
Harrop Parish, 1645-1658
Middletowne Parish, 1658-1674 (Middle Plantation and Harrop merged)
Bruton Parish, 1674-    (also York County)

Charles City Plantation Parish, 1613
Charles City County (north side of the James River)
West and Shirley Parish, c.1613-1622
Smith's Hundred, 1617-1619
(Southampton Parish, 1619-1622)
Chickahominy Parish, c.1632-1643
(Wallingford Parish, 1643-1720)
Weyanoke Parish, c.1643-1720
Wilmington Parish, 1657-1725
Westover Parish, c.1625-

Henrico Parish, 1611
Henrico County (north side of the James River)
Henrico Parish, 1611-
Varina Parish, 1680-1714 (used interchangeably with Henrico)
St. James Parish, 1720-1728    (continued as Henrico)

Elizabeth City Parish, 1619
Elizabeth City County
Kecoughtan Parish, 1610-1619    (became Elizabeth City Parish)
Elizabeth City Parish, 1619-

---

[4] Cocke presents this parish in this chronologic and geographic order. However, the evolution of the parish is as follows: York Co, 1653-1654; New Kent Co, 1654-; James City Co, 1766-. Thus the dates entered in his book and here are somewhat misleading.

Warwick Parish, 1627
Warwick County

Stanley Hundred Parish, 1627-1634
Mulberry Island Parish, 1634-1725
Waters Creek Parish, 1629-1656 (continued as Denbigh Parish)
Nutmeg Quarter Parish, 1643-1656 (continued as Denbigh Parish)
Denbigh Parish, c.1635-1725
Warwick Parish, 1725- (consolidation of above parishes)

Charles River Parish, 1634-1643
Charles River, later York Parish, 1643
York County

New Poquoson Parish, 1635-1692 (became Charles Parish)
Charles Parish, 1692-
Middle Plantation Parish, 1633-1658
York Parish, c.1638-1707
Chiskiack Parish, 1640-1643 (name changed to Hampton)
Hampton Parish, 1643-1707
Harrop Parish, 1645-1658 (became Middletown Parish)
Marston Parish, 1654-1674
Bruton Parish, 1674- (also James City County)
Yorkhampton Parish, 1707- (York and Hampton consolidated)
    (Descended therefrom through Gloucester County)[5]
Abingdon Parish, 1652-
Petsworth Parish, 1652-
Ware Parish, 1652-
Kingston Parish, 1652- (Mathews County, 1791)
    (Descended therefrom through New Kent County, 1654)
Blisland Parish, c.1653- (James City County, 1767)
Stratton Major Parish, 1655- (King and Queen County, 1691)
St. Stephen's Parish, c.1674- (King and Queen County, 1691)
St. Peter's Parish, 1679-

---

[5] There is no doubt that plantation parishes formed along the north side of the York River in the original York County. No evidence has been found that these plantation parishes, if established, were officially recognized by the General Assembly.

| | |
|---|---|
| St. John's Parish, 1680- | (King and Queen County, 1691) |
| | (King William County, 1701-) |
| St. Paul's Parish, 1704- | (Hanover County, 1720-) |
| St. Margaret's Parish, 1721- | (King William County, 1721) |
| | (Caroline County, 1728) |
| Drysdale Parish, 1723- | (King and Queen County, 1723 and Caroline County, 1728) |
| | (King and Queen County, 1780-) |
| St. Martin's Parish, 1727- | (Hanover County, 1727-) |
| St. Mary's Parish, 1677- | (Old Rappahannock County, 1677) |
| | (Essex County, 1692) |
| | (Caroline County, 1728-) |
| St. David's Parish, 1745- | (King William County, 1745-) |
| St. Asaph's Parish, 1780- | (Caroline County, 1780-) |

Lancaster Parish, 1651
(Descended therefrom Charles River, York Parishes)

| | |
|---|---|
| Unnamed Parish, 1651-1654 | (Lancaster County, 1651) |

Upper Parish and Lower Parish, 1654-1656
    Formed from the Upper Parish:

| | |
|---|---|
| Farnham Parish, 1656-1683 | (Old Rappahannock County, 1656) |
| Sittenburne Parish, 1661-1732 | (Old Rappahannock County, 1661) |
| | (Essex County, 1692-1704) |
| | (Richmond County, 1692-1732) |
| St. Mary's Parish, 1677- | (Old Rappahannock County, 1677) |
| | (Richmond County and Essex County, 1692) |
| | (Caroline County, 1727-) |
| North Farnham Parish, 1683- | (Old Rappahannock County, 1683) |
| | Richmond County, 1692-) |
| South Farnham Parish, 1683- | (Old Rappahannock County, 1683) |
| | (Essex County, 1692) |
| St. Anne's Parish, 1704- | (Essex County, 1704-) |
| Hanover Parish, 1714- | (Richmond County, 1714) |
| | (King George County, 1720-) |
| St. Paul's Parish, 1680- | (Stafford County, 1680) |
| | (King George County, 1776-) |

| | |
|---|---|
| Lunenburg Parish, 1732- | (Richmond County, 1732-) |
| Brunswick Parish, 1732- | (King George County, 1732-) |

Formed from the Lower Parish:

| | |
|---|---|
| Lancaster Parish, 1657-1666 } | |
| Piankatank Parish, 1657-1666} | (Lancaster County, 1657) |
| Christ Church Parish, 1666- | (Lancaster County, 1666-) |
| | (both sides of Rappahannock River) |
| Christ Church Parish, 1666- | (Lancaster County, 1666-) |
| Christ Church Parish, 1669- | (Middlesex County, 1669-) |

Northumberland Parish, before 1648)

| | |
|---|---|
| Chickacoan Parish, 1645-1664 | (Northumberland County, 1645) |
| Fairfield Parish, 1664-1698 | |
| St. Stephen's Parish, 1698- | |
| Wicomico Parish, 1648- | |
| Nomini Parish, 1653-c.1668 | (Northumberland County, 1653) |
| | (Westmoreland County, 1653-c.1668) |
| Appomattox Parish, c.1653-1664} | |
| Machodick Parish, c.1653-1664} | (Westmoreland County, 1653-1664) |
| Westbury Parish, 1664-c.1680 | (Westmoreland County, 1664-c.1680) |
| Washington Parish, 1664- | (Westmoreland County, 1664-) |
| Cople Parish, c.1664- | (Westmoreland County, 1664-) |
| Potomac Parish, c.1653 | (Westmoreland County, 1653) |
| | (Stafford County, 1664-) |
| St. Paul's Parish, c.1702- | (Stafford County, 1664-1777) |
| | (King George County, 1777-) |

*These parish descents should be read in conjunction with the article "The Counties of Tidewater Virginia" in Volume 1, Number 1 of Tidewater Virginia Families, in order to more clearly understand the geographic location of the parishes at any given time. One student of the colonial parishes of Virginia has observed that the confusion of names, mergers and changing boundaries makes a summary without numerous explanations and exceptions very difficult. For the serious student, the references that follow are recommended.*

\* \* \* \* \*

Parishes (By County) in 1785

Caroline County, 1728: *St. Mary's Parish (1), 1677; St. Margaret's Parish (2), 1721; St. Asaph's Parish (3), 1780.*
Charles City County, 1634: *Westover Parish, c.1625.*
Elizabeth City County, 1634 (City of Hampton, 1952): *Elizabeth City Parish, 1619.*
Essex County, 1692: *South Farnham Parish (1), c.1683; St. Anne's Parish (2), 1704.*
Gloucester County, 1651: *Abingdon Parish (1), 1652; Petsworth Parish (2), 1652; Ware Parish (3), 1652.*
Hanover County, 1721: *St. Paul's Parish (1), 1704; St. Martin's Parish (2), 1727.*
Henrico County, 1634: *Henrico Parish, 1611.*
James City County, 1634: *James City Parish (1), 1607; Blisland Parish (2), 1653; Bruton Parish (3), 1674.*
King and Queen County, 1691: *Stratton Major Parish (1), 1655; St. Stephen's Parish (2), c.1674; Drysdale Parish (3), 1723.*
King George County, 1720: *St. Paul's Parish (1), 1666; Hanover Parish (2), 1714; Brunswick Parish (3), 1732.*
King William County, 1701: *St. John's Parish (1), 1680; St. David's Parish (2), 1745.*
Lancaster County, 1651: *Christ Church Parish, 1666.*
Mathews County, 1791: *Kingston Parish, 1652.*
Middlesex County, 1669: *Christ Church Parish, 1666.*
New Kent County, 1654: *Blisland Parish (1), 1653; St. Peter's Parish (2), 1679.*
Northumberland County, 1645: *Wicomico Parish (1), c.1648; St. Stephen's Parish (2), c.1698.*
Richmond County, 1692: *North Farnham Parish (1), 1684; Lunenburg Parish (2), 1732.*
Warwick County, 1634 (City of Newport News, 1958): *Warwick Parish, 1724.*
Westmoreland County, 1653: *Cople Parish (1), 1664; Washington Parish (2), 1664.*
York County, 1643 (1634): *Charles Parish (1), c.1635; Yorkhampton Parish (2), 1707 (1638), Bruton Parish (3), 1674.*

## References:

Alexson, Edith F. *A Guide to Episcopal Church Records in Virginia*. Athens: Iberian. 1988.

Brydon, George MacLaren. *Virginia's Mother Church and the Political Conditions Under Which it Grew*. vol.1 Richmond: Virginia State Library. 1947; vol.2 Philadelphia: Church Historical Society. 1952.

Clark, Jewel T. and Elizabeth Terry Long, *A Guide to Church Records in the Archives Branch Virginia State Library*. Richmond: Virginia State Library. 1988.

Cocke, Charles Francis. *Parish Lines, Diocese of Southern Virginia*. Richmond: Virginia State Library. 1964.

Cocke, Charles Francis. *Parish Lines, Diocese of Virginia*. Richmond: Virginia State Library. 1967.

Davis, Perdue, E. Holcombe Palmer and Edward A. Coffey. *Summaries of the Parish Lines of the Diocese of Virginia, West Virginia, Southern Virginia and Southwest Virginia*. Richmond: The Diocese of Virginia. 1960-1985.

Goodwin, Edwin Lewis. *The Colonial Church in Virginia*. Milwaukee: Morehouse. 1927.

Hening, William Waller. *Statutes at Large of Virginia*. Vols.I-XIII. Richmond and New York. (various dates, beg. 1807).

Mason, George Carrington. *Colonial Churches of Tidewater Virginia*. Richmond: Whittet. 1945.

Rawlings, James Scott and Perdue Davis. *Virginia's Colonial Churches*. Richmond: Garrett. 1963.

Salmon, Emily J. ed. *A Hornbook of Virginia History*. Richmond: Virginia State Library. 1983.

## Transcriptions of Parish Registers:

**Landon C. Bell:**
*Charles Parish, York County, Virginia, History and Registers, 1648-1789*. Richmond: Virginia State Library. 1932.

**Dr. R. A. Brock:**
*The Vestry Book of Henrico Parish, Virginia, 1730-1773*. Bowie: Heritage. Rep. 1991.

**Churchill Gibson Chamberlayne:**
*The Vestry Book of Blisland (Blisland) Parish, New Kent and James City Counties, Virginia, 1721-1786*. Richmond: Virginia State Library. 1935.

*The Vestry Book of Christ Church Parish, Middlesex County, Virginia, 1663-1767*. Richmond: Virginia State Library. 1927.

*The Vestry Book of Kingston Parish, Mathews County, Virginia, 1679-1796*. Richmond: Old Dominion. 1929.

*The Vestry Book of Petsworth Parish, Gloucester County, Virginia, 1677-1793*. Richmond: Virginia State Library. 1933.

*The Vestry Book of St. Paul's Parish, Hanover County, Virginia, 1706-1786.* Richmond: Virginia State Library. 1940.
*The Vestry Book and Register of St. Peter's Parish, New Kent and James City Counties, Virginia, 1684-1786.* Richmond: Virginia State Library. 1937.
*The Vestry Book of Stratton Major Parish, King and Queen County, Virginia, 1729-1783.* Richmond: Virginia State Library. 1931.

**Beverly Fleet:**
*Virginia Colonial Abstracts.* "Northumberland County Record of Births, 1661-1810." (St Stephen's Parish Records). vol. III, 1937. Baltimore: GPC. vol.I. Rep.1988.

**George Harrison Sanford King:**
*The Registers of North Farnham Parish, 1663-1814, and Lunenburg Parish 1783-1800, Richmond County.* 1966. Easley: Southern. Rep. 1985.
*The Register of Saint Paul's Parish, King George County, 1777-1798.* 1960. Easley: Southern. Rep. 1985.

**E. R. Matheny:**
*Kingston Parish Register, Gloucester and Mathews Counties, 1749-1827.* Richmond: Private Printing. 1963. Rep. 1979.

**National Society of Colonial Dames of America in Virginia:**
*The Parish Register of Christ Church, Middlesex County, 1625-1812.* 1897, Rep. 1964, Baltimore: Genealogical. Rev. 1988.

See the *Guide to Church Records* for the listing of photostat and microfilm copies housed in the Virginia State Library Archives. Also see Perdue Davis and Rawlings, *The Colonial Churches of Virginia, Maryland and North Carolina*. 1985. pp.327-331.

Brick Church, Jamestown, 1639
Courtesy of the National Park Service

Parishes of Tidewater Virginia North of James River

## Walter Chiles, The Son

### Virginia Lee Hutcheson Davis
*Continued from Volume 1 Number 2, page 71.*

### Walter Chiles (II) of Jamestown

Mr. Walter Chiles represented James City County as Burgess in 1658.[a] He was appointed to a committee to proportion the levy in March 1660.[b] He continued to represent James City County in 1663 and 1664.[c]

Susanna Chiles[1] was listed as a headright in the land patent of William Drummond for land in James City County, dated March 26, 1662.[d] William Drummond owned land adjoining land of Walter Chiles. An earlier patent by William and George Worsnam for land in Henrico County at Old Town on the Appomattox River named Sarah and Susan Chiles[2] as headrights. It was dated February 15, 1652.[e]

Walter Chiles of Jamestown added to the Kemp House property in August 1658, when he bought a brick house from Edward Hill.[f] The house adjoined the one his father had bought.

Documentation that Walter Chiles (II) was the son of Walter Chiles (I) can be found in the transfer of the land "Black Poynt", on May 20, 1670, granted Walter Chiles, father, by right of descent to Walter Chiles, son and heir.[g]

Walter Chiles patented land April 4, 1671 in Westmoreland County on behalf of his sons, John and Henry Chiles.[h]

---

[1] An inspection of the original patent confirmed this name as correct.

[2] An inspection of the original patent confirmed the name Chiles (for each person) and the name Sarah; the name Susan was not legible.

Walter Chiles died between November 15, 1671,[i] when he made his will and November 25, 1671 when an order of the Council, through William Berkeley, granted Susanna Giles (Chiles), relict and executrix of Walter Childs 200 acres of land for ninety-nine years. *"This land to remain with John Giles [later in the document identified as John Child] the eldest son of the said Walter Giles, deceased and ye said Susanna his wife."*[j]

John Chiles witnessed a deed from George Bates to Mr. John Page on March 16, 1673/4.[k] Francis Page also witnessed the deed. Elizabeth Chiles witnessed a deed to John Page on February 4, 1673/4, also in York County.[l]

John Chiles and Mary, his wife deeded the lease from William Berkeley to Sir Edmond Andros on September 29, 1693, on account of moving. The land was not described in detail, but was identified for the remainder of the term of ninety-nine years, and in such a manner that one would conclude that it was the same granted by Wm Berkeley to Susanna Chiles.[m]

An entry dated June 25, 1684, in the York County records identified Henry Tyler as having married Elizabeth Chiles.[n]

Conclusions............
No conclusive evidence has been found as to the birth date of Walter Chiles II. It would seem from subsequent court documents that it is likely that he may have been married before the mid-1650s. From the deed witnessed by John Chiles in 1673/4, he must have been close to the age of twenty-one at that time. It appears that he must not have been of age in 1671, when William Berkeley and the Council granted Susanna Chiles a lease for 200 acres of land in her name (as executrix of the will of Walter Chiles) and in the name John Chiles. It appears the land would have gone directly to John, as son and heir, had he been of age at that time.

Contrary to most of what has been written about the Page-Chiles connection, this same document clearly identified John Chiles as the son of Susanna and Walter Chiles. From this it would appear that she was his only wife (see quote from grant, above).

It seems likely that the Susanna Chiles claimed as headright by William Drummond (1662) was the wife of Walter Chiles, given the known associations of Drummond. The headright purported to be Susan Chiles in 1652 by John Worsnan is less certain, but worthy of consideration.

No information has been found to validate the claim by Mr. Lanciano[o] that the maiden name of Susanna Chiles was Page. The same chronologies of age exist in this instance that exist in relationship to Mary Page (see John Page following). Further, there is no mention in any of the court documents or history concerning the Page family, that has been found, to identify a daughter named Susanna.

It is believed, from existing records that Susanna Chiles was the mother of the three children identified as the children of Walter Chiles (II) of Jamestown: John Chiles, Elizabeth Chiles and Henry Chiles. It is further believed that these three children were all born at an earlier date than has heretofore been considered.

## NOTES

a. Hening 1: 506.
b. Hening 2: 31.
c. Hening 2: 198, 211.
d. L P Bk 4 12; Nugent I: 400.
e. L P Bk 3 23; Nugent I: 238-239.
f. Ambler Mss #6; Duvall 4.
g. L P Bk 6 413; Nugent II: 112.
h. McIlwaine, H. R., ed. *Minutes of the Council and General Court of Colonial Virginia*. Richmond: Virginia State Library. 1979. p.245.
i. Ambler Mss #4.
j. Lee Papers, Mss1L51f673. Virginia Historical Society.
k. York County Record Book 5, p.65.
l. York: 64-65.
m. Lee Papers.
n. York County Deeds, Orders, Wills, Etc. Vol. VI, p.499.
o. Lanciano, Claude. *Rosewell, Garland of Virginia*. Gloucester: Gloucester Historical Comm. 1978. p.15.

## Colonel John Page

John Page patented land on the south side of the York River and named, among others, Alice Page, Eliza. Page and Mary Page (without further identification) as headrights.[a] No date was included in the patent. The preceding patent on the same page was dated September 11, 1653.

The inscription of John Page's gravestone gave his death date as January 23, 1692, aged sixty-five.[b] Thus he would have been born in 1627. The inscription of Alice Page's gravestone gave her death date as June 22, 1698, aged seventy-three. Thus she would have been born in 1625.[c]

Alice Page has been identified with the maiden name of Alice Lukin because of the facsimile of the Lukin family arms cut into her tombstone.[d]

John Page of Middle Plantation made his will on March 5, 1686/7. He named his wife, Alice Page and his sons, Francis and Matthew, to whom he left his substantial holdings.[e] He identified John Tyler[1] as his grandson, the son of his granddaughter, Elizabeth Tyler, and left him the sum of £50 sterling.[f] John Tyler was contingent heir to 200 acres of land in James City County, which he received after the death of Francis Page (son of John Page) in 1692.[g] John Page identified John Chiles as his grandson when he bequeathed him a mourning ring. He also bequeathed mourning rings "to his coz. Henry Tyler and his wife, and to his sister, Eliz: Diggs".

Alice Page made her will on November 12, 1696 and died on June 22, 1698.[h] She left her estate to her son, Matthew Page and his children: Mann, Alice and Mary Page. She did not name any Chiles connections as legatees in her will.

---

[1]John Tyler identified himself as the grandson of Colonel John Page when he claimed his inheritance on August 19, 1706.

Francis Page, the son of Colonel John Page, made his will on April 23, 1692[i] and died on May 10, 1692 at the age of thirty-five. His wife had already died, and he left one child, Elizabeth Page. In his will, he bequeathed mourning rings to his "cussen Tyler and his wife", among a number of other persons.

Conclusions............

John Page was twenty-six years old in 1653 when he named Alice Page, Elizabeth Page and Mary Page as headrights in a land patent. Alice seems to have been his wife and Elizabeth was evidently his sister, as he later identified Elizabeth Diggs (the wife of Edward Diggs)[j] as his sister. The identity of Mary Page is not clear. Some have thought she may have been the wife of John's brother, Matthew. She could have been an early wife; however, in a land patent of Matthew Pagge (sic) on March 19, 1662, the patent identified his wife at that time as Elizabeth Crump, the widow of John Crump.[k]

Since John Chiles served as a witness to a deed involving John Page in 1673/74 it would appear that he was close to being of age at that time. Under those circumstances he would have probably been born about the year 1655.[2] At this time, John Page, himself, would have been only about twenty-eight years old. Chronologically it is not realistic to think of Mary Page as a daughter of John Page, who married Walter Chiles, and was the mother of John Chiles. Given the known information about Walter Chiles (II), and about John Page, there is little likelihood that Walter Chiles (II) married, first, a daughter of John Page.

John Page's identification in his will of John Tyler, grandson, Elizabeth Tyler and John Chiles as granddaughter and grandson respectively, seems indicative of kinship of a different nature. Later York County records indicate a continuing relationship between the Tyler family and the Page family. Henry Tyler's mother requested the

---

[2]John Chiles may be considered to have been between the ages of eighteen and twenty-one at the time he witnessed the document. While he may not have been legally of age, there are instances where those of maturity did perform this service before legal age.

favor of John Page as her "well-beloved friend" in a document dated 1672.[m]

"Henry Tyler and wife" were named as "cousins" in both the wills of John and Francis Page, and it would seem that this may have been more related to their associations with Henry Tyler, than with his wife. The legacy left John Tyler may have been for the same reasons. As a number of researchers have observed, it may have been the namesake connection that prompted the above legacy, as well as that of the mourning ring to John Chiles, to the exclusion of his brother, Henry. The term grandson may have been used, as it was in that time, to designate a step-child relationship. Alice Page did not identify any Chiles grandchildren, nor name any of the Chiles family in her will.

It appears that John Page may well have married Alice Lukin, the widow of Walter Chiles (I). Dr. Lyon G. Tyler wrote of his conviction that this was the only logical explanation for the relationship[n] and further stated that Edward Neill in *Virginia Carolorum* erred in his identification of Captain John Page.[o] *"He meant to say that Captain John Page was the father-in-law of Walter Chiles, son of Colonel [Walter] Chiles. Father-in-law then meant stepfather and John Page's wife, Alice, was doubtless the widow of Colonel Walter Chiles."*[p]

Dr. Tyler went on to elaborate, by saying it was the only satisfactory explanation he could give to the nature of John Page's will; his consideration of his collateral relatives of the Page blood and his scant recognition of the Chiles "grandchildren". He further observed that Alice Page did not mention the Chiles children in her will.[q]

## NOTES

a. L P Bk 3 212; Nugent I: 279.
b. Page, Richard C M. *Genealogy of the Page Family*. New York: Jenkins. 1893. p.16; Gravestone, Bruton Parish Church Cemetery; Jester, Annie Lash & Martha Woodroof Hiden. *Adventurers of Purse and Person*. NJ: Princeton. 1956. p.231.
c. Jester & Hiden
d. Jester & Hiden
e. York County Will Book #9, pp.103-106.
f. York County Court Records, June 2, 1707; Tyler, Lyon Gardiner. *The Letters and Times of the Tylers*. Vol. 1. New York: DeCapo. 1970. p.49.
g. York County Deeds, Wills, Etc. #9, pp.127-129.

h. York County Record Book # 11, pp.85-86; Gravestone; G H S King Papers, Page Folder. Mss1K5823. Virginia Historical Society.
i. King Papers; Book #11 127-128.
j. Page 26.
k. L P Bk 6 298; Nugent II: 76.
l. *National Genealogical Society Quarterly*. Vol.79, No.3. p.203.
m. Weisiger, Benjamin B. *York County Records, 1672-1676*. Richmond: Weisiger. 1991. p.20.
n. Tyler, Lyon Gardiner, ed. *William & Mary Quarterly*, Series 1, Vol. VI, pp.146-147.
o. Neill, Edward D. *Virginia Carolorum*. NY: Munsell's. 1886. p.232.
p. *W & M Q* 146-147.

## A Brief History of Christ Church Middlesex County

Contributed by Carroll C. Chowning, Jr.

On January 29, 1666, a General Vestry meeting was held at the house of Sir Henry Chichley (Rosegill).

"We doe accord and agree that ye two parishes formerly call Lancaster and Peanckatanck from hense forth be united as one and called Christ Church parish.

"Item. That a Mother Church be built in ye small Indian field next ye head of Capt. Brocas his ground. It being adjudged by us to be about ye middle of ye parish.

"Item. That ye Mother church be called by name of Christ Church...building the Mother Church, in every respect to be done and finished according to the Middle Plantacon Church [in Williamsburg], to be finished in six months, glass and iron worke convenient time to be given for its transportation out of England." (Christ Church Vestry Book pp.5-6 [also see pp.x-xv, 8-9]).

This first building appears to have been of clapboard construction. It was used until 1712, when at the vestry meeting of June 9, a new church was ordered built of brick. The work was to have been completed by June 10, 1714, and we have every reason to believe it was completed by that date.

Without question, the present building occupies the identical ground of the original 1666 church, for when the new church was ordered built, directions were given also for an "arbor" (in which services might be held during construction).

There are seven graves under the church. Sir Henry Chichley, Deputy Governor of Virginia, was buried near the [present] Communion Table on February 9, 1682. Another of the graves is that of the Reverend John Sheppard, rector of Christ Church from 1668 until his death in 1683. The others are: Madam Catherine Wormley, Aylmer Wormely [sic], Edward Thompson and Mary Reeves and her son. The Thompson slab, now set in the aisle flagstones, was found under the floor of the church when the building was renovated in the 1920s.

The Communion Plate of Christ Church consists of some modern pieces given as memorials and three ancient pieces that are believed to remain from the set presented by the Honorable Ralph Wormley of Rosegill in 1687. During the Revolution the Communion Silver was placed in a bank vault in Fredericksburg where it remained for more than thirty years. On being returned to the parish, it was partially destroyed by fire. It was restored by S. Kirk and Son of Baltimore in 1855. There were originally five pieces, but after the fire they were only able to gather up enough silver to restore three pieces: a chalice, a paten and an alms plate.

The parish is most fortunate in the possession of historic records in the form of two printed volumes, *The Vestry Book of Christ Church, 1663-1767*, compiled by Dr. [Churchill Gibson] Chamberlayne from documents stored at the [Episcopal] Seminary at Alexandria, shows the early social service entrusted to vestries, and expenditures in pounds of tobacco. The other, *The Parish Register, 1653-1812*, lists births, baptisms, marriages and deaths. This may be seen in the Urbanna Library. The graveyard contains a number of table tombs of historic interest. One marks the resting place of the beloved Bartholomew Yates, who served for many years as rector, and taught at William and Mary [College]. A complete list of grave markings has been made.

In 1840 the church was revived in Middlesex. By that time the roof of Christ Church had fallen in, the woodwork had rotted and a large tree had grown in the center aisle. In 1840 the building was restored and has continued in use until the present time. In 1921 Christchurch School for boys was founded by the Rev. F. E. Warren.

This history has been presented by Mr. Chowning to guests visiting the church, and also appears on the present church bulletin. It is used with his permission, and that of the Reverend William R. Martin, presently the rector of Christ Church.

## Diagram of Old Tombs in the Yard of Christ Church

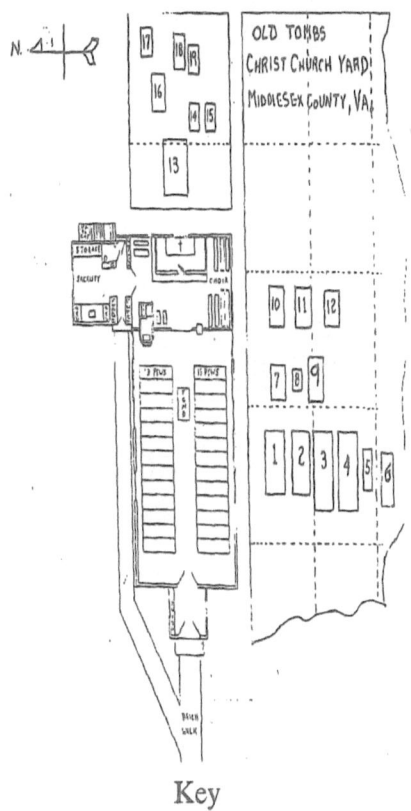

Key

1. Catherine Walker
    10/5/1730[8¹], 33 yrs.
2. Bartholomew Yates
    7/26/1734, 57 yrs.
3. John Grymes
    11/12/1748, 57 yrs.
4. Mrs Lucy (Ludwell) Grymes
    d. 3/3/1749, 57 yrs.
5. Mrs Jane (Grymes) Sayre
    d. 1/11/1806, 24 yrs.
6. Phillip Grymes
    b. 9/19/[17]75
    d. 11/9/1801
7. George Dame
    (c.1752-1805)
8. John Grymes
    d. 6/2/1746, 15 mos.

9. Dr. Henry Potter
   d. 12/20/-, 46 yrs.
10. Richard Corbin
    d. 5/20/1790, 76 yrs.
    Mrs. Betty Corbin
    d. 5/15/1781
11. Corbin Tomb from Upper Chapel
12. Corbin Tomb from Upper Chapel
13. Johannes Wormley (Latin)
    d.VII d Fe b MDCC XXVL Ann Ae XXXVII
14. John Wormley
    (1747-49)
15. No Inscription (26 yrs.)
16. Mrs. Sarah Wormley
    d. 12/2/1741
17. Dr. Geo. Dudley Micholson
    b. 12/27/1814
    d. 3/17/1883
18. Ralph Wormley
    d. 1806, 62 yrs.
19. Mrs. Eleanor
    d 2/23/1815, 60 yrs.

Plotted and identified by Carroll C. Chowning & Barton Palmer, 7/31/1962, Revised 4/21/88 by C.C. Chowning, Jr.

[1] C C Parish Register

Sketch of Christ Church, Middlesex County by Patti B. Martin

## Civil Appointments
## Elizabeth City County, 1780-1804

### Submitted by Minor Tompkins Weisiger

These Civil Appointments from the Executive Department provide information of the lives and business of the residents of Elizabeth City County. They have been selected for the counties of tidewater Virginia, and particularly those counties for which the county order books do not generally exist. There are not files for every year, or for all appointments made within a year. They are transcribed rather than presented as abstracts, to provide all of the information possible. In some cases the actual signatures of the persons writing the notation will be presented rather than a transcription of that signature.

At a Court held for Elizabeth City County August 24th. 1780

Pursuant to the Law, the Court doth Nominate and recommend to his Excellency the Governor as fit Persons to Execute the Office of Sherif of this County for the ensuing Year Worlich Westwood, Francis Mallory & Westwood Armistead Gent:

*[signature: Cary Selden]*

The Commonwealth of Virginia
To Roe Cowper Esquire greeting:
Know you that from the Special Trust and Confidence which is reposed in your Fidelity, Courage, Activity, and good Conduct, our Governor, with the Advice of the Council of State, and on the recommendation of the Worshipful Court of the county of Elizabeth City doth appoint you the said Row Cowper to be County Lieutenant of the said county of Elizabeth City to take rank as such from the 25th day of April last.
In testimony whereof these our letters are made patent.

WITNESS, Benjamin Harrison Esquire, our said Governor, at Richmond this sixth day of May in the Year of our Lord One Thousand Seven Hundred and eight-two.
(Registered in the WAR-OFFICE)                    [signed] Benj Harrison

[signed] William Davies

At a Court held for Elizabeth City County August 28th 1783
Pursuant to the Law the Court doth Nominate to his Excellency the governor as fit Persons to Execute the Office of Sherif of this County for the ensuing Year...
Viz$^t$ George Booker and John Tabb Gent

At a Court held for Elizabeth City County September the 25$^{th}$ 1783
The Court do Nominate to his Excellency the Governor as fit Persons to Execute the Office of Inspectors of Tobacco for this County
To wit. John Skinner, Joseph Cooper and John Parsons Gent.
                                        Test  Cary Selden  Clk: Cur.

D$^r$ The Sheriff of Elizabeth City in Account with the Commonwealth for Revenue of 1783

| | | |
|---|---|---|
| 1785 Apr.23 | To Judgment for balance | £102. 2.10½ |
| | 15 PCent Damages | 15. 6. 5 |
| | | £117. 9. 3½ |
| | 5 PC$^t$ Interest from 1 March 1784 | |
| | To Cost of Judgment | 3.13. 8½ |
| 1785 Oct.20 | By Costs paid L. Wood Jr | 3.13. 6 |
| | By the Treasurer | £102. 2.10½ |

Received of George Booker Esq. three pounds 6/8 for Costs of Judgment against him as Sheriff of Elizabeth City for Revenue Taxes of 1784.....

Att° fee  £ 2.10.
Clerk       . 8. 1½ 　　　　　　　　　　　　L. Wood Jr. Sol.
Notice ____. 8. 6½
          £ 3. 6. 8
Richmond Solicitors Office 12$^{th}$ Jany. 1786.

At a Court continued and held for Eliz: City County Saturday June 25$^{th}$ 1785.
Pursuant to Law the Court do Nominate and Recommend to your Excellency as fit Persons to execute the Office of Sheriff of this County the ensuing Year George Wray and John Tabb Gent.

I do Certify that the Sheriff of Elizabeth City County was very active in Collecting the Taxes due for 1783 and it was not in his power to collect the Taxes in time, Owing to the want of Cash. Given under my hand this 22$^{nd}$ October 1785

I do Certify that the Sheriff of Elizabeth City County has done his Endeavor to Collect the Revenue Tax for 1784 and cannot owning to the inability of the people. Given under my hand this 13$^{th}$ Jan: 1786.

[signed] Miles King

At a Court held for Eliz$^a$ City County Thursday the 22$^{nd}$ Day of June 1786....
Pursuant to the Law the Court do nominate and recommend to his Excellency the Governor & Council as fit Persons to execute the Office of sheriff of this county the ensuing year George Wray Gent. the present Sheriff with William Armistead and Jacob Wray Gent.; for one of them to be appointed Sheriff....

          A Copy Johnson Tabb C.C.C.

At a Court continued and held for Eliz$^a$ City County Friday July the 28$^{th}$: 1786.
> Present Wilson Miles Cary, William Armistead, Jacob Wray, Miles King, Worlich Westwood and George Booker Gent Justices

Roe Cowper, James Barron, William Moore, Wilson Cary Selden, George Latimer, and George Hope Gent are recommended to his Excellency the Governor as fit Persons to be added to the Commission of the Peace in this county....

          A Copy Johnson Tabb C.C.C.

At a Court held for Eliz$^a$ City County Thursday February 22$^{nd}$ 1787.
Present    William Armistead
       Jacob Wray
       Miles King  Gent. Justices
       Worlich Westwood
       George Booker &
       William Moore

John Parsons Gent is appointed to execute the Office of Commissioner in this County Pursuant to the Act of Assembly to amend the Act entitled an Act for ascertaining certain Taxes and Duties and for establishing a Permanent *Revenue*.

         A Copy, Test Johnson Tabb C.C.C.

At a Court for Eliza City County Thursday April 26th 1787.
Present		Wilson Miles Cary
		William Armistead    Gent Justices
		Wilson Cary Selden &
		George Hope

Pursuant to the Act of Assembly to amend the act entitled an Act for ascertaining certain Taxes and Duties, and for establishing a permanent Revenue, the Court do appoint William ap Thomas Parsons to execute the Office of Commissioner in the County in the Room of John Parsons who is unable to proceed on the Execution of the said Office by Reason of his ill State of Health.
A Copy Attest Johnson Tabb C.C.C.

[The following summary of real and personal property appears to be in the handwriting of Johnson Tabb, is undated and may be for the year 1787 or 1789. Ed.]

Elizabeth City

| | | |
|---|---|---|
| Land | [blank] | £327.17. 6¾ |
| Negroes | 866 | 433. . |
| Horses | 629 | 62.18 |
| Studs | 4 | 4. 5. 6 |
| Coach Wheels | 20 | 36. . |
| Waggon D° | 4 | 4.16. |
| Chair D° | 54 | 32. 8. |
| Ordy Licenses[1] | 5 | 25. . |
| Phys [Physicians] | 3 | 15. . |
| | | £941. 5. 0¾ |

[1] Ordinary

At a Court held for Eliza City County Thursday June 28th 1787
Pursuant to the Law the Court do nominate to his Excellency the Governor and Council as proper Persons to execute the Office of sheriff of this County the ensuing year William Armistead, Jacob Wray, and Miles King Gent for one of them to be appointed Sheriff..
A Copy Johnson Tabb C.C.C.

Elizabeth City County Court April 24th 1789.
Richard Dixon Gent being desirous of becoming Surveyor of this County, is recommended by the Court to the President and Professors of the University of William and Mary as a Person of good Character.
A Copy Teste Johnson Tabb C.C.C.

Elizabeth City County Court Friday June 26th 1789
Pursuant to the Act of Assembly in this case made and provided the Court do nominate and recommend to his Excellency the Governor and the Hon'ble the privy Council Miles King, Worlich Westwood and George Booker Gent. as proper Persons for one of them to be commissioned Sheriff of the County the ensuing Year.
A Copy Teste Johnson Tabb C.C.C.

Elizabeth City County Court Sept$^r$ 23$^d$ 1789.
Present     Wilson Miles Cary
               George Wray   Gent. Justices
               Miles King
               Worlich Westwood
               George Hope
The following Gent. are recommended & nominated by the Court to his Excellency the Governor and the Hon'ble Privy Council as proper persons to be added to the Commission of the peace and Commission of Oyer and Terminer in this county. To Wit. Cary Selden, Joseph Merideth, Robert Brough, George Wray, Junr, Charles Jennings, Michael Wing and William ap. Thomas Parsons. And the same is Ordered Accordingly.
A Copy Teste Johnson Tabb C.C.C.

Elizabeth City County Court June 23$^d$ 1791.
Pursuant to the act of assembly in the Case made and provided the Court do nominate to his Excellency the Governor and the Hon'ble privy Council Worlich Westwood and George Booker Gent for one of them to be commissioned Sheriff of this County the ensuing year. And the same is ordered accordingly.
A Copy Teste Johnson Tabb C.C.C.

Worlich Westwood esquire late Sheriff Elizabeth City has paid principal, interest & cost of a Judgment obtained against him for the taxes of 1791.

[signed] J. Pendleton

Aud.ˢ Office 24 May 1796.
At a Court held for Elizabeth City County May 26ᵗʰ 1796
Robert Armistead, Samuel Selden and Robert Armistead, Jun. are nominated to his Excellency the Governor for one of them to be commissioned Sheriff for the said County.

At a Court held for Elizabeth City County April 1799
James Davis Esqʳ is recommended to his Excellency James Wood Esqʳ Governor of the Commonwealth as a proper person to Execute the office of Coroner for this County.

Copy Teste Miles King Cl.C.C.

Dear Sir                                    Hampton 11ᵗʰ Oct 1799
Sometime ago I Recvᵈ a Coroner Commission for Mr Samuel Watts which I delivᵈ him he has not yett Qualifyᵈ nor will he do so and the County is without one. I have [illeg. word] a Recommendation for Mr Davis and will thank you to have a Commission formᵈ by our next Court I am with great Respect.

Your Most ObˢServᵗ
Miles King

Be it known to all to whom these Presents shall come, that I Augustine Moore Sheriff of Eliz City County in my full County, held at the Courthouse thereof on the 26th Day of April in the Year of our Lord 1804 by the Electors of my said County, qualified according to Law, caused to be chosen two Delegates for my said County, namely John S. Westwood & Charles K. Mallory to represent the same in general Assembly, given under my hand & seal, the Day and Year aforesaid.

[signed] Augustine Moore  Sheriff

From the records of the Executive Department, Commonwealth of Virginia. Box 3, A-E. Pre 1790. Archives and Records Division, Virginia State Library and Archives, Richmond, Virginia. Published with the kind permission of Dr. Louis H. Manarin, Virginia State Archivist.

## Will of William Sanders, 1793
## Richmond County

In the Name of God Amen
I William Sanders Senior of the Parish of Lunenburg and County of Richmond, being very sick and weak in Body but of sound perfect and disposing Mind and Memory thanks be to God therefore: and calling to Mind the mortality of my Body and knowing that it is appointed for all Men once to die; *Do* make and ordain this my last Will and Testament in manner and form following; that is to say, Principally and first of all I commend my soul into the Hands of Almighty God who gave it me and my Body I commit to the Earth to be buried in a Christian like and decent manner at the discretion of my Executor hereafter named. And as touching such Worldly State wherewith it hath pleased God to bless me with in this life; I Give devise and dispose thereof in manner and form following.

| | |
|---|---|
| Impriss: | My Will and desire is in the first place that all my Just Debts be duly paid. |
| Item | I give and Bequeath unto my Son Thomas Sanders a Suit of Virginia Cloath Cloathes. |
| Item | I give and Bequeath unto my dearly beloved Wife Mary Lewis Sanders all the residue of my Personal Estate to the whole and sole use of her my beloved Wife, Mary Lewis Sanders, for and during the Term of her Natural Life. |
| Item | I Give and Bequeath the aforesaid residue and remaining part of my Estate after my said Wifes Death to be equally divided among my following Children: to wit.. William Sanders, John Sanders, Almond, Alexander, and Thomas. |
| Lastly | I constitute appoint and ordain my Friend Daniel Willson and my beloved son William Sanders my sole Executors of this my last Will and Testament: Revoking and disannulling all other and former Wills, Legacies and Bequests by me in any wise heretofore Willed, Left and Bequeathed, Ratifying and confirming this and no other to be my last Will and Testament |

As witness my Hand and Seal this fifth Day of September in the year of Our Lord 1793.

Signed sealed and declared by
the said William Sanders Senior
to be his last Will
and Testament                 William his X mark Sanders
in the presence of
Elisha his X mark Newcomb
Daniel his X mark Jenkins

At a Court held for Richmond County the 5th day of December 1796. This last will and Testament of William Sanders Decd. was proved in open Court by the Oaths of Elisha Newcomb and Daniel Jenkins the Witnesses thereto and admitted to Record.

[This is transcribed by VLHD from a xeroxed copy of the original will. Ed.]

Richmond County. Entitled Wills. Box 34-11-E-8-1-5. Archives and Records Division, Virginia State Library and Archives, Richmond, Virginia. Published with the kind permission of Dr. Louis H. Manarin, Virginia State Archivist.

# Byrom Family Bible, 1816-1886
## Essex County

This was taken from the family Bible of Milton Byrom, 1816-1886; published for the American Bible Society by D. & G. Bruce, New York, N.Y., 1829; later in the possession of Milton's son, Rev. Robert Eli Byrom (1870-1950) of Poteet, Texas. Copied 1940. Henry H. Byrom, Mesquite, Texas. 1986.

Henry Byrom was born 28 March 1778, in South Farnham Parish, Essex Co. Va.
    died 2 November 1853, Franklin County, Tennessee.
    Married, 8 January 1803, Mecklenburg County, North Carolina to Mary Stampier Cook--born 25 September 1779, in Virginia
    died 28 August 1863, Franklin County, Tennessee.

Elizabeth Byrom was born 7 October 1803. *Died 1837.*
    *married Jake Holt*
James Byrom was born 5 August 1805. *Died young.*
William Henry Byrom was born 22 April 1807.
    *married Elizabeth Lasater & Nancy C. Fariss.*
John Calvin Byrom was born 15 July 1809. *Died 2 February 1863.*
    *married Mary Caroline Short.*
Thomas Byrom was born 10 May 1811. *Died 23 August 1864.*
    *married Agnes Fariss.*
Benjamin Byrom was born 21 December 1813. *Died March 1849.*
    *married Mary ...... and Eliza Hays.*
Milton Byrom was born 28 August 1816. *Died 11 January 1886.*
    *married Lucy Laseter, Nancy C. Arnold & Sara W. Walker.*
Mary C. Byrom was born 29 February 1820.
    *married Kindred Majors.*
Robert Cook Byrom was born 1 February 1822. *Died 27 October 1903.*
    *married Sarah Dean and Isabella Jane Heard.*
James Martin Byrom was born 20 [type-over 10] March 1825.
    *Died 16 September 1914. married Sarah Ann Edens.*
Sarah Ann Byrom was born 2 December 1826. *Died 17 April 1907.*
    *married Solomon Simion Revis.*

Note: H. H. Byrom made the notation that he had added the death dates and marriages known to him. It is likely that most of these can be verified in the Franklin County records. They are identified by italics. Ed.

Bible Records. Byrom Family Bible, 1778-1907. Essex County. Accession Number 32788. Archives and Records Division, Virginia State Library and Archives, Richmond, Virginia. Published with the kind permission of Dr. Louis H. Manarin, Virginia State Archivist.

## The Grave of Jacob Lumpkin, 1708
## Mattaponi Church

Continued from Volume 1 Number 2, page 74.
Reference was made to a stone just outside of the north doorway of Mattaponi Church with an inscription in Latin, dated 1708. This grave was identified by Dr. Alfred Bagby in *King and Queen County, Virginia*. (Baltimore: Clearfield. rep.1990. p.58).

"A marble slab, just outside the north door, covers the remains of Colonel Jacob Lumpkin, with this inscription:

JACOB LUMPKIN
*Obit 14 die September, 1708, AEtatis 64.*
*Dux Militum, Victor Hostium,*
*Morte Victus, Pax Adsit, Vives Requies,*
*Eterna Sepultis.*"

Tidewater Virginia Residents Identified in Deeds,
Northampton County, North Carolina, 1759-1774

Contributed by Dr. Claiborne T. Smith, Jr.

These selected deeds have been taken from the records of the Northampton County, North Carolina deeds abstracted by Dr. Stephen E. Bradley, Jr. Only those deeds that contain information about residents of tidewater Virginia counties are presented. All references are from the Northampton County Deed Books. It can be assumed that Northampton Co refers to the North Carolina county; that the Virginia counties named are identified without designation, and other counties will be identified by state the first time mentioned.

Charles City County:
DB3, p.381 George Morris of Northampton Co to John Brooks of Charles City Co. 21 Nov 1764; £160 gold, 160A on north side of Roanoke River, joining Canoe Creek.

Elizabeth City County:
DB4, p.68 James Faison, Jr. and his wife, Elizabeth of Northampton Co to Anthony Armistead, late of Elizabeth City Co. 7 April 1767; £500, 1 tract of 235A which had been granted by Lord Carteret to Sarah Davis 1 May 1720 on the north side of Meherrin River, joining the old county line.[1]

Gloucester County:
DB3, p.154 Mary Dawson of Gloucester Co. Kingston Parish grants power of attorney to her brother William Callis of Gloucester Co, Kingston Parish to sell 100A in Bertie Co (NC) which was purchased by father, William Dawson, decd. from Solomon Bearfield for 200A, 100 of which acres had been sold by said Dawson's sister, Elizabeth and her

---

[1] See Garber's *The Armistead Family*; the old county line was the 1710 boundary between NC and VA. CTS

husband, William Treacle. Wit. Robert Callis. Registered in Edenton (NC) 24 Nov 1760.
DB3, p.154 Mary Dawson of Gloucester Co. to Edward Rutland of Northampton Co[2]. 25 Nov 1761, £20 Va [current money], a moiety of 200A which had belonged to her father, William Dawson, which he had purchased from Solomon Barfield [sic] and descended to Mary as co-heiress. Joining Ahotshey Marsh.

### James City County
DB3, p.326 Lucas Powell of James City Co to John Newell of Brunswick Co. 5 July 1764, £15 Va, 190A on west side of Pea Hill Creek, joining the county line.

### King and Queen County
DB3, p.67 John Morris and wife Anne of Northampton Co to John Dix of King and Queen Co. 29 Jan 1760, £100 200A with a water grist mill which said Morris had purchased from Col Nathaniel Edwards.
DB3, p.117 John Dix of King and Queen Co to William Eaton of Dinwiddie Co. 2 Sept 1761, £145, 183A which said John Dix had bought of John Morris.

DB5, p.157 Philemon Shirley of King & Queen Co To William Fulks of Northampton Co. 28 Oct 1771, £40 Va, 200A which had been granted John Gully 29 Oct 1753.

### New Kent County
DB3, p.117 Noel Waddell of New Kent Co to his sister Frances Johnson & children Naomi Jones, Henry Clader and Noel Hutchins Clader, 12 March 1761, deed of gift, Negro girl Sal now in the possession of William Johnson of Northampton Co to the said children slaves Pott and her child Judith, now in possession of William Johnson of Northampton Co. Frances Johnson the mother of the said children to

---

[2] Bertie Co was mentioned in the P of A but Northampton Co had been cut off Bertie by this date. CTS

have the use of them during her lifetime. Noel Waddell. Wit. Jno. Waddell, Jr, Wm Irby, Hannah Waddell. May Court 1761.

**Warwick County**
DB3, p.147 Joseph Wood & wife Eleanor of Northampton Co to John Young, Warwick Co. 7 Aug 1760, £50 Va, 100A on Catawiskie Swamp.

DB5, p.336 John Young and Robert Young, brothers, sons of Mary Young of Warwick Co to John Cotten of Northampton Co. 17 June 1773, 100A on the south side of Cattswhiskey Swamp.

Bradley, Dr Stephen E, Jr. *The Deeds of Northampton County, North Carolina, 1759-1774*. South Boston: Private printing. 1990.

Drying Tobacco

## Losses Sustained from the British Depredations Within the Commonwealth of Virginia Gloucester County, 1782-1783

Contributed by Minor Tompkins Weisiger

*A continuation of British Depredations from Volume 1 Number 2, page 95.*

Ed. note: The following is transcribed from the original that was tabulated in chart form, with the headings: *Sufferers names / Negroes what sort & ages / Horses Cattle & Sheep hogs / Houses, Tobacco, Grain, Spirits & other property.*

William Teagle/ 1 negro woman Alice 60 y$^r$ old 1 boy Gloucester 14 y$^r$ old/ 5 Sheep, 5 Brood Sows, 7 Barrows, 12 Shoots [shoats], 7 Pigs, 2 cows and 2 calves/ 20 Bushels wheat, 30 Bushels Oats, Framing & plank for a house 20 by 28 feet, 4000 nails, a field of Corn about 52½ Barrels, 2 Barrels old Corn & mill houses, 4 large window frames & 3 small d$^o$ with sashes, 35 panes of Glass 8 by 10. a Garden destroyed & houses in a Lot damaged 6M nails of different sorts.

Ambrose Alender/ Proved by Wm Teagle/ 1 Sow & 6 Shoots 9m$^o$ old, 1 Calf 9 m$^o$ old/ 272 Barrels Corn.

John Borum by the enemy Cruison [incursion]/ 1 negro man Peter 18 y$^r$ old a Sawyer/ 3 sheep, Proved by himself/ 1 rum Case and Bottles, 1 Sword, 2 pewter Deep Dishes, 1 Bason, 2 plates & several other trifles.

Edmund Borum Sen by the enemy Cruison/ 1 negro man Harry 21 y$^r$ old, a sawyer/ 12 Sheep/ proved by John Borum.

Thomas Mason by the enemy Cruison/ proved by J. Borum/a vessel damaged by setting her on fire £20, 1 ax, 1 adze & auger. 16/6

John Elliott/ Sam a negro man 27 y$^r$ old a good house carpenter & Cooper, Joseph 24 years old/ proved by Brookes Hobday.

Brookes Hobday/ a negro man Ben 28 years old a good Pilot, Simon 24 years old/ Proved by himself.

Sir John Peyton/ a negro man Antony 21 y$^r$ old a good weaver; proved by Brookes Hobday.

James Jenkins by the enemy Cruison/ 16 Sheep 2 fattend hogs about 300 lb./ 50lb. Bacon, proved by himself.

Copy   C Pryor D. C. C.

An Account of John Fox, his Losses sustained by the enemy during the War in their Several Invasions.
Marquis about 24 y$^r$ of age. a Carpenter
Gabriel about 30 y$^r$ old an excellent weaver
York about 40 y$^r$ old
Abram about 35 y$^r$ old
Robin about 45 or 46 a good Blacksmith this fellow was left at Wmsburg by the British with the Small Pox and died in a few days with it
Mason about 21 years old. came up after the Surrender and was taken sick suppose the Goal [jail] Fever and died in a little while...
Gloucester. F$^r$.

  John Fox this day made oath before me that the above is an account of the Loss he sustaind by the Enemy during the War in their Several Invasions. Certified this 13$^{th}$ Day of September 1782.

Francis Tomkies

An Account of Charles Tomkies Estate losses sustained by the Enemy during the War in their Several Invasions.

Negroes: Ben about 46 years of age a Good hoe Negroe.
    Phebe about 25 years of age a Good House Servant
    her children Melley about 9 years old
    George about 3 years old
    Jenny about 28 years old a Good House servant who returned and died in a few days
    Mary her child about 4 years old
    London a lad 14 years of age

Issabel 16 years old a Good House Servant
A large Dressing Glass taken away
3 head of Cattle & 4 hoggs missing suppos$^d$ to be taken
103 Dunghill Fowls of Different Kinds
A Gun and the House much Damag$^d$ by the Enemy

Gloucester to Wit

Mary Tomkies this Day made oath before me that the above is an acct. of the Negroes Lost belonging to her husbands Estate and the other things taken from her by y$^e$ Enemy during the War in their several Invasions Given under my hand
May 16$^t$ Day of Sep$^t$ 1782.

*Francis Tomkies*

At a Court held for Gloucester County the 3$^{rd}$ day of July 1783 the following accounts for property lost by the Enemy were allowed..Viz. *[Listed in columns headed Owners names/negroes what sort ages, etc/Horses & other property. Ed.]*

[F]rancis Willis jun/ Daniel a negro man 30 years old, Joe a Ditto 30 years old, Moll a negro woman 30 years old and 4 Children ages from 11 downwards.

[torn,G?]uy Stevens's Estate, [in] the hands of Isaac Hobday/ Fill a man about 25 years old, Jenny a woman about 18, Will a Boy about 8, Tagey a Girl about 6, Gabriel a boy about 3, a child about 6 days old and at York.

[torn,Bu]ckner/ a negro man about 30 years old.
[El]izabeth Cooke/ a negro man about 28 years old.
John Buckner jun/ a negro man Dick about 26 y$^{rs}$ old.

Mordecai Cooke/ a negro man about 30 y$^{rs}$ old.
Anthony Davis/ a negro man 29 years old very valuable.
Ann Huggins Estate/ 2 Horses & 20 Barrels Indian Corn.

Transcribed by VLHD

From The Legislative Department, House of Delegates, Office of the Speaker. Correspondence. Losses sustained from the British. May 1783. Archives and Records Division, Virginia State Library and Archives, Richmond, Virginia. Published with the kind permission of Dr. Louis H. Manarin, Virginia State Archivist.

Gloucester County Courthouse c. 1776

## List of Marriages, 1794-1798
## York County

A list of marriages celebrated by the Reverend Thomas Camm, Rector of Charles Parish from the third of June 1794 to January 1798.

| | | |
|---|---|---|
| 3 June 1794 | | Armiger Parsons to Elizabeth Holloway Spinster both of Chas. Parish. |
| Dec 27 | | John H: Purdie to Anne Moore Spinster same Parish & County. |
| 1795 | Jany 22 | John Dewberry to Mary Saunders same Parish & County |
| | Feby 28 | John Pryson to Polly Lilburn both of Charles Parish York Cy. |
| | Feby 28 | Wills Dunsford jr of Jas. City to Sarah Kerby of same Parish & Cy. |
| | Aug. 26 | William Kerby to Sarah Kerby both of Charles Parish York Cy. |
| | Sept. 12 | Charles Leavitt to Mary Robinson of Chas. Parish York Cy. |
| | Dec. 12 | Cheley Ross to Jane Stores both of Eliza. City County. |
| 1796 | Jany 23 | Wm. Moss to Elizabeth Goodwin of Chas. Parish York County |
| | Feby 25 | Wm. Marrow to Mary Sheild Kerby of same Par: & Cy. |
| | Feby 27 | Miles Cary to Martha Sclater of same Par: & Cy. |
| | Nov. 19 | Aaron Dennis to G[2 letters illeg.]ty Roberts of same Par: & Cy. |
| | Dec. 22 | Benja. Pryson to Elizabeth Drewry both of Chas. Parish. |
| 1797 | Jany. 1 | Miles Cary of Warwk. Co. to Anne Robinson Spinster of Chas. Parish. |
| | Mar. 4 | Wm. Gilliam to Mary Moss both of Chas. Parish York Cy. |

|      |          |                                                                                      |
|------|----------|--------------------------------------------------------------------------------------|
|      | April 8  | Dudley Wright to Anne Baptist both of same City Cy & Parish.                         |
|      | July 21  | X$^r$ [Christopher?] Gayle to Molly Gayle both of same Cy & Parish.                  |
|      | Aug. 26  | Meade Wood of Warw. Cy. to Sally Jordan of Chas Parish York Cy.                      |
|      | Dec. 30  | John Tennis[1] to Frances Dixon of Charles Parish York Cy.                           |
| 1798 | March 31 | Nicholas Pryson to Sarah Minson both of same Parish & Cy.                            |
|      | June 23  | Jno. Rogers junr. to Ann Throckmorton Spinster [of] the Parish of York Hampton & Cy of York. |
|      | 21 July  | Ransome Davis to Elizabeth Gemmill widow both of Chas. Parish York Cy.               |
|      | 8 Aug.   | Job Wilson to Patsey Parsons of Charles Parish York County.                          |
|      | 1 Sept.  | Ambrose Morris to Nancy Keble of same Parish & County.                               |
|      | 6 Nov.   | Absolom Cox to Rachael Phillips of Charles Parish York Cy.                           |

I do certify that I joined together in the holy State of Matrimony according to the Rites and Ceremonies of the Protestant Episcopal Church the several Persons mentioned in the foregoing at the time specified in the margin.

[signed] Thomas Camm Rector of C Parish

Transcribed by VLHD

---

[1] A comparison with other letters indicates that this is a "T"; however, it could be an "F".

Marriages- Ministers Returns York County, 1794-1798, York County Rec. Ct. Box 14, 1802. Loose Papers, Wills from Burned Record Counties, 1729-1830. York County. Archives and Records Division, Virginia State Library and Archives, Richmond, Virginia. Published with the kind permission of Dr. Louis H. Manarin, Virginia State Archivist.

Carlton Family Bible, 1804
King and Queen County

Contributed by John R. Carlton

It is believed that these two Carlton Bible records have not been previously published. They are an especially welcome addition to the information of King and Queen County residents, because of the destruction of the county court records.

Family Record of Christopher Carlton

Chris' Carlton and Orania G Carlton his wife was married 10th day of March 1831
Christopher Carlton was born 20th day of June 1804
Robert Pollard Carlton was born the 14th day of April 1832
Harriet Ann Carlton was born 7 day of August 1834
John Atwood Carlton was born 5th day of September 1838 Died March 27 1925 Friday
Janisha Jane Carlton was born 27th day of March 1840
Charlotte Elon Carlton was born 20th[?] day of January 1843
Virginaous Singleton Carlton was born 14th day of July 1845
John Atwood Carlton departed this Life Frid[a]y March 27 1925 in the 88 year of his age
Harriet Ann Carlton daughter of Chris' Carlton died 16th day of September 1825 aged 11 years and 1 month and 9 days
Orania G Carlton the wife of Chris' Carlton departed this life 18 of September 1847
Christopher Carlton departed this life 18 of May 1859
Robert P Carlton died friday before 3rd sunday in October 1859 [October 14th]
Charlotte E Turner the daughter of Christopher & Orania G Carlton departed this life the 16 day of March 1870 in the 27 year of her age

## Family Record of Colored Children Belonging to Christopher Carlton

Names of Fanneys children when born & C
Margarid was born Oct 1837
Jacob & Esaw was born March 1839
Isaac was born March 1841
Moses & Aaron was born Jany 1$^{st}$ 1843
Thomas was born July 1844
Nelson was born 22$^{nd}$ June 1846
Francis was born April 1850

Annstead Todd Agness's son born 27 June 1849

This Bible in the possession of Mrs Elizabeth Carlton Revere, Hartfield, Virginia.

## Family Record of John A Carlton and of His Wife Manissa Susan Bulman Eubank

Ellen O Carlton was born 24$^{th}$ of Sept$^r$ 1876. Daughter of John A and Manissa Susan Carlton

Manissa Sarah Carlton was born the 1$^{st}$ day of April 1882. Daughter of John A and Manissa Susan Carlton

Ellen O Carlton married December 15$^{th}$ 1897 to Alexander G Oliver Died May 8$^{th}$ 1904

John Thomas Oliver son of A G and Ellen O Oliver was born March 25$^{th}$ 1902

Transcribed from the original by VLHD

Both of these Family Bible Records have been submitted by Mr. John R. Carlton, 617 Green Spring Drive, Bear, Delaware 19701. Manissa Sarah Carlton was his grandmother. Mr. Carlton would appreciate hearing from those descendants who have additional information about this family.

BOOK REVIEWS:

Beverly Fleet, *Virginia Colonial Abstracts*, 3 volumes, 2,087 pp. total; each volume indexed. (1937-1949), reprint 1988. The set: $150.00, Per volume: $50.00. Postage and handling $3.00, first book; each add. vol. $1.00. These much sought-after books are an addition to the researcher's library that will be a cherished possession and research tool. Beverly Fleet abstracted and published, over a period of twelve years, thirty-four volumes of early colonial records, some of them from burned record counties. Originally his work in the various counties was represented in separate and sometimes scattered volumes. The counties in which he worked are now arranged logically: Volume I has records of Accomack, Lancaster, Richmond, Northumberland and Westmoreland counties; Volume II has records of Essex and King and Queen counties and Volume III has records of York, Charles City, Henrico, Lower Norfolk and Washington counties. There is also a master index in each volume (as compared with the original thirty-four indexes). Mr. Fleet brought together vital records, using tax lists, court orders, militia lists, and wills and deeds; because of his familiarity with these counties, he was able to present information from county courthouses, municipal and state records, as well as private collections. He sometimes added his own observations, based on this same familiarity with the area, the times and the records, and interjected his own wry humor. The records provide a wealth of information, as well as being a delight to read. In many cases, additional information has come to light since his work was completed, but he provided a valuable service. With the reorganized presentation in three volumes in the recent publication, the publisher has preserved for posterity, this major collection of colonial Virginia records. Genealogical Publishing Co. 1001 N Calvert St, Baltimore, MD 21202. 1-800-727-6687.

Dr. R. A. Brock, *The Vestry Book of Henrico Parish, Virginia, 1730-1773*, 221 pp., illus., index, notes, append., paper. (n.d. bef.1914) Rep. 1991. $18.00 plus $3.00 shipping. This vestry book was transcribed from the original manuscript and contains information of genealogical value along with the transaction of the parish business. Processioning returns are included, as well as descriptions of boundary markings. Church officers are named and among the accounts of dispersal of funds are interesting identifications of persons for whom and to whom funds were dispersed. The notes following the transcription of the vestry book text relate to some well-known Henrico county families. Dr. Brock died in 1914, and some of the information he supplied has since been revised and corrected, but as always, such information provides a basis for further research. Heritage Books, Inc. 1540E Pointer Ridge Place, Suite 300, Bowie, MD 20716. Call 301-390-7709.

Nell Marion Nugent, *Cavaliers and Pioneers, Abstracts of Virginia Land Patents and Grants, 1623-1666*. (Volume I) 767 pp., illus., indexed, cloth. (1934), reissued 1991. $40.00, $3.00, postage and handling. It is exciting to find that this invaluable book has been reissued! Many researchers must have tried recently, by any means, to find a copy for their own personal use, but in vain. While this book is of interest to all researchers of early Virginia ancestors, for the readers of *Tidewater Virginia Families*, this book is an indispensable reference in identifying the origins of early tidewater Virginia ancestors. *Cavaliers and Pioneers* contains abstracts of land records dating from 1623 to 1666. In paragraph form, under the full name of the patentee, it records the earliest Virginia land grants and patents, with locations, dates of settlement and names of family members, and often refers to relationships, estates, etc. It further includes the names of thousands of headrights claimed by the land patentees. It is the primary reference of immigration to Virginia in the seventeenth century. When one obtains this book, it then becomes imperative to secure Volumes II and III. Genealogical Publishing Co. 1001 N Calvert St., Baltimore, MD 21202. 1-800-727-6687.

Louise Eubank Gray, *A Patchwork Quilt, Lifestyle in King and Queen County, Virginia, 1910-1920*. 216 pp., illus., index, soft cover. 1989. $14.95 plus $3.00 shipping. Va residents add $.045 sales tax. The patchwork quilt created by Louise Gray is one of people, their experiences and activities, their relationships worked against the fabric of their community and times. While the time frame appears almost contemporary to many, King and Queen County was a small window on the past, in that the roads were poor, there were no towns, and people lived simply, much as they had fifty years earlier; the twentieth century came late to them. The accounts of daily events and the cycles of life and nature are important to our perspective today, in understanding our heritage. The book is written with a great deal of insight, talent and love. It is both delightful and fascinating. Brunswick Publishing Corporation, Route 1, Box 1-A-1, Lawrenceville, VA 23868. 804-848-3865.

Clayton Torrence, Editor. *The Edward Pleasants Valentine Papers*. 4 Volumes. 2,768 pp., indexed, cloth. (1927) Rep. 1979. Originally $125.00, now $94.00 the set of 4 vols. Postage and handling $3.00, first book, each add. vol. $1.00. These volumes contain abstracts of 17th and 18th century Virginia records: land office, county court, chancery and general courts, parish and church; from the counties in which the families in question were found. The families include: Allen, Bacon, Ballard, Batchelder, Belson, Brassieur, Cary, Crenshaw, Dabney, Exum, Ferris, Fontaine, Gray, Hardy, Hooker, Isham, Izzard, Jordan, Langston, Lyddall, Mann, Mosby, Palmer, Pasteur, Pleasant, Povall, Randolph, Satterwhite, Scott, Smith, Valentine, Waddy, Watts, Winston, Womack and Woodson.
The abstracts are meticulously presented and represent the work, not only of Mr. Valentine, but of those who assisted him, as well as the work of the editor, Clayton Torrence. In a work of such magnitude there have to be some errors; as always the work should be compared with the originals, and it should be kept in mind that additional records have come to light since then (some have also been lost). The volumes are a treasure, a fine resource material and a very good starting point for those who have an interest in these families. Clearfield Company, 200 East Eager Street, Baltimore, MD 21202. 410-625-9004.

ANNOUNCEMENTS:

*The Lowry Quarterly: Research Newsletter of Lowry Lines (All Spellings) & Allied Connections.* A long term project is currently in progress to produce a comprehensive Lowry Family History; identifying and distinguishing the various lines and descendants. $12.00/yr. Contact Sharon Loury & Associates, 655 Beaverbrook Lane, Glendora, CA 91740.

*The Holt Herald.* A newsletter for anyone descended from Randall Holt & Elizabeth Hansford Holt of Virginia. Vol.1 No.1 now available. Non-profit, $6.00/yr, quarterly, 8 pages. Contact Andrea K Storm, 703 NE 109th Ct, Portland, OR 97220. 503-252-0402.

*The Christopher Robinson Family Association of "Hewick", Middlesex County.* A newsletter for those interested in the Robinson family, their descendants and Hewick Plantation, $12.00/2 issues (May & November). Back issues available. Helen and Ed Battleson, Hewick Plantation, P O Box 82, Urbanna, VA 23175. 1-804-758-4214.

*Magazine of Virginia Genealogy*, a quarterly publication of the Virginia Genealogical Society. Membership in the society includes a bi-monthly newsletter as well. Annual membership: Individual (including societies and libraries), $20.00; Family, $22.00. For information and membership applications, write P O Box 7469, Richmond, VA 23221.

*Keyes, The K(e)y(e)s Newsletter*, a new quarterly publication for those interested in sharing information about their Keyes ancestors. The first issue (14 pages) came out in June 1992, $8.00/year for four issues. P O Box 372205, Satellite Beach, FL 32937.

*Genealogical Research Institute of Virginia News 'n' Notes.* This is an enthusiastic and dedicated research group with a monthly newsletter, operating as a non-profit organization committed to promoting accurate genealogical and historical research. Annual dues are $10.00 per person (July 1-June 30). Contact GRIVA, P O Box 29178, Richmond, VA 23242.

*Virginia in the 1600s, An Index to Who Was There!...And Where!*
A new publication, beginning June 1992 and published quarterly, June, September, December and March. Compiled and edited by Harold Oliver. Subscription rate $18.00/year. Each issue an alphabetical listing of early immigrants, with arrival date, event and source of information. Contact D & H Publishing, 9171 Kennedy St, Riverside, CA 92509.

*Southern Baileys.* A new publication relating to the Bailey family, drawing from a database of over 30,000 family group sheets/ancestor charts. Published quarterly, September (Volume 1 Number 1, 1992), December, March and June. Subscription rate

$15.00/year, back issues $5.00 each. Contact Donna Beers, 9171 Kennedy St, Riverside, CA 92509.

*Caroline County, Virginia Chancery Court Deeds, 1758-1845*. Detailed abstracts of Caroline County deeds filed in connection with various suits in the Chancery Court. 79 pp. indexed. $12.00.
*Caroline County, Virginia Land Tax Lists, 1787-1799*. 167 pp. 8½ x 11, alphabetized, spiral bound with clear plastic covers. $14.00. Postpaid. Acid-free paper $2.00 add. each book. Order from T.L.C. Genealogy, P O Box 403369, Miami Beach, FL 33140.

*Richmond County, Virginia, Deeds and Bonds, 1721-1734*. Detailed abstract of deeds and bonds from Deed Book 8. 155 pp. 8½ x 11, indexed or alphabetized, spiral bound with clear plastic covers. $14.00. Postpaid. Acid-free paper for $2.00 add. each book. Order each from T.L.C. Genealogy, P O Box 403369, Miami Beach, FL 33140.

## SEARCH

*The queries of family researchers are very important. In the interest of accuracy and clarity: please print or type each Search question, limit each to thirty words or fewer, give year dates and identify county of residence. Multiple submissions will appear in subsequent issues.*

PUGH, Willoughby, son of Lewis and Ann Pugh b 1711 Richmond Co, d 1790 Charlotte Co. Need information. Exchange extensive Pugh research. Iris Garner, Rt 2 Box 595, Chiefland, FL 32626.

DABNEY, Mary Frances, w of Thomas Collier, Hanover Co, s of John Collier Jr, New Kent, King & Queen Cos; d 1759 Hanover Co. Need parents of Dabney and marriage date. Ed Dolan, 7403 Flint #205, Shawnee, KS 66203.

LONDON/LUNDIN/LONNON. Essex or King & Queen Cos. Deed K & Q Co 1715. Believe he is same John London found in 1730s in Augusta Co and father of John, will 1777 Halifax Co. Any info welcome. Marilyn London Winton, Rt 1 Box 50, Oakwood Dr, Coffeyville, KS 67337.

MARSH/MASH. Possibly from families of Northumberland Co. Robert Marsh in Orange Co, NC, will 1801, Chatham Co, NC. Issue: Charles, John, William, Robert, Joseph, Henry, Alexander, Elizabeth (Brantley), Barbara (Griffith), Mary (Hackney), Nancy (Dillard), Martha (Lambert), Sarah (Davis), Frances (Taylor), Eliza (Stuart) and Henrietta. Info on origin/ ancestry. U B Marsh, 5524 Apalachee Pkwy, Tallahassee, FL 32311.

HAYES, Elizabeth Whitfield Hutcheson Jones, dau of Peter Hutcheson and Elizabeth Brame. m (1)Daniel Jones d 1823 in Alabama, (2)Hiram Hayes, Clarke Co GA. Seek info. Winifred Jacob, 5200 SW Colony Ct, Beaverton, OR 97005.

HUDGINS, Mary Frances, b Mathews Co 1841. Need to know parents. Know brothers and sisters. Mary A Cannon, Box 204, Mathews, VA 23109.

WHITLOCK, John, b c.1780, (p) Henrico Co. dau Sarah Whitlock, b c.1802, d Sequatchie Co, TN, 1857; m Thomas Jefferson Hoodenpyle, s John Whitlock Hoodenpyle. Need parents, siblings, wife and issue of John Whitlock. Will exchange info. Dolores Rajca, 5156 Perry Road, Mt Airy, MD 21771.

HAYNES, Jasper, b c.1715; in Caroline Co, 1739-1760. What was maiden name of wife, Elizabeth? Wilma S Davis, 6311 Joyce Dr, Camp Springs, MD 20748.

PATE,TURNER,FREEMAN. Thomas Pate d 1774, Sussex Co. Names of parents and wife? Issue: Edmund b 1720 m Mary; Elizabeth b c.1726 m Freeman; John b 1735 m Elizabeth; Thomas b 1739 m Mary; Edward b 1742 m Lucretia; Mary b 1745 m Turner; Sarah b c.1747 m John Jones. Need given names and maiden names. Helen Pate Ross, 1801 Esic Dr, Edwardsville, IL 62025.

OSTEEN. Seek information about Osteen family of Northumberland Co. H E Osteen, P O Box 473, Trenton, FL 32693.

BROADDUS,BUCKNER,FISHER,HAILE,HUTCHINSON,JONES,MOTLEY, PITTS,POLLARD and WRIGHT. Wish to correspond with searchers of these families, or any of their connections. Will gladly exchange data. Richard M Hutchinson Jr, 731 N Stratford Rd, Winston-Salem, NC 27104.

CHAPMAN, FISHER. Seeking info on Robert Chapman, m Elizabeth; and Barksdale Fisher, wife unknown. Son William Chapman m daughter, Elizabeth Fisher, Pittsylvania Co 1816. B Jean Snedeger, 1638 Rhode Island St, Lawrence, KS 66044.

BURCHET/BURKET, Rebecca, m William Lee, son of Hugh Lee, Jr c.1715 (p) Pr George Co. Issue: Peter, William, Elizabeth, Ann, Amy and Rebecca. Need parents of Rebecca, dates and places; birth & death dates, places for Rebecca. Mrs Hope H Niedling, 1008 Third St, Stevens Point, WI 54481.

SLADDING/SLADDEN/SLAYDEN/SLATTEN/SLAYTON.Searching for Abraham and William Sladding's children, 1730's Hanover Co. Need parents of John Sladding 1711 and Arthur Slayden 1729, New Kent Co. William John Slayton, 2727 Sterling, #G, Independence, MO 64052.

LOWRY/LOURY,BRIGHT,COLE,WATTS. Also connections: LOWRY-MALLORY, ARMISTEAD,ANDERSON; BRIGHT-SINCLAIR,RIDDLEHURST,TRAVIS. Wish to exchange information with anyone researching these lines. Sharon Loury, 655 Beaverbrook Lane, Glendora, CA 91740.

DULANY, Pollard, (1780/85-1860) m 1819, Malind[a] Kelly, Culpeper/Madison Cos. d at home of son Alfred Gilmore Dulany (m Elizabeth Fink). Request names of parents of P Dulany. Ruth A Watters, Rt 2 Box 23, Miles, TX 76861.

DONALDSON. Ferry keeper of Fredericksburg (Spotsylvania Co). Seek information. Mrs Georgia Clasing, 1218 Narcissus Ave, Baltimore, MD 21237.

SELF/SELFE/SELPH. Robert Self, will rec. 1717 Westmoreland Co. Any info on this family in regard to his descendants. Jessie P Dodge, P O Box 249, Lively, VA 22507.

WHITE, Frances, b c.1720, m Battaile Harrison 1742. Father, Daniel White(?). Essex or Caroline Co(?). Request any information on White family. Ms Barbara Sturgeon, 7083 Henley Road, Klamath Falls, OR 97603.

NEALE, Christopher, b 1644 Northumberland Co m Hannah Rodham, dau Mathew Rodham. Need help with Neale & Rodham families. Will exchange info. Kim Johnson, 143 Spencer Road, Clendenin, WV 25045.

WOODRUM, John, Henrico Co late 1600s m Mary. HR of Capt Wm Randolph and servant of Phill: Childers. Later lived in Goochland Co. Seek information about port of embarkation to the colony and his wife's maiden name. Barbara Ricketts, 12464 Woodley Ave, Granada Hills, CA 91344.

MULLINS, William, will rec 1734, Hanover Co m Catherine, Issue: John, Joshua, William, James, Agnes, Mary. Believe one of the sons was father of John Mullins, b c.1758 m Nancy Gentry, 1792 Halifax Co. Moved to TN then Floyd/Perry Co KY, d 1838. Seek info and correspondence. Janallee Mullins, P O Box 135, Dwarf, KY 41739.

MCCARTY. Seek information about McCarty families, Northern Neck for upcoming book; particularly McCarty silver with the McCarty coat of arms dated 1620, last known in possession of William Page McCarty, Richmond VA d 1900 (a bachelor). William M McCarty, MD, 1 Pheasant Lane, Troy, NY 12180.

GRAVES, Francis (Sr), b c.1630-35 m 1678 in Essex Co, widow Jane, who also m John MacGuffey, a Davenport and John Doughty; d by 1691, Essex Co. Seek information about him or his son, Thomas of Essex Co and husband of Elizabeth Moody. Linda J Kummer, 8945 Matthews Ct, Laurel, MD 20708.

BROOKS, Paul, m Hester Burns 1784, Bucks Co, PA. Was his father the Paul Brooks b 1735, Middlesex Co, VA; apprenticed to a tailor 1751, Middlesex Co? Virginia Kohl, 307 N Goodhope Ave, San Pedro, CA 90732.

EIDSON/ITSON/IDSON/HITSON/EDSON, Edward, m Penelope c.1710 prob. Lancaster or Westmoreland Co. Seek her identity. Mrs Jack L Eidson, 607 W Columbia, Weatherford, TX 76086.

COX, Reuben, b 1755 along the Rappahannock River, may be brother to William and kin to Beverly Cox; all dying in South Carolina. Need to determine county of birth. Mrs Wilma C Kirkland, 145 Rutledge Rd, Greenwood, SC 29649.

DENNETT, Anne m Thomas Dennett d York Co (W.R.) 1673. She later m William Clopton lived in New Kent Co. Printed sources name father, Robert Booth d York Co (intest.). Will of William Barbar d 1668, York Co named Thomas Dennett, his son-in-law as overseer of will. Seek maiden name and parents of Anne. Jimmy L Veal, 57 Loganberry Cl, Valdosta, GA 31602.

GOOCH, Claiborne, b bet.1719-1740, d after 1792 in New Kent or King William Co. Need names of spouse and children. Winifred M Rampe, 6814 Rhode Island Trail, Crystal Lake, IL 60012.

BULLOCK, Edward, d c.1702, New Kent/Hanover/Louisa Co area. Left land to dau Lucy, wife of William Tate. Need wife and parents of Edward Bullock. Mrs Ronnie E Hall, 410 Mantooth, Lufkin, TX 75901.

ANGLE, John, d intestate, Lancaster Co, 1765, widow, Mary. John Fleet appt. guardian of children. Mary m George Edwards. Was Mary's maiden name George? Seek her maiden name. A B Angle, 10951 Johnson Blvd, #H207, Seminole, FL 34642.

OSBORNE, Capt Thomas, James City Co, early to mid 1600s. Information on parents and children, particularly daughter Jane. Elene Bennett Kottal, 11318 E Virginia Dr, Aurora, CO 80012.

*Coming in the Next Issue:*

*Losses Sustained from the British Depredations,*
*King George County*
*Additions to Christ Church Parish Register,*
*Middlesex County*
*Gloucester County Land Tax Records, 1782,*
*(Identifying Kingston Parish, Mathews County)*

# INDEX

Alender
  Ambrose 146
Alexson
  Edith F. 117
Allen
  family 155
Anderson
  family 159
Andros
  Sir Edmond 121
Angle
  John 160
  Mary 160
Armistead
  Anthony 143
  family 159
  Robert 137
  Westwood 131
  William 134,135
Arnold
  Nancy 141
Bacon
  family 155
Bagby
  Dr. Alfred 142
Ballard
  family 155
Baptist
  Anne 151
Barbar
  William 160
Barfield
  Solomon 144
Barron
  James 134
Batchelder
  family 155
Bates
  George 121
Bearfield
  Solomon 143
Beers
  Donna 157
Bell
  Landon C 117
Belson
  family 155
Berkeley
  William 121
Booker
  George
    132-134,136

Booth
  Robert 160
Borum
  Edmund 146
  Edmund, Sen 146
  J. 146
  John 146
Bradley
  Stephen 143,145
Brame
  Elizabeth 158
Brantley
  Elizabeth 157
Brassieur
  family 155
Bright
  family 159
Broaddus
  family 158
Brocas
  Capt 127
Brock
  Dr. R. A. 117,154
Brooks
  Hester 160
  John 143
  Paul 160
Brough
  Robert 136
Brydon
  George M 117
Buckner
  family 158
  John 148
Bullock
  Edward 160
  Lucy 160
Bulman
  Manissa 153
Burchet
  Rebecca 158
Burket
  Rebecca 158
Burns
  Hester 160
Byrom
  Agnes 141
  Benjamin 141
  Eliza 141
  Elizabeth 141
  Henry 141
  Isabella 141

Byrom
  James 141
  John 141
  Lucy 141
  Mary 141
  Milton 141
  Nancy 141
  Robert 141
  Sara 141
  Sarah 141
  Thomas 141
  William 141
Callis
  Mary 143
  Robert 144
  William 143
Camm
  Thomas 150,151
Carlton
  Charlotte 152
  Christopher
    152,153
  Ellen O 153
  Harriet 152
  Janisha 152
  John A 152,153
  John R 152,153
  Manissa 153
  Orania G 152
  Robert P 152
  Virginaous 152
Carteret
  Lord 143
Cary
  family 155
  Miles 150
  Wilson Miles
    134-136
Chamberlayne
  Churchill G
    117,128
Chapman
  Elizabeth 158
  Robert 158
  William 158
Chichley
  Henry 127
Childers
  Phill: 159
Chiles
  Elizabeth 121,122

Chiles
 Henry
  120,122,125
 John 120-125
 Mary 121
 Sarah 120
 Susan 120,122
 Susanna 120-122
 Walter   120-122,
  124,125
Chowning
 Carroll C
  127,128,130
Clader
 Henry 144
 Noel 144
Clark
 Jewel T 117
Clopton
 Anne 160
 William 160
Cocke
 Charles F 117
Coffey
 Edward A. 117
Cole
 family 159
Collier
 John 157
 Thomas 157
Cooke
 Elizabeth 148
 Mordecai 149
Cooper
 Joseph 132
Corbin
 Betty 130
 Richard 130
Cotten
 John 145
Cowper
 Roe 131,134
Cox
 Absolom 151
 Beverly 160
 Reuben 160
 William 160
Crenshaw
 family 155
Crump
 Elizabeth 124
 John 124
Dabney
 family 155
 Mary Frances 157

Dame
 George 129
Davenport
 Jane 159
Davis
 Anthony 149
 James 137
 Perdue 117,118
 Ransome 151
 Sarah 143,157
Dawson
 Elizabeth 143
 Mary 143,144
 William 143,144
Dean
 Sarah 141
Dennett
 Anne 160
 Thomas 160
Dennis
 Aaron 150
Dewberry
 John 150
Diggs
 Edward 124
 Eliz: 123
 Elizabeth 124
Dillard
 Nancy 157
Dix
 John 144
Dixon
 Frances 151
 Richard 136
Donaldson
 family 159
Doughty
 Jane 159
 John 159
Drewry
 Elizabeth 150
Drummond
 William 120
 William 122
Dulany
 Alfred 159
 Elizabeth 159
 Malind[a] 159
 Pollard 159
Dunsford
 Wills 150
Eaton
 William 144
Eden
 Sarah 141

Edson
 family 160
Edwards
 George 160
 Mary 160
 Nathaniel 144
Eidson
 Edward 160
 Penelope 160
Elliott
 John 146
Eubank
 Manissa 153
Exum
 family 155
Faison
 Elizabeth 143
 James 143
Fariss
 Agnes 141
 Nancy 141
Fennis
 John 151
Ferris
 Family 155
Fink
 Elizabeth 159
Fisher
 Barksdale 158
 Elizabeth 158
 family 158
Fleet
 Beverly 118,154
 John 160
Fontaine
 family 155
Fox
 John 147
Freeman
 Elizabeth 158
Fulks
 William 144
Gayle
 Christopher 151
 Molly 151
Gemmill
 Elizabeth 151
Gentry
 Nancy 159
Giles
 Susanna 121
Gilliam
 Wm. 150
Gooch
 Claiborne 160

Goodwin
  Edwin Lewis 117
  Elizabeth 150
Graves
  Elizabeth 159
  Francis 159
  Jane 159
  Thomas 159
Gray
  family 155
  Louise 155
Griffith
  Barbara 157
Grymes
  Jane 129
  John 129
  Lucy 129
  Phillip 129
Gully
  John 144
Hackney
  Mary 157
Haile
  family 158
Hansford
  Elizabeth 156
Hardy
  family 155
Harrison
  Battaile 159
  Benjamin 132
  Frances 159
Hayes
  Elizabeth 158
  Hiram 158
Haynes
  Elizabeth 158
  Jasper 158
Hays
  Eliza 141
Heard
  Isabella 141
Hening
  William W 117
Hill
  Edward 120
Hitson
  family 160
Hobday
  Brookes 146,147
  Isaac 148
Holloway
  Elizabeth 150
Holt
  Elizabeth 141,156

Holt
  family 156
  Jake 141
  Randall 156
Hoodenpyle
  John 158
  Thomas 158
Hooker
  family 155
Hope
  George 134-136
Hudgins
  Mary Frances 158
Huggins
  Ann 149
Hutcheson
  Elizabeth 158
  Peter 158
Hutchinson
  family 158
Idson
  family 160
Irby
  William 145
Isham
  family 155
Itson
  family 160
Izzard
  family 155
Jenkins
  Daniel 140
  James 147
Jennings
  Charles 136
Johnson
  Frances 144
  William 144
Jones
  Daniel 158
  Elizabeth 158
  family 158
  John 158
  Naomi 144
  Sarah 158
Jordan
  family 155
  Sally 151
Keble
  Nancy 151
Kelly
  Malind[a] 159
Kerby
  Mary Sheild 150
  Sarah 150

Kerby
  William 150
Keyes
  family 156
Keys
  family 156
King
  George H S 118
  Miles 133-137
Kirk
  S. 128
Kyes
  family 156
Lambert
  Martha 157
Langston
  family 155
Lasater
  Elizabeth 141
  Lucy 141
Laseter
  Lucy 141
Latimer
  George 134
Leavitt
  Charles 150
Lee
  Amy 158
  Ann 158
  Elizabeth 158
  Hugh 158
  Peter 158
  Rebecca 158
  William 158
Lewis
  Mary 139
Lilburn
  Polly 150
London
  family 157
  John 157
Long
  Elizabeth T 117
Lonnon
  family 157
Loury
  family 159
Lowry
  family 156,159
Ludwell
  Lucy 129
Lukin
  Alice 123,125
Lumpkin
  Jacob 142

Lundin
  family 157
Lyddall
  family 155
MacGuffey
  Jane 159
  John 159
Majors
  Kindred 141
  Mary 141
Mallory
  Charles K. 138
  family 159
  Francis 131
Mann
  family 155
Marrow
  Wm. 150
Marsh
  Alexander 157
  Barbara 157
  Charles 157
  Eliza 157
  Elizabeth 157
  Frances 157
  Henrietta 157
  Henry 157
  John 157
  Joseph 157
  Martha 157
  Mary 157
  Nancy 157
  Robert 157
  Sarah 157
  William 157
Martin
  William 128
Mash
  family 157
Mason
  George C 117
  Thomas 146
Matheny
  E R 118
McCarty
  family 159
  William 159
Merideth
  Joseph 136
Minson
  Sarah 151
Moody
  Elizabeth 159
Moore
  Anne 150

Moore
  Augustine 138
  William 134
Morris
  Ambrose 151
  Anne 144
  George 143
  John 144
Mosby
  family 155
Moss
  Mary 150
  Wm. 150
Motley
  family 158
Mullins
  Agnes 159
  Catherine 159
  James 159
  John 159
  Joshua 159
  Mary 159
  Nancy 159
  William 159
Neale
  Christopher 159
  family 159
  Hannah 159
Negro
  Aaron 153
  Abram 147
  Agness 153
  Alice 146
  Annstead Todd 153
  Antony 147
  Ben 147
  Daniel 148
  Dick 148
  Esaw 153
  Fanney 153
  Fill 148
  Francis 153
  Gabriel 147,148
  George 147
  Gloucester 146
  Harry 146
  Isaac 153
  Issabel 148
  Jacob 153
  Jenny 147,148
  Joe 148
  Joseph 146
  London 147
  Margarid 153

Negro
  Marquis 147
  Mary 147
  Mason 147
  Melley 147
  Moll 148
  Moses 153
  Nelson 153
  Peter 146
  Phebe 147
  Robin 147
  Sal 144
  Sam 146
  Simon 147
  Tagey 148
  Thomas 153
  Will 148
  York 147
Neill
  Edward 125
Newcomb
  Elisha 140
Newell
  John 144
Nugent
  Nell Marion 154
Oliver
  Alexander G 153
  Ellen O 153
  Harold 156
  John T 153
Osborne
  Jane 160
  Thomas 160
Osteen
  family 158
Page
  Alice 123-125
  Colonel John 124
  Eliza. 123
  Elizabeth 124
  Francis 121,123-125
  John 121,123-125
  Mann 123
  Mary 122-124
  Matthew 123,124
Pagge
  Matthew 124
Palmer
  Barton 130
  E. Holcombe 117
  family 155
Parsons
  Armiger 150

Parsons
  John 132,134,135
  Patsey 151
  Thomas 135,136
  William 135,136
Pasteur
  family 155
Pate
  Edmund 158
  Edward 158
  Elizabeth 158
  John 158
  Lucretia 158
  Mary 158
  Sarah 158
  Thomas 158
Pendleton
  J. 137
Peyton
  Sir John 147
Phillips
  Rachael 151
Pitts
  family 158
Pleasant
  family 155
Pollard
  family 158
Potter
  Henry 130
Povall
  family 155
Powell
  Lucas 144
Pryor
  C 147,149
Pryson
  Benja. 150
  John 150
  Nicholas 151
Pugh
  Ann 157
  Lewis 157
  Willoughby 157
Purdie
  John H: 150
Randolph
  Capt Wm 159
  family 155
Rawlings
  James Scott
    117,118
Reeves
  Mary 127

Revere
  Mrs E C 153
Revis
  Sarah 141
  Solomon 141
Riddlehurst
  family 159
Roberts
  G--ty 150
Robinson
  Anne 150
  Christopher 156
  Mary 150
Rodham
  family 159
  Hannah 159
  Mathew 159
Rogers
  Jno. 151
Ross
  Cheley 150
Rutland
  Edward 144
Salmon
  Emily J 117
Sanders
  Alexander 139
  Almond 139
  John 139
  Mary 139
  Thomas 139
  William 139,140
Satterwhite
  family 155
Saunders
  Mary 150
Sayre
  Jane 129
Sclater
  Martha 150
Scott
  family 155
Selden
  Cary 132,136
  Samuel 137
  Wilson Cary
    134,135
Self
  Robert 159
Selph
  family 159
Sheppard
  John 127
Shirley
  Philemon 144

Short
  Mary 141
Sinclair
  family 159
Skinner
  John 132
Sladden
  family 158
Sladding
  Abraham 158
  John 158
  William 158
Slatten
  family 158
Slave
  Judith 144
  Pott 144
Slayden
  Arthur 158
Slayton
  family 158
Smith
  Claiborne T. 143
  family 155
Stampier
  Mary 141
Stevens
  [torn]uy 148
Stores
  Jane 150
Stuart
  Eliza 157
Tabb
  John 132,133
  Johnson 134-136
Tate
  Lucy 160
  William 160
Taylor
  Frances 157
Teagle
  William 146
  Wm 146
Tennis
  John 151
Thompson
  Edward 127
Throckmorton
  Ann 151
Tomkies
  Charles 147
  Francis 147,148
  Mary 148
Torrence
  Clayton 155

165

Travis
  family 159
Treacle
  Elizabeth 143
  William 144
Turner
  Charlotte 152
  Mary 158
Tyler
  Elizabeth 123,124
  Henry
    121,123-125
  John 123-125
  Lyon G 125
Valentine
  family 155
Waddell
  Frances 144
  Hannah 145
  John 145
  Noel 144,145
Waddy
  family 155
Walker
  Catherine 129
  Sara 141
Warren
  F. E. 128
Watts
  family 155,159
  Samuel 137

Weisiger
  Minor T. 131,146
Westwood
  John S. 138
Worlich
    131,134,136
White
  Daniel 159
  family 159
  Frances 159
Whitlock
  John 158
  Sarah 158
Willis
  Francis 148
Willson
  Daniel 139
Wilson
  Job 151
Wing
  Michael 136
Winston
  family 155
Womack
  family 155
Wood
  Eleanor 145
  James 137
  Joseph 145
  L. 132,133
  Meade 151

Woodrum
  John 159
  Mary 159
Woodson
  family 155
Wormley
  Aylmer 127
  Catherine 127
  Johannes 130
  Ralph 128
Worsnam
  George 120
  William 120
Worsnan
  John 122
Wray
  George
    133,134,136
  Jacob 134,135
Wright
  Dudley 151
Yates
  Bartholomew
    128,129
Young
  John 145
  Mary 145
  Robert 145

# *TIDEWATER VIRGINIA FAMILIES:*
## *A Magazine of History and Genealogy*

### TABLE OF CONTENTS

| | |
|---|---:|
| From Virginia | 168 |
| Virginia Land Tax Records | 169 |
| The Will of Lot Higby, 1854, Henrico County | 174 |
| The Will of William Cole, 1729, Warwick County | 175 |
| The Williams Family of Mathews County | 178 |
| Orphans and Their Guardians, 1757-1763, Northumberland County | 182 |
| Vauter's Church, St. Anne's Parish, Essex County | 187 |
| Tithables List, 1678, Henrico County | 191 |
| Civil Appointments, 1779-1799, Hanover County | 193 |
| Christ Church Parish Register, 1754-1763, Middlesex County | 200 |
| Losses Sustained from the British Depredations, 1782, King George County | 204 |
| Land Tax Records, 1782, Gloucester County | 208 |
| Wills of Edgecombe County, North Carolina, With Reference to Tidewater Virginia, 1793-1794 | 210 |
| Book Reviews | 211 |
| Search | 213 |
| Index | 218 |

Volume 1 Number 4　　　　　　　　　　February/March 1993

From Virginia.........

It is time to renew your subscription when you receive this February-March issue of *TIDEWATER VIRGINIA FAMILIES*.

An envelope, already addressed, is included with this copy of your magazine for your convenience; you will only need to insert your check.

Your subscription rate will remain at $20.00 ($25.00 Canada and overseas) a year. Be sure to renew early to continue to receive your magazine without interruption. Volume two will begin with issue one of May-June 1993.

Some of the plans for Volume two.........

> New Kent, King William, James City counties and Williamsburg: early records, a part of the Jones Collection, made available by the Jones family of Northumberland and Richmond counties.
> King and Queen County: family papers and cemetery records made available by the King and Queen County Historical Society.
> Northumberland County: early court records, not committed to microfilm, and not previously published.
> Some wills from burned record counties.
> The journal of a horseback traveler, 1823, from Caroline County to Kentucky and Tennessee.
> Early lists of tithables, Lancaster, Middlesex and Northumberland counties.
> Transcriptions, verbatim, of earliest Land Tax Records.
> Gloucester and Mathews counties: family records
> Middlesex County: a continuation of the Christ Church Parish Register additions.
> A balanced geographic and content presentation of material.

*TIDEWATER VIRGINIA FAMILIES: A Magazine of History and Genealogy* began as *An exciting new publication*........ it continues to be an exciting experience, a tribute to both subscribers and contributors.

## *RENEW YOUR SUBSCRIPTION TODAY!*

# Virginia Land Tax Records

## Compiled by Conley L. Edwards

### Using Land Tax Records

In 1782 the General Assembly of Virginia enacted a major revision of the tax laws of the Commonwealth. The act provided for state-wide enumeration on the county level of land and certain personal property. The act created a permanent source of revenue for the operation of government in Virginia.

Copies of annual lists of land owners for each county and city from 1782 (or the date of formation of the county if after 1782) to the present are available for research in the Archives. These land tax records are one of four copies required by law. Prior to 1928, one copy of each tax book was to be sent to the Auditor of Public Accounts. With the creation of the Department of Taxation in March 1928, the land tax book for each locality was sent to that department. The land tax records now in the collection come from these two agencies. There are more that 19,600 volumes, which comprise one of the oldest continuous series of records in the Archives.

Various revenue acts passed by the General Assembly established the tax rates and procedures for the collection of land taxes. At first, justices of the local court were designated to collect the taxes. By 1786, the county courts were directed to divided each locality into precincts and to appoint "commissioners" to collect the tax. Taxes were assessed between March and April of each year and were payable by the end of December. The commissioners prepared four "fair and correct" copies of the land tax books. Copies were prepared for the commissioner, county clerk, sheriff and Auditor of Public Accounts.

Original land tax records for those Virginia counties that are now part of West Virginia were given to the West Virginia auditor's office by direction of an act passed by the General Assembly in February 1892. The General Assembly passed an act in 1808 ordering the commissioners not to compile lists of taxpayers or collect taxes. In March 1864 the General Assembly suspended the revenue act of 1864 because there were adequate funds already in the treasury. Therefore, no land tax records exist for the years 1808 and 1864.

Form of Land Tax Records

The form of Virginia land tax records varies from manuscript lists dating from the eighteenth century to modern computer generated lists and lists produced directly on microfilm. The earlier manuscript lists are small booklets that record the names of property owners arranged by the initial letter of the surname. There is a separate volume for each district within the county, if the county was so divided. The district may be identified by the name of the commissioner for that district or by a geographical designation, such as "upper district" or "lower district". Local militia designations such as "First battalion", or "District of Colonel Clay" were also used. Descriptions of tax districts may sometimes be recorded in the county court order books. By 1845, preprinted forms were developed for recording land tax information and their use continues into this century. More recent computer produced lists have pages of smaller size with information recorded in a more compact form. Modern lists use districts corresponding to existing subdivisions within the locality, such as wards, magisterial districts, or sanitary districts. Usually, the boundaries of these districts can be located on contemporary maps.

Content of Land Tax Records

Information recorded in Virginia land tax records changes relatively little from 1782 to the present. The early laws required the tax commissioner in each district to record in "a fair alphabetical list" the names of persons owning land or town lots, the quantity of land owned, the value of the land or lots, and the amount of tax owed. Each tract or lot owned by an individual was to be entered separately.

Later laws required additional descriptive information. A brief description of the location of the land was required by 1814. The distance and direction from the courthouse was included on lists beginning the same year. An act passed in 1786 required that alienation, alteration, or changes in ownership during the preceding year be recorded where appropriate. The amount of tax due was reported in pounds, shillings, and pence on the early land tax lists. Amounts were reported in dollars and cents by 1810.

By the 1850s, the land tax records included the following entries arranged in columns:

> Name of owner and residence;
>
> Estate (whether held in fee simple, for life, etc.) as well as number of acres and name of tract;
>
> Description of the land, as to water courses, mountains and contiguous tracts;
>
> Distance and bearing from the courthouse;
>
> Value of the land per acre, including buildings, sum added to the land on account of buildings and the total values of the land and buildings;
>
> Amount of tax on the whole tract at the legal rate and amount of tax for county purposes;
>
> Explanation of alterations during the preceding year, especially from whom transferred and when and how the owner derived the land.

In the later part of the nineteenth century, certain lands were exempted from taxation. These lands included property owned by the state and any county, city, town or school district. Land owned by church or religious bodies were exempted, as were public and private "burying grounds". Benevolent and charitable organizations and certain preservation organizations received exemptions for their property. Land owned by railroad and steamship companies was exempt also.

Land owned by blacks began to be listed separately within each district in 1891. Preprinted pages were marked "white' and "colored". The distinction remained through the mid-twentieth century.

Modern land tax records include the post office address of owners and tax information on timber, trees, minerals, and mineral lands. In addition to the amount of tax due, the description of each parcel may include references to the parcel on local tax maps, deed book references to transfer to the current owner, and the value of the land, building(s) and total assessment.

Use of Land Tax Records

The most frequent use of land tax records is for the direct information recorded; name of the property owner, quantity of land owned, location of land, amount of tax imposed, or changes in ownership. Comparative analysis of land tax records from year to year may lead to conclusions about social, economic and agricultural history, as well as the status of certain individuals or groups of land owners within a locality.

For genealogical researchers land tax records may help distinguish between individuals by the same name in a locality at the same time. John Jones living in the upper district will be distinct on the tax records from the John Jones living in the lower district or owning different acreage.

Land tax records are a substitute for records in those counties where destruction of the original deeds, wills and other records has occurred. By studying the lists from year to year, the researcher may trace an ancestor to determine the date of departure from the locality, or possibly the year of death. The name of a taxpayer will continue on the tax list, noted as "deceased' or "estate", until the estate is settled. Careful reading of marginal notes and the entries for other taxpayers who might have inherited or received land from the deceased's estate can help support evidence about genealogical relationships gathered from other sources.

Land tax records also are used to help date structures. Beginning in 1820 and continuing thereafter a column was added to the tax list for "Sum added to land on account of buildings". An increase in figures reported in this column from one year to the next may indicate the addition of a new building or improvements to an existing structure. Such information from the land tax records, used in conjunction with physical evidence from the structure itself and other evidence, may lead to conclusions about the period during which a structure was erected.

Availability of Records for Research

Land tax records in the Archives are available for use without prior arrangements. The surviving records for each county for the period 1782 through 1850 are available on microfilm. Also, microfilm copies for this period circulate through the interlibrary loan system of local libraries. A list, available upon request, shows microfilm reel numbers and dates covered for each county. Original land tax records for the period 1782 to 1850 have been withdrawn from circulation since microfilm copies are available.

Original land tax records dating from 1851 to the present are available for use in the Archives Research Room. The research archivist will instruct researchers how to obtain the records. Please use extreme care in handling original records as many of them are fragile.

Form of keeping the Book containing the Land Tax
by the Commissioner:

List of the Land Tax within the District of [Commissioner name]
in the County of [name]

[Categories]
Persons names owning land
Number of lots
Yearly rent of lots
Quantity of land
Rate of land per acre
Total amount of value of land exclusive of lots
Amount of tax at one and a half percent

Instructions to commissioners on the form of the land books for 1786. From William Waller Hening, ed., *The Statutes at Large: Being a Collection of All the Laws of Virginia, from the First Session of the Legislature, in the Year 1619.*

The preceding article was compiles by Conley L. Edwards, Head, Archives Public Services Section, Archives and Records Division, Virginia State Library and Archives, Richmond, Virginia. Published with his permission and the kind permission of Dr. Louis H. Manarin, Virginia State Archivist.

## The Will of Lot Higby, 1854
## Henrico County

In the name of God, Amen. I Lot Higby a free Man of Color of the County of Henrico, in the State of Virginia, being of sound & disposing mind & body, do make this to be My last will & testament, as follows: that is to say, I desire that my body may be buried at the descretion of my executor, hereinafter named, and I direct that all my just debts be paid out of my estate as soon after my decease as may be convenient.

    First, I give & bequeath unto my sons Lot & David all the property which I may die seized of both real & personal, to be equally divided between them. And it is my desire that out of the said property my said sons Lot & David Higby, do give to my daughter Mourning the sum of one hundred dollars. I appoint my son David my executor & desire that no security be required of him.

    Witness my hand & seal this 4th day of October 1854.

                                        Lot his X Mark Higby Seal

Witness N.[?] J. Lackland
          B. W. Starke

Will not probated.
This will was filed under Henrico County Wills as "Will not Probated". It was placed in an envelope entitled "Higby L's will...Handed me by Henry A Atkinson Jr Esq. and is to be held for proof.
Mr Starke lives in Pike County Alabama"

                                        Transcribed by VLHD

Henrico County Wills, Will not Probated. Archives and Records Division, Virginia State Library and Archives, Richmond, Virginia. Published with the kind permission of Dr. Louis H. Manarin, Virginia State Archivist.

## The Will of William Cole, 1729
## Warwick County

In the name of God Amen I William Cole of the County of Warwick Gent. being very sick and weak in Body but of perfect memory and understanding Do make this my last will and Testament in form and manner following Imprimis I give and bequeath my mortal soul into the hands of Almight God my heavenly Father hoping for remission of all my sins through the merits of Jesus Christ my Savior and my body to the Earth to be discretely intered at the discretion of my Executors here in after named.

And as for my worldly Estate, Wherewith it has pleased God to bless me after my Just debts and funeral expenses are paid I dispose of the same as followeth. I give and devise all my Lands lying and being in the County of Goochland to my three Sons John Cole, Roscow Cole, and James Cole, and their Heirs for ever to be equally divided between them. Item I give and bequeath to my loving wife Mary Cole forever two Negroes named Will and Sarah & above and besides her Dower in any Lands and Negroes as also one ninth Part of my personal Estate. Item I give and bequeath to my loving Son William Cole for ever one Negro boy named Lewis; And whereas my late Brother James Roscow Esq$^r$ by his last Will bequeathed to my Son, John Cole one hundred pounds to be laid out in Negroes for the use of the said John Cole which said hundred pounds I have Received of the Executor of the said James Roscow and have appropriated two Negro boys named Gaby and Bob and two Negro Girls named Moll and Betty for that use I do hereby give and bequeath to my said Son John Cole for ever the said Negroes Gaby, Bobb, Moll, and Betty, in lieu of the said hundred pounds.

Item all the rest and residue of my Negroes and personal Estate of what kind or nature so ever; I give and bequeath to my Children William Cole, John Cole, Roscow Cole, James Cole, Mary Cole, Martha Cole, Jane Cole & Susannah Cole; for ever to be equally divided among them the Survivors or survivor Share and Share alike my Will also is and I do hereby order that my Executors do work all my Negroes (except those particularly bequeathed)) on my Lands at their discresion until my son William arive to the age of twenty one years and the profits of the said

Lands and Negroes to be equally divided among all my Children as aforesaid  And in case my Son William Shall hinder molest Sue for or demand amount of my said Executors from or for using or working the entailed Lands that then and in such case I give and bequeath all the residue of my said Negroes and personal Estate to my Children John Cole, Roscow Cole, James Cole, Mary Cole, Martha Cole, Jane Cole and Susannah Cole  My will also is and I do hereby desire my Executors if my Estate will afford it that they do bring up my Children in my house under the care of my Schoolmaster  Lastly I do hereby constitute and appoint my loving friends Cole Diggs Esq$^r$ Lewis Burwell Gent. and my loving wife Mary Cole (to whom I also give and devise the Guardianship and Tuition of all my Children) Executors of this my last will and Testament and my loving friend William Roscow Gent. to be trustee thereof hereby revoking and annulling all former or other wills and testaments by me made  *In Witness* whereof I have hereunto set my hand and Seal this first day of November in the third year of the Reign of our now Sovereign Lord George the second and in the year of our Lord One Thousand Seven hundred and Twenty nine

And in case my loving wife Mary Cole should be now with Child and such Child should be born alive then I give and bequeath to such Child an equal part with the others of my personal Estate and Negroes.

W$^m$ Cole  SS

Signed Sealed Published and delivered to his last
Will and testament by the said William Cole
and the witnesses under written.  Subscribed their names in the presence of the said testator (the word)
(Lands and) between the fifteenth and sixteenth lines the words (for ever between the Sixteenth and seventeenth lines the words (Survivor or Survivors) between the twenty ninth and thirtieth lines the word (the word (amount) between the thirty fifth and thirty sixth lines and the [illeg] the twenty Sixth line first interlined and made.
William Roscow, William Hopkins, James Pedin
Virginia so.

  (The General Court held at the Capitol November the first MDCCXXIX.

This will was presented in Court by Lewis Burwell Gentleman one of the Executors therein named who made oath to it according to Law and William Roscow and James Pedin two of the Witnesses to it made oath that on the first day of October last they saw the said William Cole sign seal and publish it as his will and that he was then in perfect sense & memory whereupon the said will was admitted to Record.

           Teste   R Hickman   C G C
        A Copy   Teste   John Brown   C G C

                Transcribed by VLDH

Loose Papers, Wills from Burned Record Counties, 1729-1830. Warwick County [General Court] 1729. From Albemarle County 430-5, Accession Number 33216. Archives and Records Division, Virginia State Library and Archives, Richmond, Virginia. Published with the kind permission of Dr. Louis H. Manarin, Virginia State Archivist.

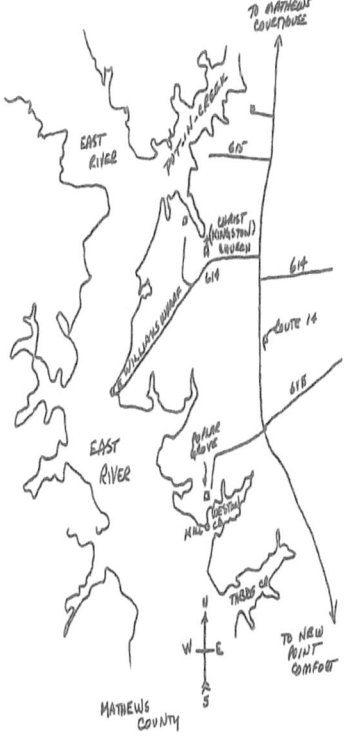

## The Williams Family of Mathews County

### Contributed by Mr. Milton Murray II

*The Williams family of Mathews County had its origins in the colony of Virginia on the Eastern Shore. Mr. Murray is descended from the fourth great granddaughter of Michael Williams. He is the grandson of Cordelia Cary Williams who married Heron Campbell Murray; he has researched this family extensively. The direct line of Mr. Murray is indicated by an asterisk. The vital records of the later generations have been taken from family Bible records, copies of which Mr. Murray has graciously shared with this researcher.*

Michael Williams* sailed from Gravesend, England on the ship *George*, August 21st, 1635; he was then eighteen years old. He landed in Virginia (Hotten, p.124). He apparently returned to England and then returned to Virginia with his wife and son (LP Book 2, p.75 VASL). This patent was on the Eastern Shore of Virginia, near Franktown on Nassawadox Creek, Northampton County; he called it "Holly Grove". Before December 28th, 1650, Michael Williams had died and his wife Sarah had married Stephen Horsey, who on that date made out a deed to Michael Williams' children (Michael, Jr., Thomas* and Sarah) for all of the Williams' holdings (Northampton Co. Orders, Deeds, Wills &c. Book 4 {red ink IV} 1651-54, p.193, rec. 21 Jan. 1654). In 1653 Stephen Horsey was fined 300 pounds of tobacco as a nonconformist. He then left Northampton County for Somerset County, Maryland, with his wife, stepchildren and children. On August 16th, 1660 he received a patent for 600 acres of land, naming headrights: Stephen Horsey, Sarah Horsey his wife, Stephen Horsey, Jr., John Horsey, Samuel Horsey, Mary Horsey, Abigall Horsey, Michael Williams, Thomas Williams*, Sarah Williams, John Rocke, Benjamin Summer and Thomas Whitfield. He called his patent "Coulbourne" (Patents Liber 4, f.580, MD Hall of Records). For an account of Stephen Horsey see Torrence, *Old Somerset on the Eastern Shore of Maryland*. 1935.

On August 12th, 1662, Stephen Horsey took out a patent for Michael Williams, orphan for 300 acres (Patents Liber 5, f.209) and the same date for Thomas Williams*, orphan for 300 acres (Patents Liber

5, f.210). On September 4th, 1663, Thomas Williams repatented his land which was on Annemessex Creek in Somerset Co.(Patents Liber 6, f.139), and called it "Williamston".

Thomas Williams married June 17th, 1684, Frances Robinson (Somerset Co Land Records Liber I.K.L. f.285, MD HofR). Their children: Thomas Williams, born 1684/5
Sarah Williams, born 1686
Hannah Williams, born 1688, m. [blank] Turpin
John Williams*, born 2/20/1692/3, m. 1 Sarah Beauchamp,
    2 Mary Fountain*, 3 Elizabeth Polk
Elizabeth Williams, born [blank], m. [blank] Herne
Mary Williams
(Somerset Co. Land Records Liber I.K.L. f.287, MD HofR)

Thomas Williams* made his will on April 14th, 1720 and it was probated May 5th, 1720 (Wills Liber 16, f.103-105, MD HofR).

His son, John Williams* was born February 20th, 1692/3 and married Sarah Beauchamp on 16th October 1717; they had one son, Jacob Williams, born 10/24/1718. John Williams* married Mary Fountain* on 12th November 1724 and had two children by his second wife: Samuel Williams*, born 11/25/1725 and Hannah Williams, born 12/5/1727. John Williams married a third time, Elizabeth Polk on 10th April 1733; their children: Prissellia Williams, born 1/17/1733/4; Mary Williams, born 1/25/1736/7; John Williams, born 5/28/1739; Josiah Williams, born 7/3/1742 and Benjamin Williams, born 5/12/1747. (Coventry Parish Register, 1714-1828, f.63, MD HofR).

John Williams* made his will on November 29th, 1760 and it was probated December 27th, 1760 (Wills Liber 31, f.247-249, MD HofR).

Samuel Williams*, his son was born November 25th, 1725, moved to Northampton County, Virginia and married, first, November 7th, 1753, Sarah Haggoman*, the daughter of John and Sarah Powell Haggoman (Coventry Parish Register, f.63; Northampton Co Marriage Register, 1706-1853). They had three sons:

John Williams, born 8/17/1754, m. 1 Edith Nottingham 8/12/1775

2 Margaret Granville 8/17/1787, 3 Margaret Goffigon 6/12/1793
William Williams, born 4/9/1759, m. 1 Mary Nottingham 4/29/1786, 2 Leah Goffigon 8/3/1795
Thomas Williams*, born 5/5/1762, m. 1 Susanna Billups 5/15/1793, 2 Mary Lilly Billups* 10/18/1804

Samuel Williams married second, December 4th, 1764, Sarah Dunton, the daughter of Levin Dunton and had two daughters: Pollie Williams, born 10/18/1765, m. Capt. Gabriel Hughes; Margaret Williams, bap. 1/9/1776, m. Levin Gayle.

Samuel Williams married third, December 12, 1772, Margaret Nottingham (d.10/1/1810), daughter of Thomas and "Scarbrough" Nottingham. They had six daughters: Sarah Scarbrough Williams m. Colonel Christopher Billups; Elizabeth Williams m. John Dixon Jarvis; Hannah Williams m. Dr. Briggs; Susan Williams m. Captain Francis Bright; Annie Williams m. Dr. Deans; Mary Fountain Williams m. Dr. Seth Sheppard.

Samuel Williams* sold his plantation, "Holly Brook" on the Eastern Shore of Virginia, just north of Eastville on September 13th, 1774 and moved to Williams Wharf in what was then Gloucester County [later became Mathews County]. He died in Kingston Parish, Gloucester County on May 19th, 1789 and was buried in the Williams Cemetery at Williams Wharf. His great-great granddaughter, Mary H (Murray) Vawter made a copy of his will from an extant copy in 1946. Samuel had made his will on February 19, 1788. His will was proved on the first day of Ju[illeg], 1789.

Thomas Williams, the son of Samuel and Sarah Haggoman Williams was born on May 5th, 1762 and married, first May 15th, 1793. His wife Susanna Billups was the daughter of Robert and Elizabeth Eddings Billups, and was born on January 31st, 1770 and died May 31st, 1804. They had three children: Elizabeth Williams, born 7/28/1794, m. James Ransone; Sarah Williams, born 2/7/1797, unmarried; Samuel Williams, born 9/14/1799, m. Mary A Harper. (Williams Family Bible, Acc. #26008, VSL).

Thomas Williams* married, second, Mary Lilly Billups* on October 18th, 1804. Mary was the daughter of Joseph and Joice Respess

Billups, and was born on January 21st, 1785 and died June 23rd, 1857. They had eight children: (Williams Family Bible)

    William Williams*, born 10/26/1805, m. Delely Borum* 1/7/1830
    John Williams, born 6/18/1807, m. Palina Herbert
    Joice Williams, born 9/18/1809, m. Captain Thomas G. Weston
    Hannah Williams, born 6/12/1811, m. Sterling Borum, Sr.
    Josiah Williams, born 10/11/1813, m. Emma Rains
    Thomas Columbus Washington Jackson Perry Cary Williams, [called Thomas] born 6/11/1816, m. Mary Louisa Smith
    Drusilla Williams, born 8/16/1818, m. John A. Weston
    Benjamin Williams, born 10/11/1821, unmarried

Thomas Williams* died September 19th, 1823 in Kingston Parish and was buried in the Williams Cemetery at Williams Wharf.

    William Williams*, the son of Thomas Williams* was born October 26th, 1805 and married January 7th, 1830, Delely Borum*. She was born December 15th, 1812, and died June 29th, 1887. She was the daughter of John and Mary Smith Borum. They had seven children (Williams Family Bible and gravestone inscriptions):

    Louisa Williams, born 1/30/1831, died 10/4/1843
    Sarah Elizabeth Williams, born 4/4/1833, died 2/24/1907
    Columbia Williams, born 4/4/1835, died 6/8/1899, m. 3/23/1886, Lemuel James, born 7/10/1827, died 7/27/1899
    Eugenia Williams, born 6/27/1837, died 1/23/1919
    Mary Lilly Williams, born 12/3/1839, died 3/11/1923
    Cordelia Cary Williams*, born 11/9/1845, died 3/18/1907, m. 10/26/1868, Heron Campbell Murray, born 5/17/1811, died 10/10/1880
    Lucy Williams, born 12/23/1848, died 4/1/1854

William Williams* died July 23rd, 1885 and Delely [Delelia] Borum Williams* died on June 29th, 1887. They were buried in the Williams Cemetery. The family cemetery is at Williams Wharf on the East River in Mathews County [Williams Wharf {Landing} is on County Road 614, west of Route 14, south of Mathews Courthouse].

## Orphans and Their Guardians, 1757-1763
## Northumberland County

### Contributed by Robert N. McKenney

In each instance where a father who died left an estate to which his child was an heir; whether the child's mother was living or not, the court was required to appoint a guardian to the minor child or children of that father. The guardian was appointed to look after (or protect) the estate of the child, and only incidentally to see to the welfare of the child himself. If things went well the court's initial appointment probably was left in force until that minor reached the age of twenty-one. Entries are made indicating the settlement of an estate, thus the minor children would have all reached the age of majority (twenty-one), or the girls would have married. If the minor was of the age of fourteen it was accepted by common law that he could choose his own guardian, or if he reached that age and his guardian did not or could not serve his best interests, he was allowed by court to choose another guardian. It was generally entered in the records that the orphan "made choice of...", thus designating who he would have serve as his guardian.

The law was very clear as to the duties of the guardian, in keeping accounts of the estate of the minor children and reporting the same to the court. The mother of the child may have assumed guardianship of the child's person (if the father so willed it), but a guardian of the estate was generally an impartial person, who could protect the child's inheritance if the mother should marry again, and marry improvidently. It is of note that the guardian was bonded for a designated number of pounds of tobacco and had to provide the court with securities who would see to it that the legal requirements were met.

Minor children were "bound out" by the court when there was no estate left them and no one to provide for them materially. This meant that a guardian was appointed and they usually were required to work in some manner for their guardian in return for their keep. In some cases the parish assumed the responsibility of paying for the keep of the orphan. A guardian may also have been appointed to teach a minor a trade; in addition the person to whom the minor was bound was required to teach him/her to read and write and cipher up to a point. It is assumed that the person to whom the minor was bound was himself a craftsman in the trade named. Most noted crafts included shoemaker, cooper, house carpenter, bricklayer, joiner and tailor. There is one instance where merchandizing and business was involved and one where seamanship was involved; however no mention is made of agriculture and related tasks associated with it.

Information of a genealogical nature that can be obtained from the guardian and orphan records include: identification of parents and their issue, the approximate date of death of the father or parents, the approximate ages of the orphans, which children were of age and which were not, identification of other siblings and relatives, identification of associates and information about the family's social and economic status in the community.

The following is an enumeration of those orphans found in the Northumberland County Minute Book beginning in 1757. The enumeration has followed the exact citation as found in the original with the exception of abbreviations. In this case the Christian names and other abbreviations are spelled out.

AT A COURT HELD FOR NORTHUMBERLAND COUNTY 8 AUGUST 1757

Judith Mott is appointed guardian to Betty Mosley, and Molly Mott orphans of Mosely Mott deceased.

Frances Beatly is appointed guardian to E[---] Beatley orphan of John Beatley. On the petition of John Beatley, Giles Webb, Beverley Keeve, John Webb or any two are appointed to divide the estate of John Beatly deceased to settle ye same and possess the orphans with their proportionable part of the said estate.

George Hunt's orphans account returned by John Hunton

Caty Mott orphan of Mosly Mott came into court and made choice of Thomas Cotterel her guardian

James Lamkin appointed guardian to Samuel, Nanny and Sarah Oldham orphans of John Oldham deceased

William Taite, Thomas Williams, Thomas Jones are appointed to settle all accounts and possess James Lamkin with the orphans estate of John Oldham deceased in the hands of James Foushee

AT A COURT HELD FOR NORTHUMBERLAND COUNTY 9 AUGUST 1757

Thomas Cotrell is appointed guardian to William Mott orphan of Mosly Mott deceased and was also chose and appointed guardian to John Mott orphan of the said Mosley Mott deceased

Richard Hull gent produced accounts of the estate of Rodham Kenner orphan of Rodham Kenner deceased and made oath to the same

AT A COURT HELD FOR NORTHUMBERLAND COUNTY 14 NOVEMBER 1757

Thomas Mahanes orphan of Thomas Mahanes deceased made choice of David Lattimore as his guardian

Eliza Walker orphan of Leonard Walker deceased made choice of Mary Stott for her guardian

John Harvey and Sarah Harvey orphans of John Harvey deceased made choice of David Lattimore as their guardian

Richard Hudnall, John Palmer and William Barrat are appointed to possess David Lattimore with John and Sarah Harvey's estate in the hands of Robert Balvard

Tignor Fallen, John Corbell, Elisha Harcum and William Harcum to appraise [the estate of Stephen Stott] and divide the said estate and to possess Mary Stott with Eliza Walker's estate and to possess her with her 3rd part Stott's estate and also to possess John Stott with the orphan's part thereof

AT A COURT HELD FOR NORTHUMBERLAND COUNTY 15 NOVEMBER 1757

Ordered the churchwardens of Wiccomico Parish bind out Chloe Swanson orphan of John Swanson deceased according to law

On the petition of Judith Mott with the consent of the executors of her deceased husband Mosley Mott; Jacob Haynie, Samuel Davis, David Pickering and William Haynie or any three of them are appointed to divide the corn and fodder on the plantation and possess the said Judith with her part as also Mosely, Betty and Molley's part of the same as guardian according to the will of the said deceased and make report

AT A COURT HELD FOR NORTHUMBERLAND COUNTY 12 DECEMBER 1757

Hannah Singer orphan of John Singer deceased made choice of John Butler her guardian

John Boyd orphan of John Boyd deceased made choice of Richard Thomas

Report of possessing Mary Stott with Eliza Walker's estate and for possessing her with her dower of her husband's estate

John Mott orphan of Mosley Mott deceased made choice of Elisha Betts for his guardian who is approved

William Thomas, Dennis Conway and William Blackerby are appointed to possess Richard Thomas with John Boyd's estate in the hands of George Boyd

Joseph Ball, Jacob Haynie, Samuel Davis and John Gaskins or any three are appointed to possess Elisha Betts with John Mott's estate in the hands of the executors of Mosley Mott

Cloe Angell orphan of Robert Angell deceased made choice of Charles Pritchard for her guardian

Joseph Ball, Jacob Haynie, Samuel Davis and John Gaskins or any three are appointed to possess Judith Mott with the negro left to her by the will of her deceased husband as also with the negroes given to Betty, Mosley and Molly Mott orphans of the said deceased Mosley Mott
*To be continued*

Mr. McKenney found in his research that the minute books of Northumberland County contained information about court proceedings that cannot be found in the order books, so although the orders books have been abstracted, there is considerable information that has not been made available to the public. It is his endeavor to provide this additional information. Ed.

These entries have been researched and compiled by Mr. Robert N. McKenney, Executive Director of the Northumberland County Historical Society, Heathsville, Virginia 22473. They have been taken from the Northumberland County Minute Book, August 8, 1757 to August 8, 1763 and are presented with the permission of the Clerk of the Circuit Court of Northumberland County.

Vauter's Church Circa 1719
John Moll

## Vauter's Church, St. Anne's Parish
## Essex County

Vauter's, in the present era of rapid change, stands as reassuring evidence of continuity of service and purpose, a visible reminder of the force and permanence of the Church. Located in Essex County, Virginia, not far from the Rappahannock River, it is the Upper Church of St. Anne's Parish of the Protestant Episcopal Church. According to authorities, it seems certain that the original portion of Vauter's was standing in 1719 and enlarged in 1731 by the addition of the south wing. [Note: The 1969 renovation of the church interior conclusively revealed that the church was built in its entirety in 1731]. Its brick walls, two feet thick throughout, are laid in Flemish bond with glazed headers, and its two doorways are in the classic pedimented style. It appears to have retained its original doors, sash windows, and shutters, with most of the hand-wrought hardware. It also retains, among its congregation today, representatives of a number of families it has served since first it became established in this tidewater section.

Subsequent to the American Revolution, Vauter's Church passed out of service, a fate common to many colonial church buildings. Vandalism threatened to destroy it during this period of practical abandonment, but it was saved by Mrs. Muscoe Garnett, of *Elmwood*, who claimed the building as standing on her property. The foundation of her claim lay in the fact that although the church was built on land originally adjoining that of the Vauter family, Mr. James Garnett had purchased, from that family before the middle of the eighteenth century, the land next to the church property. Mrs. Garnett was successful in giving Vauter's her protection.

Although Vauter's continued closed for many years except on rare occasions, the never-waning interest of the parishioners is shown by a hand-bill advertising a lottery held in 1792 to raise "the sum of three hundred pounds, for the purpose of repairing the Churches and Glebe of St. Ann[e]'s Parish..." Muscoe Livingston, William Waring, Sr., William Waring, Jr., and Robert Baylor were the managers of the lottery.

Revival of organization of church affairs was evidenced in 1814 when records show that Mr. Thomas Matthews and the Honorable James Hunter were delegates from this parish to the Diocesan Council; in 1817, the Honorable James Garnett; in 1820, Mr. Robert Beverley. The year 1822 saw a resumption of regular services at Vauter's for the first time since 1776. The interior was repaired and remodeled in 1827 under the rectorship of the Reverend John Peyton McGuire, the high, box pews being reduced in height and the chancel moved from the east to the north wall. A new, two-story pulpit replaced the colonial, three-story one.

In 1724, the Reverend John Bagge responded to "Queries to be Answered by Every Minister." He reported to the Bishop of London that Divine Service was performed in his church every Sunday, on Christmas Day, and on Good Friday. Such services continue to be held in St. Anne's Parish having been interrupted only in the years of confusion and poverty that followed the American Revolution.

The church stands today on the east side of Route 17 near Loretto, about twenty miles north of Tappahannock, amidst well-kept lawns and old cedar and holly trees. It is on the edge of a hardwood forest and adjoining fertile farmland. The cemetery surrounds two sides of the church building with several old tabletop gravestones near the church. While the whole of the cemetery gives the appearance of age with the large boxwood plantings, most of the stones commemorate residents of the late 1800s to mid 1900s. Only the earlier inscriptions have been copied.

### The Cemetery

Table top gravestones, north side of the church:

| | |
|---|---|
| Here Lies the Body | The Society of the |
| of Paul Micou who | Cincinnati 1783 |
| Departed this Life the | William Miller |
| 23 of May 1736 in the 78 | Captain-Lieutenant |
| Year of his Age | 1st Regiment Continental |
| Brass Plaque | Artillary Served in the |
| To honor the memory of | Revolutionary War |
| Dr. Paul Micou | July 1775-Jan 1783 |
| Huguenot Immigrant | Died 1793 |
| from Nantes, France 1690 | Original Member |

Placed by the Huguenot Society　　　　　　Society of Cincinnati
Founders of Manakin in the　　　　　　Placed by his descendants
Colony of Virginia 17 May 1969　　　　　　and others 1979

## Table top gravestones, east side of the church:

Underneath this stone　　　　　　John Miller
is buried the remains of　　　　　　of Glasgow
Mr Andrew Anderson　　　　　　was born
Marchant　　　　　　17th of April, 1772
A Native of Scotland　　　　　　and died
Who died the 23rd of　　　　　　3rd of August, 1761
September, 1764, in the
55th year of his age
He was eminently endued [sic]
with every Divine, humane　　　　　　Copy of inscriptions
and social virture　　　　　　on [these] two gravestones
which earned him the love　　　　　　at
and esteem of all his　　　　　　Vauter's Church
relations and of those who　　　　　　Made in 1890
came to be acquainted　　　　　　By
with him　　　　　　Lucy Brooke Catlett

## These five stones placed side by side:

Robert P Baylor　　　　　　Richard Baylor
Born June 14 1840　　　　　　son of Richard and Isabella T
Died June 2, 1872　　　　　　Baylor
　　　　　　September 27, 1883
Ann Waring Baylor　　　　　　November 22, 1953
September 4 1835
September 26 1901　　　　　　Mary Baird Baylor
　　　　　　wife of
Isabella　　　　　　Richard Baylor
Daughter of　　　　　　April 26, 1877
Rich$^d$ & I T　　　　　　January 19, 1971
Baylor
Born Oct. 12, 1880
Died Aug. 3, 1882

These six stones placed side by side:

| | |
|---|---|
| Henry Latane Baylor<br>Born at Kinloch<br>July 21, 1853<br>Died at Edenetta<br>Dec. 9, 1930 | Virginia Barron Baird<br>wife of<br>Henry Latane Baylor<br>Born at Epping Forest<br>Dec. 13, 1868<br>Died at Edenetta<br>Dec. 26, 1959<br>He maketh me to lie<br>down in Green Pastures<br>He leadeth me<br>Beside the still waters |
| Henry Latane Baylor<br>son of<br>Henry Latane and Virginia<br>Baylor<br>Born at Edenetta<br>Jan. 22, 1903<br>Died<br>Feb. 20, 1937 | |
| | Richard Baylor<br>February 25, 1803<br>November 25, 1862 |
| Lucy Baylor<br>wife of Richard Baylor<br>September 2, 1814<br>March 5, 1862 | Elizabeth Payne Baylor<br>May 30, 1844<br>November 25, 1863 |

Shaft:   James Barron      John Lawrence Brooke
         1849-1914         Nov. 1, 1847
                           June 17, 1938
         Kate Barron       Company D 13th
         1851-1927         Virginia Infantry CSA

Alexander Tunstall Brooke           Maria Battaile Brooke
Aug. 22, 1855 - Feb. 21, 1927              Nee
and his wife                             Garnett
Harriet Thornton Catlett             Aug. 15, 1846
June 2, 1949 - Jan. 1, 1924          May 13, 1930

The history is taken from the brochure of Vauter's Episcopal Church; the sketch of the church from that executed by John Moll. Both have been submitted by Mrs. L. David Butler and used with the kind permission of the senior warden, Ms. Frances Ellis and the rector, the Reverend Phillip Haug.

## Tithables List, 1678
## Henrico County

An account of ye several fortye Tythables ordered by this Worth<sup>y</sup> Court to fitt out men horse armies &c according to act./Vizt.

| | | | | | |
|---|---|---|---|---|---|
| In Bermuda Hundred | | M<sup>r</sup> Jn<sup>o</sup> Goode | 4 | Abrah Womecke | 2 |
| Mr Martin Elam | 6 | Edw<sup>d</sup> Jones | 2 | Edw<sup>d</sup> Bowman | 3 |
| Tho: Shippey | 3 | Edw<sup>d</sup> Deeley | 2 | Att M<sup>n</sup> Skermes | 3 |
| Edw<sup>d</sup> Stratto[n]J<sup>r</sup> | 3 | Henry Preut | 1 | M<sup>r</sup> Henry Lownds | 3 |
| Sam<sup>l</sup> Knibbe | 2 | W<sup>m</sup> Blackman | 2 | M<sup>r</sup> W<sup>m</sup> Clerke | 3 |
| Mr ffra<sup>s</sup> Epes | 9 | Gilbert Jones | 1 | M<sup>r</sup> Tho: Poldon | 4 |
| Jos Royall | 3 | Henry Sheerman Sn | 4 | M<sup>r</sup> Gilbert ElamS<sup>r</sup> | 5 |
| Att M<sup>n</sup> Ishams | 6 | Rich<sup>d</sup> Peirce | 1 | M<sup>r</sup> Henry Gee | 2 |
| George Browninge | 5 | M<sup>r</sup> Rich<sup>d</sup> Wardson | <u>5</u> | Jn<sup>o</sup> Bowman | 2 |
| Mr Kennon | 3 | | 44 | Tim Allen | 1 |
| Jn<sup>o</sup> Worsham | <u>4</u> | Coll W<sup>m</sup> Byrd is | | M<sup>r</sup> Gilbert Platt | <u>5</u> |
| | 44 | ordered to give notice to | | | 44 |
| Mr Epes is ordered | | these &c | | M<sup>r</sup> Rich<sup>d</sup> Lygon is | |
| to give notice to | | | | ordered to give | |
| these &c | | Edward Hatcher | 3 | notice to these &c | |
| | | Rob<sup>t</sup> Bullington | 4 | | |
| | | Michael Turpin | 3 | M<sup>r</sup> Peter ffeild | 7 |
| Turkey Island | | Jn<sup>o</sup> ffarrar | 4 | M<sup>r</sup> Charles | |
| M<sup>r</sup> Rich<sup>d</sup> Cocke | 5 | W<sup>m</sup> ffarrar | 2 | ffetherstone | 3 |
| Capt<sup>n</sup> Wm Randolph | 5 | W<sup>m</sup> Basse | 4 | Jn<sup>o</sup> Baugh | 3 |
| Giles Carter | 6 | Batt Roberts | 1 | Majo<sup>r</sup> | |
| John Aust | 2 | Jn<sup>o</sup> Lisle | 1 | Chamberlaine | 4 |
| Thomas Cocke | 8 | Jn<sup>o</sup> Cox Sen | 5 | Rich<sup>d</sup> Holmes | 1 |
| John Gunter | 2 | M<sup>r</sup> W<sup>m</sup> Elam | 2 | James Gates | 1 |
| W<sup>m</sup> Humphreys | 2 | Rich<sup>d</sup> Rabone | 1 | Tho: Puckett | 2 |
| W<sup>m</sup> Cocke | 2 | | | Jn<sup>o</sup> Puckett | 1 |
| Anthony Tall | 1 | | | W<sup>m</sup> Beven | 3 |
| Jn<sup>o</sup> Lewis | 3 | John Davis | 4 | Tho: Wells | 2 |
| Henry Watkins | 3 | Jn<sup>o</sup> Burton Jun | 5 | M<sup>n</sup> Morris | 3 |
| Rob<sup>t</sup> Evans | 3 | Thomas Davis | 2 | Tho: Lockett | 1 |
| Peter Harris | 1 | Sam<sup>ll</sup> Bridgewater | <u>3</u> | Evan Owen | 1 |
| Tho: East | <u>1</u> | | 44 | George ffreeman | 1 |
| | | Coll ffarrar is | | M<sup>n</sup> Lygon | 2 |
| | | ordered to give | | Majo<sup>r</sup> W<sup>m</sup> Ligon | 3 |
| | 44 | notice to these &c | | Robert Man | 1 |
| Capt<sup>n</sup> W<sup>m</sup> Randolph | | | | M<sup>n</sup> Hancocke | 1 |
| is ordered to give | | Tho Newcombe | 1 | James Eakin | 2 |
| notice to these &/c | | Peter Ashbrooke | 3 | W<sup>m</sup> Puckett | <u>2</u> |
| | | M<sup>r</sup> W<sup>m</sup> Baugh | 5 | | 44 |
| Coll W<sup>m</sup> Byrd | 20 | Tho: Burton | 1 | M<sup>r</sup> Peter ffeild is | |
| W<sup>m</sup> Dancy | 2 | Rich<sup>d</sup> Lygon | 1 | | |

| | | | | | |
|---|---|---|---|---|---|
| ordered to give notice to these &/c | | Wᵐ Theobalds | 1 | Mʳ George Worsham | 3 |
| | | Robᵗ Woodson | 5 | Ess[ex] Bevill | 4 |
| | | John Woodson Sʳ | 3 | Mʳⁿ Tho: Batte | 4 |
| John Millner | 6 | Jnᵒ Woodson Junr | 2 | Jnᵒ Davis | 1 |
| Henry Pue | 1 | Mʳ Jnᵒ Pleasants | 13 | Godfᵉ Ragsdal Sen | 1 |
| John Pledge | 1 | Mʳ Jnᵒ Ball | 1 | Wᵐ Dodson | 1 |
| Tho: Wood | 1 | Edwᵈ Goode | 1 | James ffrancklin | 1 |
| Samˡˡ Moody | 2 | Edwᵈ Lester | 1 | Charles Clay | 1 |
| at Mʳ | | Henry Brazeelle | 1 | John Steward | 4 |
| Hatcher's sen | 5 | Jnᵒ Greenhaugh | 1 | | 44 |
| Mʳ Radford | 5 | Ben: Hatcher | 1 | Mʳ Essex Bevill is | |
| Jnᵒ Steward | 3 | Wᵐ Hewes | 1 | ordered to give notice to | |
| Jnᵒ Huddlesen | 2 | Lewis Watkins | 1 | these &c | |
| Nich Perkins | 1 | Thᵒ Holmes | 1 | | |
| Richᵈ Parker | 2 | Sally Indian | 1 | Abell Gower | 7 |
| Wᵐ Wheatly | 1 | | 44 | Mʳ Tho: Branch Sʳ | 2 |
| Wᵐ Giles | 4 | Mʳ Ben: Hatcher is | | Xtopher Branch Jʳ | 3 |
| Jnᵒ Leadd | 1 | ordered to give | | James fforest | 2 |
| Lemon Childres | 1 | notice to these &c | | Mʳ Tho: Osborne | 7 |
| Tho: Wooles | 1 | | | Tho: Bottom | 1 |
| Robᵗ Clerke | 1 | John Ellis | 1 | Mʳ Edwᵈ Osborne | 3 |
| John Watson | 1 | George Archer | 2 | Phillip Turpin | 3 |
| Wᵐ Porter sen | 4 | Wᵐ Harris | 1 | Att Esqʳ Places | |
| Charles Matthews | 1 | Tho: Webster | 1 | quarter | 6 |
| | 44 | Tho Gregory | 1 | Richᵈ Perrin | 3 |
| John Millner is ordered | | Mʳⁿ Chandler | 5 | Tho: Perrin | 1 |
| to give notice | | John Willson Sen | 1 | Joshua Stapp | 2 |
| to these &c | | Jnᵒ Willson Jun | 2 | John Baly | 1 |
| | | Richᵈ Dobbs | 1 | Tho: Risbee | 3 |
| Curls | | Nich Dison | 1 | | 44 |
| Abrah Childres | 2 | Tho: ffitzherbert | 4 | Mʳ Abell Gower is | |
| Rich Marsh | 6 | Jnᵒ ffarloe | 1 | ordered to give notice to | |
| John Howard | 2 | Peter Rowlett | 3 | these &c | |
| | | | | Transcribed by VLHD | |

*Transcribed by VLHD using both the original record book, microfilm Reel 4 and the transcription found on Reel 4a. The transcription of this record book was made under the Act of the General Assembly to provide for copying and preserving the old records of certain counties in the state of Virginia, March 1892, transcribed by Charles M Wallace. Certified by James P Waddell, Clerk Henrico County Court.*

Henrico County Deeds, Wills, 1677-1692, pp.102-103. Also Henrico County Records, Reel 4 and 4a, Archives and Records Division, Virginia State Library and Archives, Richmond, Virginia. Published with the kind permission of Dr. Louis H. Manarin, Virginia State Archivist.

## Civil Appointments, 1779-1799
## Hanover County

### Submitted by Minor Tompkins Weisiger

These Civil Appointments from the Executive Department provide information of the lives and business of the residents of Hanover County. They have been selected for the counties of tidewater Virginia, and particularly those counties for which the county order books do not generally exist. There are not files for every year, or for all appointments made within a year. They are transcribed rather than presented as abstracts, to provide all of the information possible. In some cases the actual signatures of the persons writing the notation will be presented rather than a transcription of that signature.

At a Court continued and held for Hanover County on Friday the 3d day of September 1779
Bartelot Anderson Gent: produced a Commission under the hand of his Excellency Thomas Jefferson Esq[r] Governor of this Common-Wealth dated the seventeenth day of August last appointing him Escheator for this County Whereupon the said Bartelot Anderson together with Garland Anderson & Thomas Garland Gent[n] his securitys entered into and acknowledged a Bond according to Law, and had the Oath of Fidelity, as also the oath of the said office of Escheator Administered to him

At a Court held for Hanover on Thursday the 7[th] day of February 1782

John Blackwell John Stanley William Richardson & William Tinsley Gent[n] are recommended to his Excellency the Governor as proper persons to Execute the Office of Inspectors at Meriwether's Warehouse

At a Court held for Hanover County on Thursday the 7$^{th}$ day of February 1782

Thomas Clarke Nathaniel Talley Ambrose Lipscombe & William Gardner Gent$^n$ are recommended to his Excellency the Governor as proper persons to Execute the Office of Inspectors at Pages Warehouse
A Copy   W Pollard Jun$^r$ CHC

At a Court continued and held for Hanover County on Friday the 8th day of March 1782 It is Ordered that the clerk of this Court do Certifie to his Excellency the Governor that John Snelson, Essex William Winston, Meriwether Skelton, Benjamin Anderson and Robert Carter Page, Gent$^n$ named in the Commission of the Peace for the said County, are dead, that Samuel Meriwether Gent$^n$ a Justice of the peace for the said County has removed therefrom, that Charles Crenshaw, John Pendleton and George Dabney, late Justice of the said County have resigned their office, that Nathaniel West Dandridge, John Meriwether, William Macon, John Starke, Thomas Garland, John Robinson, Isaac Winston, Charles Dabney, Robert Page, John Thompson, William Dandridge, Halsenby Dixon, Davis Anderson jun$^r$, Elisha White, William Darracott, John Price and Dabney Minor, Gent$^n$, also named in the said Commission have refused to Act as Justices and Max Wilson, Miles Cary, Richard Chapman, John Winston, William Johnson, George Clough, William Anderson j$^r$ Parke Goodall & James Bullock Gent$^n$ are proper persons to be Added to the said Commission/
A Copy   W Pollard j$^r$ CHC

At a Court held for Hanover County on Thursday the 4$^{th}$ day of April 1782
William Richardson who Stands as assistant Inspector at Meriwethers Warehouses, is recommended to his Excellency the Governor as a proper person reputed to be skilful in tobacco for the Execution of the office of inspector at the said Warehouses in the room of John Blackwell, dec$^d$, John Jones & Charles Hundley are also recommended as proper persons reputed to be skilful in tobacco for the Execution of

the office of Assistant inspectors at the aforementioned Warehouses in the room of the said William Richardson and William Tinsley deceased.

A Copy W Pollard Jun[r] CHC

At a Court held for Hanover County on Thursday the 3[d] day of October 1782
Geddes Winston John Lawrence and W[m] Overton Winston Gent[n] are recommended to his Excellency the Governor for him to Commissionate one of them to execute the Office of sheriff for this county the ensuing Year.

A Copy W[m] Pollard jun[r] CHC

At a Court held for Hanover County on Thursday the 1st day of May 1783
Richard Chapman & William Johnson Gent[n] named in the last commission of the peace as also in the last commission of Oyer and Terminer for this County came into Court and took the oath of Fidelity to this Commonwealth as also the oath by law appointed to be taken by Justices

A Copy William Pollard CHC

Hanover County Sirs
This day John Garland came before me a Magistrate for the above County & made oath that he received the enclosed certificate of John Wood on the morning of the 13[th] Inst[t] and that the said Wood summoned him as a Grand Juryman to attend Ap[l] Gen[l] Court 1782 and promised, for the reason set forth in his certificate to excuse him and he further declares that he knew nothing of the final utitile[?] after October Gen[l] Court 1782, he expecting from the promise of the Sheriff that no ~~such~~ process would isshur [issue] against him,
Given under my hand the 15[th] day of October 1783.

*Nelson Anderson jr*

At a Court held for Hanover County of Thursday the 6th day of November 1783

Elisha White Gent$^n$ named in the Commission of the peace for this County came into Court and was sworn a Justice of the Peace according to Law

A Copy   William Pollard CHC

At a Court continued and held for Hanover County on Friday the 7th day of November 1783

Garland Anderson, William Overton Winston and William Johnson Gent$^n$ are recommended to his Excellency the Governor as proper persons for him to Commissionate to execute the office of Coroners in this County

A Copy   W$^m$ Pollard j$^r$ CHC

At a Court held for Hanover County on Thursday the 5th day of August 1784

John Lawrence William O Winston and Ambrose Lipscombe Gent$^n$ are recommended to his Excellency the Governor for him to Commissionate one of them to execute the office of Sheriff in this County the ensuing Year.

*A Copy W Pollard j$^r$ CHC*

At a Court for Hanover County on Thursday the 5th day of May 1785
Present
Gentlemen Justices

| | |
|---|---|
| John Syme | Bartelot Anderson |
| Geddes Winston | Richard Chapman |
| William O Winston | John Winston |
| Ambrose Lipscombe | George Clough |
| Elisha White | William Anderson j$^r$ |
| Thomas Trevilian | & Parke Goodall |

Ordered that it be Certified to his Excellency the Governor that William Jones one of the Gentlemen named in the last Commission of the Peace for this County is unable, being very infirm, to execute the office of a majestrate; that William Johnson another Gent$^n$ named in the said Commission refuses to act for reasons set forth in his letter to the Court; which letter is in these words to wit "Gen$^t$ By the Sheriff I received your Summons requesting my reasons for not qualifying as a Majestrate of the County, At the time I left the Bench I moved for such repairs to the prison as I thought necessary to guard the Court ag$^{st}$ Insolvent Debtors in which I was overruld, under the present Law concerning Prisons I conceive our Court are answerable to the Sheriff for every Debtor who breaks Jail and until I see such a Prison in Hanover County, as the law directs I must beg leave to persist in my resolution of not acting as a Majestrate in the County I am Gen$^t$ with much respect your most obedient Humble Servant William Johnson 5 May 1785"

And that David Anderson Gent$^n$ also named in the said Commission refuses to qualify himself to execute the office of a Justice of the Peace. Ordered that it be also Certified that Garland Anderson, John Garland, John Thompson, James Turner, John Anderson, Chapman Austin, William Barrett, Thomas Tinsley, John Dandridge, and Samuel Overton Gent$^n$ are proper persons to be added to the said Commission, and that the said Garland Anderson ought to stand the 2$^d$ in Commission, that being his place before he resigned the office of Justice of the peace.

And in consequence of the reasons set forth in the letter aforesaid of the sd Johnson the Court do Order that it be further Certified that it is their Opinion that there is a good and sufficient Prison.

                            A Copy    William Pollard j$^r$ CHC

At a Court held for Hanover County on Thursday the 2$^d$ of June 1785 William Lawrence Deputy Sheriff on behalf of John Lawrence Gent$^n$ Sheriff of this County, came into Court and protested against the sufficiency of this County Prison for the safe keeping prisoners

                                    A Copy    Tho. Pollard dC

To whom it may concern: Whereas William Johnson and David Anderson Gentlemen named as Justices of the peace for the County of Hanover by Commission bearing date the 25th Day of October 1784, have been charged with refusing to qualify and act, which said Charge upon due inquiry hath been sufficiently supported: *KNOW* ye that by virtue & authority of the Act of Assembly entitled "An Act to extend the powers of the Governor and Council", I do, with the advise of the Council of State, remove the said William Johnson and David Anderson from the Commission of the peace for the said County, and they are hereby removed accordingly *In Witness* whereof I have hereunto set my name and caused the seal of the Commonwealth to be affixed, at Richmond this second Day of June one thousand seven hundred & eight five

            Seal  P Henry
      A Copy William Pollard jr CHC

At a Court continued and held for Hanover County on Friday the $3^d$ day of June 1785.
    William O Winston, Haldenby Dixon and William Anderson jun$^r$ Gent$^n$ or any two of them are appointed to advertize in the *Virginia Gazette* the letting to the lowest bidder at next Court the building a Prison for the use of this County, and then to let the same in such manner as shall at that day be agreed on by the Court accordingly
           A Copy Tho. Pollard dC

At a Court held for Hanover County of Thursday the $1^{st}$ day of June 1786
    William O Winston Ambrose Lipscombe and Thomas Trevilian Gent$^n$ are recommended to his Excellency the Governor for him to Commissionate one of them to execute the office of Sheriff in this County for the ensuing year And it is Ordered that the clerk do certify to his Excellency, that the reason they did not recommend Elisha White Gent$^n$ who is named in the Commission of the peace for this County before Thomas Trevilian Gent$^n$ is, that the said White did not Qualify 'til three years and upwards after the said Trevilian
         A Copy W$^m$ Pollard j$^r$ CHC

At a Court held for Hanover County on Thursday the 1st day of February 1787

Present
Gent<sup>n</sup> Justices

| | |
|---|---|
| John Lawrence | Bartelot Anderson |
| Ambrose Lipscombe | Richard Chapman & |
| Elisha White | George Clough |

Pursuant to an Act of Assembly intituled [entitled] "An Act to amend the Act intituled an Act for ascertaining certain taxes and duties, & for establishing a permanent Revenue" The Clerk of the Court laid the said Act before the Court     A Copy  W<sup>m</sup> Pollard j<sup>r</sup> CHC

*To be continued*

From the records of the Executive Department, Commonwealth of Virginia. Civil Appointments. Archives and Records Division, Virginia State Library and Archives, Richmond, Virginia. Published with the kind permission of Dr. Louis H. Manarin, Virginia State Archivist.

Hanover Court Courthouse c. 1735

## Christ Church Parish Register, 1754-1763
## Middlesex County

The Parish Register of Christ Church, Middlesex County, 1653-1812, was first transcribed and published as a project of the National Society of Colonial Dames of America in the State of Virginia. It was published in Richmond in 1897. It has been reprinted by the Genealogical Publishing Company, Baltimore in 1964, 1975 and again in 1990. It, along with the parish vestry book, provides perhaps the most complete and comprehensive record of an early parish. It has been long known that the original index was not complete and a page by page search was necessary to be sure of finding a particular individual. The Southern Historical Press published an edition in 1988 in which these omitted names are indexed. This edition also contains, in pagination order, a correction of names that had not been transcribed (spelled) quite as written in the original. The same pagination has been retained in all of the publications.

The following typed transcription was found inserted in the back of an 1897 edition of the transcription of the register; the copy held by the Urbanna Public Library. In so far as has been determined, these names, or at least the majority of these names, have not been included in any of the published transcriptions that are available.

The explanation of the insert is as follows: [page 1, typed copy] "The following nine pages of the old Christ Church Parish Register were, for some unaccountable reason, omitted from the published volume done by the Colonial Dames in 1897. The folder, or file, of this material was discovered in later years by Carroll C. Chowning [Sr.], of Urbanna, Va., and a photostatic copy made for Christ Church Parish. A copy of the latter was made and is being bound herewith for use in our Urbanna Library. This is a strictly Church of England record.

There is also in the Virginia State Archives, Richmond, Virginia, the original Parish Register and Vestry Book covering the period of the Protestant Episcopal period immediately following the Colonial period. Although the minutes of the meetings were few and brief, it forms an interesting record of the activities of the Protestant Episcopal Church in Middlesex County after the Church of England went down after the Revolution and the revival of the modern congregation."

The Virginia State Library Archives holds the photostatic copy of the original Parish Register and included in that book, but not bound with it, are photostatic copies of these pages. They are accessioned separately under the number 20095. The description states that the majority of these births, deaths and marriage records are not included in the register. To quote: "The said records appear to be transcripts, but the source has not been established. It may be that the register included all the records at one time. Negative photostats [were] made from manuscript lent to the library by the clerk of Middlesex County. August 26, 1929."

*The following is transcribed (by VLHD) from the typewritten text as it, in turn, was transcribed by Mr. Chowning. Wherever there is a blank noted, or the reader has a question it is suggested that the photocopy of the original at the Virginia State Library be consulted.*

[page 2]
Charles, son of Alexander and Elizabeth Meaderias, was born Feb. 13, 1754.
Benjamin, son of Jacob and Eliza. Jacobes, born February 2nd, 1755.
Christian, daughter of George and Ann Sanders, born March 18, 1755.
Fanny, daughter of Jacob and Susannah Blake, born March 23, 1755.
John, son of William and Eliz. Healy, born April 25th, 1755.
Ruben, son of John and Mary Brooks, born May 20th, 1755.
Lewis, son of Charles and Ann Roan, born June 1st, 1755.
Linsey, son of Robt. and Margaret Clark, born June 23rd, 1755.
John, son of John and Margaret Yarrington, born August 8th, 1755, Bapt.21.
Thacker, son of Henry and Ann Washington, born Aug. 28th and bapt. Sept. 13, 1755.
Catherine, daughter of William and Susanna Daniel, born Aug 29th, 1755.
Alexander, son of David and Dinnah Barrick, born September 21st, 1755.
Johnson, son of John and Judith Wake, born September 25th, 1755.

William, son of John and [blank] Patterson, born October 4th, 1755.
Alexander, son of John and Mary Sanders, born November 2nd, 1755.
Roleson, son of John and Eliz. Boss, born November 17th, 1755.
William, son of William and Sarah Stiff, born November 30th, 1755.
Richard, son of Richard and Phebe Burke, born January 5th, 1756.
Thomas, son of Reuben and Mary Shelton, born January 6th, 1756.
Thomas Beard, son of [blank], born January 6th, 1756.
Charles, son of James and [blank] Green, born January 26th, 1756.
Margeret, daughter of Tobias and Margret Allen, born January 28th, 1756.
William, son of Edmd. and Mary Field, born January 29th, 1756.
Rachel, daugher of Benjamin and Averille, born January 31st, 1756.
James, son of Robt. Clemons and Jane Warren [Clemons][1], born February 5th, 1756.
Curtis, son of John and Agatha Hardee, born February 18th, 1756.
Elizabeth, daughter of Ralph and Hannah Watts, born February 27th, 1756.
David, son of Curtis and Anner Hardee, born February 15th, 1756.
William, son of John and Frances Berry, born February 29th, 1756.
Mary, daughter of John and Betty Bryant, born March 9th, 1756.

[page 3]
*Note: The entries on this one page concern the Thacker family and are found in the transcribed publications and in the indexes of these books. Ed.*


Henry, son of Henry and Eltonhead Thacker, was born the 9th day of August, 1663.
Edwin [Edward] Thacker, the son of Henry and Eltonhead Thacker, born [Jan] 7, 1665, and died Feby. 16, 1719.
Martha, daughter of Henry and Eltonhead Thacker, born Dec. 5th, 1667.

---

[1]The name Jane Warren is listed under the name Clemons in the index of the 1988 edition of the parish register. She and Robt. Clemons are listed along with [E]lizabeth [b 1753] on p289.

Alice, daughter of Henry and Eltonhead Thacker, born Dec. 30th, 1671, mar. Wm. Gough, May 31, 1688.

Lettice, daughter of Henry and Eltonhead Thacker, born February 27, 1669.

Chicheley Corbin Thacker, the son of Henry and Eltonhead Thacker, was born Jan. 4th, 1673.

Elizabeth Thacker, daughter of Henry and Eltonhead Thacker, born Dec. 3, 1694.

Frances, dau. of Henry and Eltonhead Thacker, born Dec. 19, 1696, mar. Thomas Vivien Jany. 2, 1719.*

Edwin Thacker, son of Edwin and Frances Thacker, was born July 3rd, 1695.

Anne, daughter of Edwin and Frances Thacker, was born 27th of Sept. 1696.

John Thacker, son of Edwin and Frances Thacker, born January 15, 1697.

Henry, son of Henry and Elizabeth Thacker, born the 9th of October, 1698.

Martha Thacker, daughter of Henry and Elizabeth Thacker, born Dec. 27th, [1701]. mar. Richard Curtis [blank] Dec. 26th, 1723.*

Chicheley Thacker, son of Henry and Elizabeth Thacker, born Mar. 26th, 1704.

Lettice Thacker, dau. of Henry and Elizabeth Thacker, born Feb. 16, 1704. mar. Thomas Todd June 7th, 1728.*

Anne Thacker, dau. of Henry and Elizabeth Thacker, born Oct. 16, 1709.

Mrs. Elizabeth Thacker, widow, died May 22, 1714.

Ann Thacker [died] August 26th, 1715.

[ ] these notations were taken from the printed copy of the *Christ Church Parish Register*
* indicates that the information could not be found in the printed copy of the register.

*Additions to the Register will be continued*

## Losses Sustained from the British Depredations, 1782
## King George County

### Contributed by Minor Tompkins Weisiger

Transcriptions of losses claimed from the British invasions are presented for the burned record counties to help researchers identify residents of those counties, where other information is lacking. The losses claimed also provide information about the economic and social status (and property) of the claimants. Clues to relationships can be found in the names of those submitting the claims for others, and in those proving the claims. The approximate dates of estates not settled may also be identified. It is understood that this information may be used to establish eligibility for some hereditary societies.

The General Assembly of Virginia enacted the following law in May 1782: *"Be it enacted by the General Assembly, That the courts of the several counties within this state shall and they are hereby empowered and required wither to hold special courts, or to appoint so many of their own body as to them shall seem most proper, to collect and state, from the best proof the nature of the case will admit of, the various losses and injuries, both public and private, which have been sustained within their respective counties during the war, from the depredations of the enemy in their several invasions, and to state the same under so many different heads as such losses or injuries may consist of, and return their proceedings herein, together with the proofs made in support thereof, to the governor and council, to be by them laid before the next assembly."*[2]

At a Court held for King George County the 7th day of Novem' 1782. The Court proceeded to inquire into the Losses Sustained by the Inhabitants of this County, by the Depredations of the Enemy Agreeable to an Act of Assembly intitled an Act to Assertain the Losses and Injuries Sustained from the Depredations of the Enemy within this Commonwealth as followeth.......

---

[2]Hening, William Waller. *The Statutes At Large, A Collection of All of the Laws of Virginia.* Vol.11, Richmond: Cochran. 1823. p.27.

Col Francis Thornton produced an Acct. of 22 Negros taken by the Enemy & made oath to the same & further prov'd by the Oath of his Son William Thornton, & Valued as followeth Negro

| | | | |
|---|---|---|---|
| Cully | Aged 30 | An active and Genteel Waiting Man | £120.00. |
| Charles | 20 | An excellent House Servant | 140.00. |
| Bristol | 22 | a Strong and active Planter | 100.00. |
| Sampson | 30 | a Carpenter | 120.00. |
| Billy | 25 | a Planter | 100.00. |
| Frank | 19 | An extraordinary Plough-man | 100.00. |
| Nanny | 36 | An excellent cook | 80.00. |
| Judy | 21 | a fine Spinster & her Child Milly 2 years old Valued to | 100.00. |
| Nan | 19 | a labourer & her Child Pegg 3 years old Valued to | 110.00. |
| Grace | 17 | a fine House Servant | 100.00. |
| Kate | 22 | a Labourer & her Child Valued to | 120.00. |
| Dick | 4 | Years old | 45.00. |
| Jenny | 14 | ditto | 80.00. |
| Sam | 10 | ditto | 65.00. |
| Nanny | 3 | ditto | 40.00. |
| Charles | 2 | ditto | 30.00. |
| Thier a mulatto | 26. | An excellent Seemstress & children | 125.00. |
| Sarah | 10 | years of age Valued to | 30.00. |
| Virgin | 6 | ditto | 25.00. |
| Billy | 3 | ditto | 15.00. |

Francis Thornton & William Thornton made Oath that Daniel MᶜCarty Genᵗ Lost two Negros taken by the Enemy to wit

| | | |
|---|---|---|
| Charles Aged 15 Years a Planter Valued to | | 80.00. |
| Phill Aged 12 ditto | ditto ditto | 70.00. |

John Shinker Esqʳ made Oath that he had one Negro taken by the Enemy, a Good Skipper Valued to 140.00.

Laurance Washington made Oath to one Negro taken by the Enemy Valuable Shoemaker Valued to £140 140.00.

Thomas Massey's Estate by the Oath of Segismond Massey Lost four Negros Planters Valued to £250 250.00.

John Storke made Oath to three Valueable Negros

| | |
|---|---:|
| he had taken by the Enemy Valued to £330 | 330.00. |
| Henry Washington made Oath to one Negro taken by the Enemy belonging to the Estate of Col Jn° Washington. De$^d$ Valued to £100 | 100.00. |
| Segismond Massey made Oath that Nehemiah Mason Lost one Negro Valued to £100 (taken by the Enemy) | 100.00. |
| Laurance Washington made Oath that Robert Stith Lost three Negros taken by the Enemy Valued to £300 | 300.00. |
| Baldwin Dade made Oath that he Lost two Negroes taken by the Enemy Valued to £180 | 180.00. |
| Henry Ward made Oath that the Estate of Henry Smith de$^d$ Lost one Negro taken by the Enemy Valued to £100 | 100.00. |
| Henry Ward made Oath that Col. Henry Fitzhugh Lost five Negroes taken by the Enemy Valued to £500 | 500.00. |
| Laurance Washington made Oath that Townshend Dade lost one Negro taken by the Enemy a Good Blacksmith & Carpenter Valued to £150 | 150.00. |

Jos: Robinson  C:K.G.Co

At a Special Court held at the house of Jos. Rodgers the 14th day of November 1782: for the Purpose of making further Inquirey into the Losses Sustained by the Inhabitants of King George County by the Depridations of the Enemy-"-"-"-"

| | |
|---|---:|
| Thacker Washington made Oath that he Lost three Slaves that went on board the Enemy's ships which we Value to | £285.00.0 |
| Henry Alexander Ashton made Oath that he lost five Negroes that went on board the Enemy's ships in the year 1785 which we Value to | 275.00.0 |
| William Tyler made Oath that he Lost one Negro Man Slave that went on board the Enemy's ship the 18th Ap$^l$ 1781. which we Value to | 85.00.0 |
| Philip Alexander made Oath that he Lost two Negro men Slaves that went on board the Enemy's ships in the Year 1777. which we Value to | 130.00.0 |

Philip Alexander made Oath that William Thornton
Alexander lost a Valuable Ship Carpenter that went on
board the Enemy's ships in the year 1777. which we value     150.00.0
William Thompson made Oath that Alven Moseley lost two
Negro women Slaves by the Enemy which we value to     135.00.0
William Thompson made Oath that the Este. of Maj$^r$
Richard Hooe lost four Slaves that went on board the
Enemy's ships in the year 1777. which we Value to     205.00.0
John Berryman made Oath that Sarah Berryman lost by
the Enemy two Negr's that went on board their ships
which we Value to     190.00.0
Gerrard Hooe made Oath that he lost Three Slaves
that went on board the Enemy's ships the 5$^{th}$ Ap$^l$
1781. which we value to £270. & also Sundry Household
Goods &c which we Value to £275.06.6     545.06.6
Robert Washington made Oath that he Lost three
Negros which went on board the Enemys ships which we Value
to £260. also that he Lost Sundry Household Goods &c
which we Value to £67.06.     327.06.0
John Christie made Oath that he Lost Sundry household
goods &c by the Enemy which we value to     7.07.3
Francis Berry made Oath that W$^m$ Lord had taken by
the Enemy Sundry household Goods &c which we value to     6.12.0
William Fitzhugh of Marmion made Oath that he Lost four
Negroe Men Slaves that went on board the Enemy's ships
which we Value to     430.00.0
Benjamin Grymes made Oath that William Fitzhugh of
Chatham lost eight Slaves that went on board the Enemy's
ships which we Value to     360.00.0

                 Cop: Test    Jos: Robinson C:K.G.Co
                                    Transcribed by VLHD

From The Legislative Department, House of Delegates, Office of the Speaker. Correspondence. Losses sustained from the British. May 1783. Archives and Records Division, Virginia State Library and Archives, Richmond, Virginia. Published with the kind permission of Dr. Louis H. Manarin, Virginia State Archivist.

## Land Tax Records, 1782
## Gloucester County

The Land Tax Records for Gloucester County are transcribed as they were written, one colume to a page in the journal. The names were entered in alphabetical order according to the letter of the alphabet, but not in complete alphabetical order. It can be seen that names of individuals who lived in the same area are generally listed consecutively. This provides valuable information about these earlier land owners. Other lists have been transcribed, but have been presented in alphabetical order, which destroys some of the information that can be gleaned from the original lists. Those names in brackets are given as they have been found in other records, and are believed to be the correct identification, where the original record is either torn (identified by an "*") or illegible. The land owner's name and the number of acres of land are given here. The original record also showed the amount of tax due in pounds, shillings and pence. **Those persons who could be identified as living in Kingston Parish from the 1791 Mathews County Land Tax Records, where the acreage of land remained the same, are identified by the letter "K".** The records are badly worn at this date, but the original should be consulted where there are questions as to the accuracy of this transcription.

Land Owners of Gloucester County and Amount of Land Owned for the Year 1782

| | | | |
|---|---|---|---|
| *[Amb]rose Adams [K] | 55 | *[Ro]bert Armistead [K] | 113 |
| *[Willi]am Allard | 50 | *[Geo]rge Armistead [K] | 300 |
| *[John] Ash | 200 | *[Zacha]riah Adams [K] | 42 |
| *[Matt]hew Anderson [K] | 240½ | *[John] Allerman [K] | 100 |
| *[Chur]chill Armistead [K] | 856 | *[Doro]thy Armistead [K] | 167 |
| *[Willi]am Armistead [K] | 3000 | *[Will]iam Buckner [K] | 88 |
| *[Currell] Armistead Est[K] | 79 | *[Hen]ry Buckner | 87 |
| *[Jos]eph Ashbury [K] | 50 | *[Richar?]d Billups [K] | 289 |
| *[Rich]ard Anderson | 66 | *          Ditto | 186½ |
| *[?]n Anderson [K] | 85 | *[John] Beveridge | 103½ |
| *[Jn]° Armistead Est [K] | 376 | *[Jam]es Bentley | 240 |

| | | | |
|---|---|---|---|
| *[B]aldwin Buckner | 55 | Aaron Belvin | 47 |
| *[J]udith Buckner | 30 | William Busby's Estate | 95 |
| Ditto | 40 | Lewis Burwell | 1000 |
| *[T]homas Bates | 47 | Ditto | 6800 |
| *[Pinny?] Burton | 830 | [Maj Tho⁸] Burwell | 263 |
| *[J]n° Browning | 450 | William Blake [K] | 40 |
| *[J]n° Baytop | 220⅓ | Elizabeth Brammil [K] | 50 |
| *[Sarah?] Baytop | [illeg] | Christopher Brown [K] | 100 |
| *Richard Bonall | 220½ | Ditto | 54½ |
| Ditto for B Tomkins | 695 | Samuel Bonafield | 375 |
| *[J]oseph Bellamy | 80 | Mary Blacknall [K] | 400 |
| *[J]no Blassingham | 150 | Richard Bassett [K] | 68 |
| *[Geo]rge Booth | 637 | James Booker [K] | 385 |
| *[E]lizabeth Baker | 150 | Mary Bailey [K] | 153 |
| *Edm ᵈ Berkley | 450 | Matthew Bailey [K] | 150 |
| *[S]amuel Buckner | 448 | William Buckner [K] | 177 |
| James Baytop | 332 | Humphrey Billups [K] | 100 |
| Lewis Booker | 541 | Robert Billups [K] | 320 |
| John Buckner | 550 | Joseph Billups [K] | 174 |
| Thomas Buckner | 200 | George Billups [K] | 40 |
| Samuel Buckner | 200 | Jn° Billups Captⁿ [K] | 725 |
| Robert Buckner | 400 | William Bohannon [K] | 74 |
| George Booth Est | 740 | George Brown [K] | 246 |
| Ditto | 400 | Robert Brown [K] | 55 |
| Thomas Booth | 400 | Thomas Billups [K] | 375 |
| Thomas Booth Sen | 350 | Thomas Blake [K] | 83⅓ |
| Jn° Boswell | 308 | Edmund Borum [K] | 460 |
| William Briggs | 2 Lots | Peter Bernard [K] | 230 |
| Edward Busby | 1 Lot | | |

*To be continued*

These land tax records were transcribed by VLHD before it was known that Clearfield Company was planning to reprint *Records of Colonial Gloucester County, Virginia, A Collection of Abstracts from Original Documents Concerning the Lands and People of Colonial Gloucester County*, Polly Cary Mason, (1946-48). Rep. 1992. This reprint is now available from the publisher.

Gloucester County Land Tax Records, 1782, Reel 117. Archives and Records Division, Virginia State Library and Archives, Richmond, Virginia. Published with the kind permission of Dr. Louis H. Manarin, Virginia State Archivist.

## Abstracts of Wills Probated in Edgecombe County, North Carolina Which Refer to Tidewater Virginia

### Abstracted by David B. Gammon

WILLIAM GILL of Northumberland Co., VA  19 Sep 1794  Nov Ct 1794
"...being very sick and weak in body..." Sister MARY GILL - Negroes Sarah and Winne.  Brother RICHARD GILL - Negro Isaac and my saling boat named "Betsee Vecommecoe".  Brother WINDER GILL - Negro Jude. Ex. brothers GEORGE GILL and WINDER GILL.
Wit. John Willeford, Martin Pitman, Edward (X) Pitman.
Edgecombe County (NC) Will Book C, p.288.

WILLIAM NORTHEN  18 July 1790  Feb Ct 1793  Northen
Sons EDMUND NORTHEN, WILLIAM NORTHEN, MYNTA NORTHEN, JOHN NORTHEN, GEORGE NORTHEN - ten shillings each as their full part of my estate. Daughter SARAH NORTHEN - 100 silver dollars, and if she should die, this sum shall fall to her first child to arrive at the age of twenty-one, but if she leaves not issue this shall fall to my daughters CATEY, NELLY and LUCY NORTHEN. Daughters MARGARET NORTHEN, ANN NORTHEN, MARY NORTHEN, son RUBEN NORTHEN and daughter LUANER NORTHEN - ten shillings each as their full part of my estate. Son PETER NORTHEN - all my lands in Richmond County, Virginia, also all my stock, Negro Siner and her children;, Negro George, all my money. Sons MERIMON NORTHEN and KILBEY NORTHEN - ten shillings each as their full part of my estate. Daughters CATEY, NELLY and LUCY NORTHEN - all my land in Edgecombe county, as well as Negroes in Edgecombe and Negroes in Virginia, to be divided when CATEY is twenty-one. Daughter ELIZABETH NORTHEN - ten shillings as her full share of my estate.
Ex. friends Jacob Sessums, Thomas Hodges
Wit. Alexander Sessums, Alice Sessums, Rebekah Sessums, Polley Sessums.
Edgecombe County (NC) Will Book C, p.218.

David B. Gammon, 119 Brooks Avenue, Raleigh, NC 27607, contributed these wills found in the records of Edgecombe County, North Carolina (1732-1910). They will be included in the book he is publishing of Edgecombe County Wills.

BOOK REVIEWS:

Ann S. Lainhard, *State Census Records*. 116 pp. cloth. 1992. $17.95, $3.00 postage and handling. This is the first comprehensive listing of state census records to be published. These state census records are distinct from the federal censuses, as they follow a proscribed chronology of every ten years, with uniform listing for each state (where the records have survived). The state censuses were taken randomly, and it is valuable to know not only when they were ordered, but the information collected with each census record. Each state is presented with the years of the state census listed, and the information required for that census. These census records rank with the federal census records as a major genealogical resource. Research in states other than one's own is difficult at best, and this is a major contribution to the genealogist in determining what information is available. This book opens opportunities heretofore virtually unknown. Genealogical Publishing Co, 1001 N Calvert St., Baltimore, MD, 21202.

Lloyd DeWitt Bockstruck, *Virginia's Colonial Soldiers*. 443 pp. index, cloth. 1988, Second printing 1990. $30.00, $3.00 postage and handling. Mr. Bockstruck has done an outstanding job of identifying and assembling the names and information of the early Virginia colonial militia. The militia was established by law as a defense of the colonists against Indian attacks and invasion by hostile powers. The records of those citizens who participated are scattered and incomplete. For this reason this book is a prized source of information to genealogists in identifying a particular person, placing him as to time and residence. The author has covered the periods of the militia from the time of inception in each county, where information could be obtained. This is a **must** reference book. Genealogical Publishing Co, 1001 N Calvert St., Baltimore, MD, 21202.

Blanche Adams Chapman, *Wills and Administrations of Elizabeth City County, Virginia, 1688-1800*. 1989 pp. index, cloth. 1941, Reprint 1980. $17.50, $3.00 postage and handling. The original wills and administrations that have survived, as well as records from deed and order books have been methodically abstracted and compiled. Not only is all of the pertinent information presented, but much other information about early Elizabeth City County. Included are a quit rent roll, polls for election of burgesses, public claims, tithables, marriage licenses, and other records of value to researchers. Genealogical Publishing Co, 1001 N Calvert St., Baltimore, MD, 21202.

Augusta B. Fothergill, *Wills of Westmoreland County, Virginia, 1654-1800*. 229 pp., index, cloth. 1925, Reprint 1990. $17.50, $3.00 postage and handling. Mrs. Fothergill's purpose was to improve upon earlier compilations of Westmoreland County will abstracts where pertinent information had been left out and the volume 1665-1677 was omitted entirely from the work by Crozier. She performed a much needed service in presenting in chronological order abstracts of the will of early Westmoreland County, and including legatees, legacies and other genealogical information. While other works have been subsequently abstracted, this is a valuable contribution by a knowledgeable genealogist. #1995. Clearfield Co, 200 East Eager St, Baltimore, MD 21202.

Peter Wilson Coldham, *English Adventurers and Emigrants, 1609-1660*. 219 pp. index, cloth. 1984, Reprint 1991. $29.50, $3.00 postage and handling. Records of the High Court of Admiralty yield information about many companies and individuals involved in trade and emigration to America. With both a name index and a place index it is possible to identify Virginia residents. By the time of the colonization of America the HCA had assimilated from the Chancery Court almost all civil and criminal cases affecting ships and merchandise at sea, so there is considerable information not available elsewhere. #9489. Clearfield Co, 200 East Eager St, Baltimore, MD 21202.

*Note: On all books ordered from GPC and Clearfield, the postage and handling for the first book is $3.00, and for additional books in the same order, for each additional book, add $1.00. Maryland residents add sales tax. Payment can be made by Mastercard or Visa. 1-800-727-6687.*

William Carter Stubbs, PhD. *The Descendants of John Stubbs of Cappahosic, Gloucester County, Virginia, 1652.* 1902, Reprint, 1991, A Heritage Classic. 120 pp. index, paper. $15.00, $3.00 ship. Dr. Stubbs included a chapter of the Origin of the Stubbs Family with gleanings from England; however, the preponderance of his work concerns the Stubbs family of Gloucester County and their descendants throughout the South. The presumed children of John and Susannah Stubbs are identified and presented, with Richard Stubbs, a son, believed to be the one found in Bath County, North Carolina, and his descendants in South Carolina. Several of the lines of Stubbs daughters are carried forward for several generations and data are presented for the families of: Baytop, Booth, Boswell, Carter, Catlett, Coleman, Robins and Taliaferro. Dates and documentation are lacking in many instances, but the book is a good starting point for research of a family from a burned record county. Copies of the original edition are quite sought after. #S780. **Heritage Books, Inc 1540-E Pointer Ridge Place #300, Bowie, MD 20716.**

Guida M. Jackson-Laufer, PhD. *Virginia Diaspora, Southern Bensons and Related Families.* 1992. xviii, 148 pp. index, charts, illus., bibliog., app., paper. $17.00, $3.00 ship. Also included in the book are the Civil War memoirs of Lt. Peru Hardy Benson, CSA and Lt. J. J. Dunkle's list of six hundred Confederate prisoners mistreated by Federals (published 1869). They were sent from Fort Delaware to Morris Island to be punished in retaliation for the reported mistreatment of Union soldiers at Andersonville. The list gives their home county and state as well as date and place of capture, and is annotated by Dr. Laufer. The genealogical section of the book deals with the descendants of Robert Benson, born circa 1685 and his wife, Frances Prou, both of Virginia. Approximately seven generations, including the daughters are covered. The allied families of McCracken, Dickson, Scruggs, Clack, Foster, Davis, Youngblood, Patterson, Harwell, Hume and Fowler are presented. Peru Hardy Benson is a direct descendant of Robert and Frances, born in 1829 in Tennessee. His account of the Civil War includes his experiences in Yankee prisons. It is required reading for those who have heard only "the other side". #J014. **Heritage Books, Inc, 1540-E Pointer Ridge Place #300, Bowie, MD 20716.**

Alfred Sumner Winston III, *The Winstons of Hanover County, Virginia and Related Families, 1666 to 1992.* 1992. xiv, 945 pp., index, app., bibliog., hard cover. $49.50, postpaid. This is a handsomely bound compilation of over 10,000 descendants of the early Winstons of New Kent, Hanover and Henrico counties. The author states that the book is meant to be a bank of information on the Winston family and to offer some clues for additions or corrections. The book catalogues, but does not individually document the descendants carrying the Winston surname; it also identifies, in the same manner, over 1600 family names from the daughters of the Winston sons. There are additional vital records available. Narrative accounts of each of the early lines are included as an introduction to the listing of the descendants of each generation to the present time. There are records now available that clarify some of the misconceptions of earlier research of the early Winston family; new research could have been presented that brings together and corrects some of this earlier research. If one claims a Winston ancestor the link is likely to be found; however, one should then proceed to seek documentation for ones own line. **Alligator Book Co, 314 Seabrook Dr, Hilton Head Island, SC 29926.**

Gibson Jefferson McConnaughey, *Amelia County, Virginia Deed Books 12, 13 & 14, (Deeds 1773-1778)*. 1992. 149 pp. index, soft cover. $24.50, postpaid. These abstracts are made from the original records in the Amelia County clerk's office. They are very well organized, and assembled in a consistent and concise manner, with all of the pertinent information presented in a readable form. Contained in these deeds are those for the county of Nottoway, cut of from Amelia in 1789. The names of the grantors and grantees are identified in bold numerals in the index, a real aid in research. Abstracts of Deed Books 1 through 11 may also be obtained, some as single volumes, and others with two or three books per volume, and priced accordingly. **Mid-South Publishing Co, P O Box 659, Amelia, VA 23002.**

Dr. Stephen E. Bradley, Jr., *Prince George County, Virginia Federal Censuses 1810, 1820, 1830, 1840*. 1991, 92 pp. index, 8½x11, soft cover. $16.00, $1.00 ship. Each of these census compilations includes the names of the heads of households, and information about the household. All columns which could be correlated are included. Order from **Dr S E Bradley Jr, P O Box 22, Keysville, VA 23947.**

Dr. Stephen E. Bradley, Jr., *The 1850 Federal Census Prince George County, Virginia (All Schedules)*. 1990. 205 pp. index, 8½x11, soft cover. $15.00, $1.00 ship. The census of 1850 names and gives information about each of the residents of a household, as well as about the head of the household. Additional schedules give information about individuals under the headings of: Mortality, Slaves, Agriculture and Industry. Order from **Dr S E Bradley Jr, P O Box 22, Keysville, VA 23947.**

### SEARCH

*The queries of family researchers are very important. In the interest of accuracy and clarity: please print or type each Search question, limit each to thirty words or fewer, give year dates and identify county of residence. Multiple submissions will appear in subsequent issues.*

COLLIER, William, York Co, c.1665-1670. Merchant and tailor, emigrated from London; s Charles m Mary Eyers in (p) New Kent Co. Records on this family needed. Ed Dolan, 7403 Flint #205, Shawnee, KS 66203.

PITTS, Henry, b Isle of Wight Co 1738; d Newberry Co SC 1803; m 1757 Hannah Collier, moved to SC same year. Seek source of this information. Judith Dixon, 124 Valley View Dr, Joplin, MO 64804.

DUNKLEY, John (wife, Martha), d 1770-80s Halifax Co(p); sons Henry and Moses, dau. Elizabeth m Isaiah London 1782. Any info welcome. Marilyn London Winton, Rt 1 Box 50, Oakwood Dr, Coffeyville, KS 67337.

PEEBLES,IVY,ADAMS,PATE. Thomas Pate b 1739. Issue: Thomas, Drewry and Suky Pate Ivy; moved to GA, then TN or AL. Did Freemans, Turners, Jones move with Pates? Peebles & Lydia Pate Ivy moved to GA. Did John & Mary Pate Adams move also? Want to hear from Pate relations. Helen Pate Ross, 1801 Esic Dr, Edwardsville, IL 62025.

MARSHALL, Ezekiel, b April 1756/57 Pr George Co m Lucy. He died 1842 Summer Co TN. Need parents of Ezekiel and Lucy and all dates. Mrs Hope H Niedling, 1008 Third St, Stevens Point, WI 54481.

PRESLEY, Peter, b 1693 Northumberland Co m Elizabeth Thompson, dau Richard & Ursula (Bish) Thompson. Interested in family of dau Ursula who m Daniel Neale. Kim Johnson, 143 Spencer Road, Clendenin, WV 25045.

MULLINS, Booker, b c.1795 m Nancy. In Franklin Co, 1791 where dau Ollie b. In Floyd Co, KY 1810; d c.1865 Wise Co, VA. Seeking parents and siblings, will exchange info. Janallee Mullins, P O Box 135, Dwarf, KY 41739.

CORBIN, William, b 1769 VA m Ann(e) Burnett, Shelby Co, KY 1816, d 1862, Anderson Co, KY. Who were his parents? Virginia Kohl, 307 N Goodhope Ave, San Pedro, CA 90732.

BRANCH, Edward, d c.1810/15, wife Elizabeth. Issue: Edward, Bolling, Fanny (m Roberts), Patsy (m Cheatham), listed in great aunt, Sarah Bacon's will (who was she?), Chesterfield Co, 1810. Need identity of Edward Branch, birth, marriage and death. Mrs Ronnie E Hall, 410 Mantooth, Lufkin, TX 75901.

BOHAME, HEPINSTALL, MATTHEWS, WILKINS. Need help with following families: Moses Matthews (parents?) m 1772 Alice Heptinstall; James Heptinstall m by 1750, Judith Wilkins (dau of Wm b 1728 Northumberland Co?); James Heptinstall m 1727 Rebecca Bohame (parents?). Origin of these families? Allen H Norris, 2405 Countryside Drive, Silver Spring, MD 20905.

CHILES. Polly Chiles, born 1780-90, m Stephen Houchins Nov 1810 in Louisa Co. Seeking parents of Polly Chiles Houchins. Dan McGuire, 2202 Guildmore Road, Reston, VA 22091; 703-620-9879.

DOSS. Would like to contact Doss researchers working pre-1752, Virginia. Will exchange information and answer all correspondence. Barbara Doss McKinlay, 2740 La Cuesta Dr, Los Angeles, CA 90046.

BALLARD, Bland, c.1700-1791 of Spotsylvania Co. Wish to correspond with anyone researching 17th & 18th century Ballard families. Stephen M Ballard, 1339 Fourteenth St, NW Apt #5, Washington, DC 20005.

WILSON, BURT, FLEMING, TALLEY. Seek information about William Wilson of Elizabeth City Co; Richard Burt of York Co; William Fleming of Hanover Co; George Talley of Louisa Co. Margaret C Smith King, 104 Montclair Court, East Peoria, IL 61611.

RANDOLPH, Capt William, land patent Henrico Co late 1600s. Seek info concerning his voyage to the colony of VA. Barbara L Woodrum Ricketts, 12464 Woodley Ave, Granada Hills CA 91344.

SMITH, Elizabeth, m Lovell Harrison, 1789, King George Co. Seek parents of Elizabeth. Would like to contact persons working on the Smith family. Ms Barbara D Brassell, 3700 Meadowwood Cl. Guntersville, AL 35976.

WILLIAMS, Judge John, Granville Co, NC. Seeking parents, siblings, dates and documentation citations for him. How was he related to John Williams (late 1600s) York Co and his wife, Mary Keeling, dau of George Keeling? Mrs L Winifred Jacob, 5200 SW Colony Ct, Beaverton, OR 97005.

POWERS, John, c.1710-1767, King William Co. Need maiden name of wife, Ann. Sons: William and Major Powers, possible sons: Julius, Bernard, David and Thomas. Tressie Nealy, 509 SE 70th St, Oklahoma city, OK 73149.

FOUQUET, Guillaume, m Jane Eyre c.1687, Charles City Co. Subsequently had four confirmed children: William, Joseph, Giles and Ralph. Need info on Guillaume's parents, siblings. Frank Fuqua, 9460 Yale Lane, Highlands Ranch, CO 80126.

CALLENDER, Samuel, b 1756 in VA, d 1830 in PA. Enlisted 1776 in 9th VA Regiment (Gloucester area), m Martha Slawson (b 1755, d 1836). Seek info on parents and siblings. Robin S Arvickson, 1335 W 8th St, Erie, PA 16502.

UPSHAW Family. Need info about any Upshaw family cemeteries in Caroline, Essex or King & Queen cos. Also need Upshaw Bible records. Send your Upshaw family group sheets for check of my computer files; I will send computer (PAF) sheet in return. Ted Brooke, 408 Colchester Dr, Stone Mountain, GA 30088.

CLARK, Christopher mentions his Great Bible in his will probated Louisa Co 1754. Does anyone know its whereabouts or that of notes of Miss Sue Terrell of Lynchburg regarding it? Linda S Starr, 2642 Brentwood Drive, Norman, OK 73069.

HOFFMAN, HOOFMAN, Adam, m 1782 in New Orleans, LA; gave parents as Adam and Marie Barbara Mayer/Meyer and former residence as Virginia. His first s was Nicholas Adam Hoffman. Need to find locality of his parents' Virginia home. Norma Rose, Rt 7, Box 284-T, Longview, TX 75602.

PIPPEN/PIPPIN, Richard, d c.1702, Gloucester Co. m Mary. Seek information of relatives. Frances I Harvey, 4803 Galena Dr, Colorado Springs, CO 80918.

SAMUEL, Anthony, Essex Co, early 1700s; Caroline Co after 1727. Seek information. Joseph B Lambert, 1956 Linneman St, Glenview, IL 60025.

ARRINGTON, William Anderson, b c.1818 VA, m 1847, Halifax Co, Perlina Harriet Buntin, dau Irby G and Nancy C (Dewberry) Buntin. Lived Halifax Co 1847-1869, d 1892, Granville Co NC. Served Co E, 1st Reg VA Reserves. Seek to prove his parents, and correspond with Arrington researchers. Marie Arrington Hinton, 4700 Hiddenbrook Dr, Raleigh, NC 27609.

GAINES, Henry, d 1784, probably in a tidewater VA county. Uncle of Helena Maria Theresa Timberlake (w of Henry Timberlake) of London. Seek name of son of Henry and Helena, as well as info about Henry Gaines. John A Duncan, 395 Redding Rd, #3, Lexington, KY 40517.

ADDISON, JARRETT, MIMS, MARTIN, PRUETT, WELDY. Need birth, death dates, parents, ancestors for the following: Alice Addison b c.1730, may have been dau of Thomas & Ann

Addison. Devereux Jarrett b c.1700 prob New Kent Co, m Elizabeth. Thomas Mims b c.1640, England; Mellyanne Martin b c.1680 m Thomas Mims Jr. John Pruett b c.1730, d 1788 Goochland Co. William Weldy b c.1680. All of the families lived in New Kent, Middlesex and Goochland cos. Will exchange info. Barbara Moore, Rt 12 Box 378, New Braunfels, TX 78132.

CHAMBERLAYNE, WILLIAMSON. Seek information about relationship of Cornelius Williamson, m Rhonda Stone, dau of Benjamin and Anna Asbury Stone, to John Williamson m Rebecca Chamberlayne of New Kent Co. Descendants lived in Henrico and James City cos, but need to make the connection. Evelyn Warren, 13335 SW 16th Ave, Ocala, FL 34473.

WILLOUGHBY, MORELAND. Thomas Willoughby c.1610, Elizabeth City; James Thomas Moreland, c.1660, probably York Co. Seek information. Mrs Ruth Thomas, 2336 47th Ave SW, Seattle, WA 98116.

HIGHTOWER, Joshua, b 1696, Richmond Co d 1772, Amelia Co m Susannah Taverner, 1720; dau. Ann m Capt John Hammond. Seek ancestry of the Hightower family. Mrs. Harvey C Vance, 2335 Atkinson Rd, #1-2, Biloxi, MS 39531.

SATTERWHITE/MITCHELL. Need parents, birthplace, birth date of Michael Satterwhite who m Amy Mitchell; settled in Granville Co NC c.1759. May have been b in Prince George Co. Velma W Pelley, 1426 Parker Lane, Henderson, NC 27536.

MINTER, William H(undley), b c.1812, Northumberland Co, d 1857 Richmond City; m in Richmond 1837 Jane Puryear; 1846/7 Elizabeth ___. Was John J Minter, a Richmond resident, a brother or first cousin? Seek information on these Minters and relatives. Mrs S C Rosapepe, 6900 Apamatica Ln, Chesterfield, VA 23832.

SAVAGE, Thomas, c. 1610. Settled in Accomack/Northampton cos. Seek information about his descendants. Ms Dorothy Ingham, P O Box 1778, Clarksville, VA 23927.

BAILEY. Need parents and wife of John Bailey/Bayly, b 1748, Northumberland Co. In Pittsylvania Co by 1767 & Lincoln Co KY by 1784. He was a Baptist minister. Miss Maxine Alcorn, 1038 Althea, Houston, TX 77018.

MOORE, Mary Henry, b 1821, d 1857 Henrico Co, buried Hollywood Cemetery, m 1842 Benjamin Medlicott of Gloucester Co. Seek parents. Anne Maling, 434 Harvard St #2, Norfolk, VA 23505.

*For those subscribers who have submitted multiple SEARCH queries, or questions after the magazine had gone to the consultant, your queries will be continued in the first issue of Volume 2.*

*Coming in the Next Issue:*

*Losses from British Depredations, Warwick County*
*Christ Church Parish Register Additions*
*Civil Appointments, Hanover County*
*Guardians and Orphans, Northumberland County*
*Virginia Personal Property Tax Records*

# TIDEWATER VIRGINIA FAMILIES

## By Virginia Lee Hutcheson Davis

Covering an incredible 375 years, from the arrival of the *George* in 1619 to contemporary times, this book sets forth the genealogical history of some forty families who have their roots in Tidewater Virginia. Starting with the earliest colonial settler, the origins of the following Tidewater families are presented: Bell, Binford, Bonner, Butler, Campbell, Cheadle, Chiles, Clements, Cotton, Dejarnette(att), Dumas, Ellyson, Fishback, Fleming, Hamlin, Hampton, Harnison, Harris, Haynie, Hurt, Hutcheson, Lee, Mosby, Mundy, Nelson, Peatross, Pettyjohn, Ruffin, Short, Spencer, Tarleton, Tatum, Taylor, Terrill, Watkins, Winston, and Woodson.

With the benefit of myriad sources both in print and manuscript, and with the expert assistance of numerous county archivists, Mrs. Davis has developed a microcosmic genealogy of Tidewater Virginia, an area until now sadly lacking in well-documented genealogical compilations. Counties covered are Amherst, Caroline, Charles City, Chesterfield, Dinwiddie, Elizabeth City, Essex, Fairfax, Fauquier, Gloucester, Goochland, Hanover, Henrico, Isle of Wight, James City, King William, Lancaster, Mathews, Middlesex, New Kent, Northampton, Northumberland, Prince William, Prince George, Spotsylvania, Surry, Sussex, and York.

*"A significant contribution to our genealogical understanding of the Tidewater. . . . Family histories of this calibre are rare, so rare that* TIDEWATER VIRGINIA FAMILIES *has deservedly become an 'overnight' best seller in the field."*—Newsletter of the Virginia Genealogical Society.

*"A bench mark for all future publications of this genre."*—Western New York Genealogical Society Journal

8 1/2 x 11. 730 pp., indexed, cloth. 1990. ISBN 0-8063-1283-1. **$75.00** plus $3.00 postage & handling. Maryland residents add 5% sales tax; Michigan residents add 4% sales tax.

## Genealogical Publishing Co., Inc.
### 1001 N. Calvert St., Baltimore, Md. 21202

# INDEX

NFN  No first name given; NLN  No last name given

Adams
  Ambrose 208
  John 213
  Mary 213
  Zachariah 208
Addison
  Alice 215
  Ann 216
  Thomas 216
Alexander
  Philip 206, 207
  William T 207
Allard
  William 208
Allen
  Margaret 202
  Tim 191
  Tobias 202
Allerman
  John 208
Anderson
  Andrew 189
  Bartelot 193, 196, 199
  Benjamin 194
  David 197, 198
  Davis 194
  Garland 193, 196, 197
  John 197
  Matthew 208
  Richard 208
  William 194, 196, 198
  [?]n 208
Angell
  Cloe 186
  Robert 186
Archer
  George 192
Armistead
  Churchill 208
  Currell 208
  Dorothy 208
  George 208
  John 208
  Robert 208
  William 208
Arrington
  Perlina 215
  William 215

Asbury
  Anna 216
Ash
  John 208
Ashbrooke
  Peter 191
Ashbury
  Joseph 208
Ashton
  Henry A 206
Atkinson
  Henry A 174
Aust
  John 191
Austin
  Chapman 197
Bagge
  John 188
Bailey
  Mary 209
  Matthew 209
Bailey/Bayly
  John 216
Baird
  Mary 189
  Virginia B 190
Baker
  Elizabeth 209
Ball
  Jno 192
  Joseph 185, 186
Ballard
  Bland 214
Balvard
  Robert 184
Baly
  John 192
Barrat
  William 184
Barrett
  William 197
Barrick
  Alexander 201
  David 201
  Dinnah 201
Barron
  James 190
  Kate 190
  Virginia 190
Basse
  Wm 191

Bassett
  Richard 209
Bates
  Thomas 209
Batte
  Tho: 192
Baugh
  Jno 191
  Wm 191
Baylor
  Ann 189
  Elizabeth P 190
  Henry L 190
  Isabella 189
  Isabella T 189
  Lucy 190
  Mary B 189
  Richard 189, 190
  Robert 187
  Robert P 189
  Virginia 190
Baytop
  family 212
  James 209
  John 209
  Sarah 209
Beard
  Thomas 202
Beatley
  E[---] 183
  Frances 183
  John 183
Beauchamp
  Sarah 179
Bellamy
  Joseph 209
Belvin
  Aaron 209
Benson
  family 212
  Frances 212
  Peru H 212
  Robert 212
Bentley
  James 208
Berkley
  Edmund 209
Bernard
  Peter 209
Berry
  Frances 202

218

Berry
  Francis 207
  John 202
  William 202
Berryman
  John 207
  Sarah 207
Betts
  Elisha 185, 186
Beven
  Wm 191
Beveridge
  John 208
Beverley
  Robert 188
Bevill
  Essex 192
Billups
  Christopher 180
  Elizabeth 180
  George 209
  Humphrey 209
  John 209
  Joice 181
  Joseph 181, 209
  Mary 180, 181
  Richard 208
  Robert 180, 209
  Sarah 180
  Susanna 180
  Thomas 209
Bish
  Ursula 214
Blackerby
  William 185
Blackman
  Wm 191
Blacknall
  Mary 209
Blackwell
  John 193, 194
Blake
  Fanny 201
  Jacob 201
  Susannah 201
  Thomas 209
  William 209
Blassingham
  John 209
Bockstruck
  Lloyd D 211
Bohame
  Rebecca 214
Bohannon
  William 209

Bonafield
  Samuel 209
Bonall
  Richard 209
Booker
  James 209
  Lewis 209
Booth
  family 212
  George 209
  Thomas 209
Borum
  Delelia 181
  Delely 181
  Edmund 209
  Hannah 181
  John 181
  Mary 181
  Sterling 181
Boss
  Eliz. 202
  John 202
  Roleson 202
Boswell
  family 212
  John 209
Bottom
  Tho: 192
Bowman
  Edwd 191
  Jno 191
Boyd
  George 185
  John 185
Bradley
  Stephen E 213
Brammil
  Elizabeth 209
Branch
  Bolling 214
  Edward 214
  Elizabeth 214
  Fanny 214
  Patsy 214
  Tho: 192
  Xtopher 192
Brazeelle
  Henry 192
Bridgewater
  Samll 191
Briggs
  Dr. 180
  Hannah 180
  William 209

Bright
  Francis 180
  Susan 180
Brooke
  Alexander T 190
  John L 190
  Maria 190
Brooks
  John 201
  Mary 201
  Ruben 201
Brown
  Christopher 209
  George 209
  John 177
  Robert 209
Browning
  John 209
Browninge
  George 191
Bryant
  Betty 202
  John 202
  Mary 202
Buckner
  Baldwin 209
  Henry 208
  John 209
  Judith 209
  Robert 209
  Samuel 209
  Thomas 209
  William 208, 209
Bullington
  Robt 191
Bullock
  James 194
Buntin
  Irby 215
  Nancy 215
  Perlina 215
Burke
  Phebe 202
  Richard 202
Burnett
  Ann 214
Burt
  Richard 214
Burton
  Jno 191
  Pinny 209
  Tho: 191
Burwell
  Lewis 176 177 209
  Thomas 209

Busby
  Edward 209
  William 209
Butler
  John 185
  L David 190
Byrd
  Wm 191
Callender
  Martha 215
  Samuel 215
Carter
  family 212
  Giles 191
Cary
  Miles 194
Catlett
  family 212
  Harriet T 190
  Lucy B 189
Chamberlaine
  Major 191
Chamberlayne
  Rebecca 216
Chandler
  Mrs 192
Chapman
  Richard 194-196, 199
Cheatham
  Patsy 214
Childres
  Abrah 192
  Lemon 192
Chowning
  Carroll C 200
Christie
  John 207
Clack
  family 212
Clark
  Christopher 215
  Linsey 201
  Margaret 201
  Robert 201
Clarke
  Thomas 194
Clay
  Charles 192
Clemons
  James 202
  Jane 202
  Robert 202
Clerke
  Robt 192

Clerke
  Wm 191
Clough
  George 194, 196, 199
Cocke
  Richd 191
  Thomas 191
  Wm 191
Cole
  James 175, 176
  Jane 175, 176
  John 175, 176
  Martha 175, 176
  Mary 175, 176
  Roscow 175, 176
  Susannah 175, 176
  William 175-177
Coleman
  family 212
Collier
  Charles 213
  Hannah 213
  Mary 213
  William 213
Conway
  Dennis 185
Corbell
  John 184
Corbin
  Ann 214
  William 214
Cotrell
  Thomas 183, 184
Cox
  Jno 191
Crenshaw
  Charles 194
Curtis
  Richard 203
Dabney
  Charles 194
  George 194
Dade
  Baldwin 206
  Townshend 206
Dancy
  Wm 191
Dandridge
  John 197
  Nathaniel W 194
  William 194
Daniel
  Catherine 201
  Susanna 201

Daniel
  William 201
Darracott
  William 194
Davis
  family 212
  Jno 192
  John 191
  Samuel 185, 186
  Thomas 191
Deans
  Annie 180
  Dr. 180
Deeley
  Edwd 191
Dewberry
  Nancy C 215
Dickson
  family 212
Diggs
  Cole 176
Dison
  Nich 192
Dixon
  Haldenby 198
  Halsenby 194
Dobbs
  Richd 192
Dodson
  Wm 192
Doss
  family 214
Dunkle
  J J 212
Dunkley
  Elizabeth 213
  Henry 213
  John 213
  Martha 213
  Moses 213
Dunton
  Levin 180
  Sarah 180
Eakin
  James 191
East
  Tho: 191
Eddings
  Elizabeth 180
Edwards
  Conley L 169
Elam
  Gilbert 191
  Martin 191
  Wm 191

Ellis
  Frances 190
  John 192
Epes
  Fras 191
Evans
  Robt 191
Eyers
  Mary 213
Eyre
  Jane 215
Fallen
  Tignor 184
Farloe
  Jno 192
Farrar
  Coll 191
  Jno 191
  Wm 191
Feild
  Peter 191
Fetherstone
  Charles 191
Field
  Edmd. 202
  Mary 202
  William 202
Fitzherbert
  Tho: 192
Fitzhugh
  Henry 206
  William 207
Fleming
  William 214
Forest
  James 192
Foster
  family 212
Fountain
  Mary 179
Fouquet
  Giles 215
  Guillaume 215
  Jane 215
  Joseph 215
  Ralph 215
  William 215
Foushee
  James 184
Fowler
  family 212
Francklin
  James 192
Freeman
  George 191

Gaines
  Henry 215
Gammon
  David B 210
Gardner
  William 194
Garland
  John 195, 197
  Thomas 193, 194
Garnett
  James 187, 188
  Maria 190
  Muscoe 187
Gaskins
  John 185, 186
Gates
  James 191
Gayle
  Levin 180
  Margaret 180
Gee
  Henry 191
Giles
  Wm 192
Gill
  George 210
  Mary 210
  Richard 210
  William 210
  Winder 210
Goffigon
  Leah 180
  Margaret 180
Goodall
  Parke 194, 196
Goode
  Edwd 192
  Jno 191
Gower
  Abell 192
Granville
  Margaret 180
Green
  Charles 202
  James 202
Greenhaugh
  Jno 192
Gregory
  Tho 192
Grymes
  Benjamin 207
Gunter
  John 191
Haggoman
  John 179

Haggoman
  Sarah 179, 180
Hammond
  Ann 216
  John 216
Hancocke
  Mrs 191
Harcum
  Elisha 184
  William 184
Hardee
  Agatha 202
  Anner 202
  Curtis 202
  David 202
  John 202
Harper
  Mary 180
Harris
  Peter 191
  Wm 192
Harrison
  Elizabeth 214
  Lovell 214
Harvey
  John 184
  Sarah 184
Harwell
  family 212
Hatcher
  Ben: 192
  Edward 191
  Mr 192
Haug
  Phillip 190
Haynie
  Jacob 185, 186
  William 185
Healy
  Eliz. 201
  John 201
  William 201
Henry
  Patrick 198
Heptinstall
  Alice 214
  James 214
  Judith 214
  Rebecca 214
Herbert
  Palina 181
Herne
  Elizabeth 179
  NFN 179

Hewes
　Wm 192
Hickman
　R 177
Higby
　David 174
　Lot 174
Hightower
　Joshua 216
　Susannah 216
Hodges
　Thomas 210
Hoffman
　Adam 215
　Nicholas 215
Holmes
　Richd 191
　Tho 192
Hooe
　Gerrard 207
　Richard 207
Hopkins
　William 176
Horsey
　Abigail 178
　John 178
　Mary 178
　Samuel 178
　Sarah 178
　Stephen 178
Howard
　John 192
Huddlesen
　Jno 192
Hudnall
　Richard 184
Hughes
　Gabriel 180
　Pollie 180
Hull
　Richard 184
Hume
　family 212
Humphreys
　Wm 191
Hundley
　Charles 194
Hunt
　George 183
Hunter
　James 188
Hunton
　John 183
Ishams
　Mrs 191

Ivy
　Lydia 213
　Peebles 213
Jackson-Laufer
　Guida M 212
Jacobes
　Benjamin 201
　Eliza. 201
　Jacob 201
James
　Columbia 181
　Lemuel 181
Jarrett
　Devereux 216
　Elizabeth 216
Jarvis
　Elizabeth 180
　John 180
Jefferson
　Thomas 193
Johnson
　William 194-198
Jones
　Edwd 191
　Gilbert 191
　John 194
　Thomas 184
Keeling
　George 215
　Mary 215
Keeve
　Beverley 183
Kenner
　Rodham 184
Kennon
　Mr 191
Knibbe
　Saml 191
Lackland
　N J 174
Lainhard
　Ann S 211
Lamkin
　James 184
Lattimore
　David 184
Lawrence
　John 195-197, 199
　William 197
Leadd
　Jno 192
Lester
　Edwd 192
Lewis
　Jno 191

Ligon
　Wm 191
Lipscombe
　Ambrose　194,
　　196, 198, 199
Lisle
　Jno 191
Livingston
　Muscoe 187
Lockett
　Tho: 191
London
　Elizabeth 213
　Isaiah 213
Lownds
　Henry 191
Lygon
　Mrs 191
　Richd 191
Macon
　William 194
Mahanes
　Thomas 184
Man
　Robert 191
Marsh
　Rich 192
Marshall
　Ezekiel 213
　Lucy 213
Martin
　Mellyanne 216
Mason
　Nehemiah 206
Massey
　Segismond　205,
　　206
　Thomas 205
Matthews
　Alice 214
　Charles 192
　Moses 214
　Thomas 188
Mayer/Meyer
　Adam 215
　Marie 215
McCarty
　Daniel 205
McConnaughey
　Gibson J 213
McCracken
　family 212
McGuire
　John P 188

McKenney
  Robert N 182, 186
Meaderias
  Alexander 201
  Charles 201
  Elizabeth 201
Meriwether
  John 194
  Samuel 194
Micou
  Paul 188
Miller
  John 189
  William 188
Millner
  John 192
Mims
  Mellyanne 216
  Thomas 216
Minor
  Dabney 194
Minter
  Elizabeth 216
  Jane 216
  John 216
  William 216
Mitchell
  Amy 216
Moll
  John 190
Moody
  Samll 192
Moreland
  James 216
Morris
  Mrs 191
Moseley
  Alven 207
Mott
  Betty   183, 185, 186
  Caty 183
  John 184-186
  Judith   183, 185, 186
  Molly   183, 185, 186
  Mosley 183-186
  William 184
Mullins
  Booker 214
  Nancy 214
  Ollie 214
Murray
  Cordelia 181

Murray
  Heron 181
  Mary 180
  Milton 178
Neale
  Daniel 214
  Ursula1 214
Negro
  Betty 175
  Billy 205
  Bob 175
  Bristol 205
  Charles 205
  Cully 205
  Dick 205
  Frank 205
  Gaby 175
  George 210
  Grace 205
  Isaac 210
  Jenny 205
  Jude 210
  Judy 205
  Kate 205
  Lewis 175
  Milly 205
  Moll 175
  Nan 205
  Nanny 205
  Pegg 205
  Phill 205
  Sam 205
  Sampson 205
  Sarah 175, 210
  Siner 210
  Thier 205
  Virgin 205
  Will 175
  Winne 210
Newcombe
  Tho 191
NLN
  Averille 202
  Benjamin 202
  Rachel 202
Northen
  Ann 210
  Catey 210
  Edmund 210
  Elizabeth 210
  George 210
  John 210
  Kilbey 210
  Luaner 210
  Lucy 210

Northen
  Margaret 210
  Mary 210
  Merimon 210
  Mynta 210
  Nelly 210
  Peter 210
  Ruben 210
  Sarah 210
  William 210
Nottingham
  Edith 179
  Margaret 180
  Mary 180
  Scarbrough 180
  Thomas 180
Oldham
  John 184
  Nanny 184
  Samuel 184
  Sarah 184
Osborne
  Edwd 192
  Tho: 192
Overton
  Samuel 197
Owen
  Evan 191
Page
  Robert 194
  Robert C 194
Palmer
  John 184
Parker
  Richd 192
Pate
  Drewry 213
  Lydia 213
  Mary 213
  Suky 213
  Thomas 213
Patterson
  family 212
  John 202
  William 202
Payne
  Elizabeth 190
Pedin
  James 176, 177
Peirce
  Richd 191
Pendleton
  John 194
Perkins
  Nich 192

Perrin
  Richd 192
  Tho: 192
Pickering
  David 185
Pippen
  Mary 215
  Richard 215
Pitman
  Edward 210
  Martin 210
Pitts
  Hannah 213
  Henry 213
Place
  Esqr 192
Platt
  Gilbert 191
Pleasants
  Jno 192
Pledge
  John 192
Poldon
  Tho: 191
Polk
  Elizabeth 179
Pollard
  Thomas 197, 198
  William 194-199
Porter
  Wm 192
Powell
  Sarah 179
Powers
  Ann 215
  Bernard 215
  David 215
  John 215
  Julius 215
  Major 215
  Thomas 215
  William 215
Presley
  Elizabeth 214
  Peter 214
Preut
  Henry 191
Price
  John 194
Pritchard
  Charles 186
Prou
  Frances 212
Pruett
  John 216

Puckett
  Jno 191
  Tho: 191
  Wm 191
Pue
  Henry 192
Puryear
  Jane 216
Rabone
  Richd 191
Radford
  Mr 192
Ragsdal
  Godfe 192
Rains
  Emma 181
Randolph
  William 214
  Wm 191
Ransone
  Elizabeth 180
  James 180
Respess
  Joice 180
Richardson
  William 193-195
Risbee
  Tho: 192
Roan
  Ann 201
  Charles 201
  Lewis 201
Roberts
  Batt 191
  Fanny 214
Robins
  family 212
Robinson
  Frances 179
  John 194
  Jos: 206, 207
Rocke
  John 178
Rodgers
  Jos. 206
Roscow
  James 175
  William 176, 177
Rowlett
  Peter 192
Royall
  Jos 191
Samuel 209
Sanders
  Alexander 202

Sanders
  Ann 201
  Christian 201
  George 201
  John 202
  Mary 202
Satterwhite
  Amy 216
  Michael 216
Savage
  Thomas 216
Scruggs
  family 212
Sessums
  Alexander 210
  Alice 210
  Jacob 210
  Polley 210
  Rebekah 210
Sheerman
  Henry 191
Shelton
  Mary 202
  Reuben 202
  Thomas 202
Sheppard
  Mary 180
  Seth 180
Shinker
  John 205
Shippey
  Tho: 191
Singer
  Hannah 185
  John 185
Skelton
  Meriwether 194
Skermes
  Mrs 191
Slawson
  Martha 215
Smith
  Anthony 215
  Elizabeth 214
  Henry 206
  Mary 181
Snelson
  John 194
Stanley
  John 193
Stapp
  Joshua 192
Starke
  B W 174
  John 194

Steward
  Jno 192
  John 192
Stiff
  Sarah 202
  William 202
Stith
  Robert 206
Stone
  Anna 216
  Benjamin 216
  Rhonda 216
Storke
  John 205
Stott
  John 185
  Mary 184, 185
  Stephen 184
Stratton
  Edwd 191
Stubbs
  John 212
  Richard 212
  Susannah 212
  William C 212
Summer
  Benjamin 178
Swanson
  Chloe 185
  John 185
Syme
  John 196
Taite
  William 184
Taliaferro
  family 212
Tall
  Anthony 191
Talley
  George 214
  Nathaniel 194
Taverner
  Susannah 216
Terrell
  Sue 215
Thacker
  Alice 203
  Ann 203
  Anne 203
  Chicheley 203
  Edward 202
  Edwin 202, 203
  Elizabeth 203
  Eltonhead  202, 203

Thacker
  Frances 203
  Henry 202, 203
  John 203
  Lettice 203
  Martha 202, 203
Theobalds
  Wm 192
Thomas 209
  Richard 185
  William 185
Thompson
  Elizabeth 214
  John 194, 197
  Richard 214
  Ursula 214
  William 207
Thornton
  Francis 205
  Harriet 190
  William 205, 207
Timberlake
  Helena 215
  Henry 215
Tinsley
  Thomas 197
  William 193, 195
Todd
  Thomas 203
Tomkins
  B 209
Trevilian
  Thomas 196, 198
Turner
  James 197
Turpin
  Hannah 179
  Michael 191
  NFN 179
  Phillip 192
Tyler
  William 206
Upshaw
  family 215
Vauter
  family 187
Vawter
  Mary 180
Vivien
  Thomas 203
Waddell
  James 192
Wake
  John 201
  Johnson 201

Wake
  Judith 201
Walker
  Eliza 184, 185
  Leonard 184
Wallace
  Charles 192
Ward
  Henry 206
Wardson
  Richd 191
Waring
  Ann 189
  William 187
Warren
  Jane 202
Washington
  Ann 201
  Henry 201, 206
  John 206
  Laurance 205, 206
  Robert 207
  Thacker 201, 206
Watkins
  Henry 191
  Lewis 192
Watson
  John 192
Watts
  Elizabeth 202
  Hannah 202
  Ralph 202
Webb
  Giles 183
  John 183
Webster
  Tho: 192
Weisiger
  Minor T 193, 204
Weldy
  William 216
Wells
  Tho: 191
Weston
  Drusilla 181
  John 181
  Joice 181
  Thomas 181
Wheatly
  Wm 192
White
  Elisha 194, 196, 198, 199
Whitfield
  Thomas 178

225

Wilkins
  Judith 214
  William 214
Willeford
  John 210
Williams
  Annie 180
  Benjamin 179, 181
  Columbia 181
  Cordelia 178, 181
  Delely 181
  Drusilla 181
  Edith 179
  Elizabeth 179, 180
  Emma 181
  Eugenia 181
  Frances 179
  Hannah 179-181
  Heron 178
  Jacob 179
  John 179, 181, 215
  Joice 181
  Josiah 179, 181
  Leah 180
  Louisa 181
  Lucy 181

Williams
  Margaret 180
  Mary 179-181, 215
  Michael 178
  Palina 181
  Pollie 180
  Prissellia 179
  Samuel 179, 180
  Sarah 178-181
  Susan 180
  Susanna 180
  Thomas 178-181, 184
  William 180, 181
Williamson
  Cornelius 216
  John 216
  Rebeccaa 216
  Rhonda 216
Willoughby
  Thomas 216
Willson
  John 192
Wilson
  Max 194
  William 214

Winston
  Alfred S 212
  Essex W 194
  family 212
  Geddes 195, 196
  Isaac 194
  John 194, 196
  William O 195, 196, 198
Womecke
  Abrah 191
Wood
  Tho: 192
Woodson
  John 192
  Robt 192
Wooles
  Tho: 192
Worsham
  George 192
  Jno 191
Yarrington
  John 201
  Margaret 201
Youngblood
  family 212

Heritage Books by Virginia Lee Hutcheson Davis:

*Henrico County, Virginia Deeds, 1750–1774*
Virginia Lee Hutcheson Davis and Gary Murdock Williams

*Tidewater Virginia Families: A Magazine of History and Genealogy:*

*Volume 1, May 1992–February 1993*

*Volume 2, May 1993–February 1994*

*Volume 3, May 1994–February 1995*

*Volume 4, May 1995–February 1996*

*Volume 5, May 1996–February 1997*

*Volume 6, May 1997–February 1998*

*Volume 7, May 1998–February 1999*

*Volume 8, May 1999–February 2000*

*Volume 9, May 2000–February 2001*

*Volume 10, May 2001–February 2002*

*Volume 11, May 2002–February 2003*

*Volume 12, May 2003–February 2004*